PALGRAVE STUDIES IN THEATRE AND PERFORMANCE HISTORY is a series devoted to the best of theatre/performance scholarship currently available, accessible, and free of jargon. It strives to include a wide range of topics, from the more traditional to those performance forms that in recent years have helped broaden the understanding of what theatre as a category might include (from variety forms as diverse as the circus and burlesque to street buskers, stage magic, and musical theatre, among many others). Although historical, critical, or analytical studies are of special interest, more theoretical projects, if not the dominant thrust of a study, but utilized as important underpinning or as a historiographical or analytical method of exploration, are also of interest. Textual studies of drama or other types of less traditional performance texts are also germane to the series if placed in their cultural, historical, social, or political and economic context. There is no geographical focus for this series and works of excellence of a diverse and international nature, including comparative studies, are sought.

The editor of the series is Don B. Wilmeth (EMERITUS, Brown University), Ph.D., University of Illinois, who brings to the series over a dozen years as editor of a book series on American theatre and drama, in addition to his own extensive experience as an editor of books and journals. He is the author of several award-winning books and has received numerous career achievement awards, including one for sustained excellence in editing from the Association for Theatre in Higher Education.

Also in the series:

Undressed for Success by Brenda Foley
Theatre, Performance, and the Historical Avant-garde by Günter Berghaus
Theatre, Politics, and Markets in Fin-de-Siècle Paris by Sally Charnow
Ghosts of Theatre and Cinema in the Brain by Mark Pizzato
Moscow Theatres for Young People by Manon van de Water
Absence and Memory in Colonial American Theatre by Odai Johnson
Vaudeville Wars: How the Keith-Albee and Orpheum Circuits Controlled the Big-Time and Its Performers by Arthur Frank Wertheim
Performance and Femininity in Eighteenth-Century German Women's Writing by Wendy Arons
Operatic China: Staging Chinese Identity across the Pacific by Daphne P. Lei
Transatlantic Stage Stars in Vaudeville and Variety: Celebrity Turns by Leigh Woods
Interrogating America through Theatre and Performance edited by William W. Demastes and Iris Smith Fischer
Plays in American Periodicals, 1890–1918 by Susan Harris Smith

Representation and Identity from Versailles to the Present: The Performing Subject by Alan Sikes

Directors and the New Musical Drama: British and American Musical Theatre in the 1980s and 90s by Miranda Lundskaer-Nielsen

Beyond the Golden Door: Jewish-American Drama and Jewish-American Experience by Julius Novick

American Puppet Modernism: Essays on the Material World in Performance by John Bell

On the Uses of the Fantastic in Modern Theatre: Cocteau, Oedipus, and the Monster by Irene Eynat-Confino

Staging Stigma: A Critical Examination of the American Freak Show by Michael M. Chemers, foreword by Jim Ferris

Performing Magic on the Western Stage: From the Eighteenth-Century to the Present edited by Francesca Coppa, Larry Hass, and James Peck, foreword by Eugene Burger

Memory in Play: From Aeschylus to Sam Shepard by Attilio Favorini

Danjūrō's Girls: Women on the Kabuki Stage by Loren Edelson

Mendel's Theatre: Heredity, Eugenics, and Early Twentieth-Century American Drama by Tamsen Wolff

Theatre and Religion on Krishna's Stage: Performing in Vrindavan by David V. Mason

Rogue Performances: Staging the Underclasses in Early American Theatre Culture by Peter P. Reed

Broadway and Corporate Capitalism: The Rise of the Professional-Managerial Class, 1900–1920 by Michael Schwartz

Lady Macbeth in America: From the Stage to the White House by Gay Smith

Performing Bodies in Pain: Medieval and Post-Modern Martyrs, Mystics, and Artists by Marla Carlson

Performing Bodies in Pain

Medieval and Post-Modern Martyrs, Mystics, and Artists

Marla Carlson

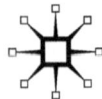

PERFORMING BODIES IN PAIN
Copyright © Marla Carlson, 2010.
Softcover reprint of the hardcover 1st edition 2010 978-0-230-10386-3
All rights reserved.

First published in 2010 by
PALGRAVE MACMILLAN®
in the United States—a division of St. Martin's Press LLC,
175 Fifth Avenue, New York, NY 10010.

Where this book is distributed in the UK, Europe and the rest of th world, this is by Palgrave Macmillan, a division of Macmillan Publishers Limited, registered in England, company number 785998, of Houndmills, Basingstoke, Hampshire RG21 6XS.

Palgrave Macmillan is the global academic imprint of the above companies and has companies and representatives throughout the world.

Palgrave® and Macmillan® are registered trademarks in the United States, the United Kingdom, Europe and other countries.

ISBN 978-1-349-28827-4   ISBN 978-0-230-11148-6 (eBook)
DOI 10.1057/9780230111486
Library of Congress Cataloging-in-Publication Data

Carlson, Marla.
    Performing bodies in pain : medieval and post-modern martyrs, mystics, and artists / Marla Carlson.
        p. cm.—(Palgrave studies in theatre and performance history)
    Includes bibliographical references.

    1. Pain in the theater. 2. Violence in the theater. 3. Theater—United States—History—21st century. 4. Performance art. 5. Theater—France—History—Medieval, 500–1500. 6. French drama—To 1500—History and criticism. 7. Mysteries and miracle-plays, French—History and criticism. I. Title.
PN2272.5.P35C37 2010
792.02′8—dc22   2010001967

A catalogue record of the book is available from the British Library.

Design by Newgen Imaging Systems (P) Ltd., Chennai, India.

First edition: August 2010

Transferred to Digital Printing in 2012

For Tony and Eli

Contents

List of Illustrations	ix
Acknowledgments	xi
Introduction	1
1. Feeling Torture	25
2. Imagining Death	49
3. Enduring Ecstasy	77
4. Whipping Up Community	103
5. Containing Chaos	131
Conclusion	155
Notes	167
Bibliography	201
Index	219

Illustrations

1. Photograph of John Kani and Winston Ntshona in *The Island* at the Brooklyn Academy of Music, April 2003. © Richard Termine. Courtesy: BAM Archives.   25
2. Flagellation of Saints Denis, Rustique, and Eleuthere from the *Légende de Saint Denis: Reproduction des Miniatures du Manuscrit Original Présenté en 1317 au Roi Philippe le Long*, ed. Henry Martin (Paris: Champion, 1908).   26
3. Saint Denis picks up his head, with two angels to guide him, while Larcie watches, from *Légende de Saint Denis*.   49
4. Film still of Marina Abramović performing *Lips of Thomas* at the Solomon R. Guggenheim Museum, New York, November 14, 2005, from the film *Seven Easy Pieces*, dir. Babette Mangolte. © Marina Abramović. Courtesy: Sean Kelly Gallery, New York.   77
5. Jean Fouquet (ca. 1415/20-1481), *The Martyrdom of St. Apollonia* from *Le Livre d'Heures d'Etienne Chevalier: The Suffrage of the Saints*, MS 71, fol 39. Photo: R. G. Ojeda, Musée Condé, Chantilly, France. Photo Credit: Réunion des Musées Nationaux/Art Resource, NY.   78
6. Photograph of Ron Athey atop wooden pyramid in performance *Judas Cradle*, Ljubljana, 2004. © Manuel Vason.   103
7. Giovanni del Biondo (fl. 1356–1399), *Martyrdom of Saint Sebastian and Scenes from His Life*. Triptych. Museo dell'Opera del Duomo, Florence, Italy. Photo credit: Scala/Art Resource, NY.   104
8. Photograph of Reed Birney (Ian) and Marin Ireland (Cate) in Sarah Kane's *Blasted*, Soho Rep., New York, 2008. © Simon Kane 2008.   131

Acknowledgments

This book had its seeds in the dissertation I wrote for the Ph.D. Program in Theatre at the City University of New York Graduate Center under the direction of Marvin Carlson. I thank him and the other members of the committee—Jill Dolan, Judith Milhous, and Pamela Sheingorn—for their encouragement, provocations, and inspiration both during and after the dissertation process. Don Wilmeth has provided crucial support ever since I submitted an earlier, quite different manuscript to Palgrave Macmillan, and the detailed comments by that manuscript's two anonymous readers enabled me to reconceptualize the project in the form of this book. Ken Cerniglia and Derek Matson provided valuable support and critique during the earlier stage of the project.

I thank the organizers, my copanelists, and the audiences for the many conference sessions during which I tried out portions of this material: ASTR seminar organizers Stanton Garner, Jr. ("Theatre and Medicine," 2006), Jean Graham-Jones and Adam Versenyi ("Tasting the Limits," 2004), Laurie-Beth Clark and Michael Peterson ("Performance Art Documentation," 2003), and Rhonda Blair and John Lutterbie (Cognitive Studies Working Group, 2008); Chase Bringardner for inviting me to participate in the ATHE Theory and Criticism Focus Group roundtable "Risking Theory/Theorizing Risk" in 2009, and Gad Guterman for organizing the panel "Theatre vs. Law," ATHE 2008; David Savran and the ASTR 2002 program committee for the opportunity to present material in a plenary session; Jill Stephenson for including me on the panel "Cognitive Theory and Medieval Performance" at the International Congress for Medieval Studies in 2009; and the program organizers for the *Société Internationale pour l'Étude du Théâtre Médiéval* in 2001, 2004, and 2007. I also thank the Medieval Studies group, the Institute for Women's Studies, and the Theatre and Film Studies Department at the University of Georgia for the opportunity to present portions of this work during its process. I wrote a large portion of this book at the Brooklyn Writers Space, that blessed sanctuary that Scott Adkins and Erin Courtney have created.

Catherine Jones, Graham A. Runnalls, and Robert L.A. Clark gave generous and invaluable help with translations from the Middle French, and Steven Smith helped with the Latin. Jessica Boon read many chapters and Chris Sieving the entire manuscript during the final stages of its development, and their comments have strengthened the argument and organization. Arnab Banerji and Alicia Corts painstakingly checked all of my citations. I am humbled by the many mistakes that they discovered and take full responsibility for any that remain. I thank Daniel Gundlach for preparing the index. Finally, Tony and Eli Dardis have been part of this project since its inception, and I thank them for sharing its pains and pleasures.

Chapter 4 incorporates a large portion of my essay "Whipping up Community: Reworking the Medieval Passion Play, from Ron Athey to Mel Gibson," published in *The Renaissance of Medieval Theatre*, ed. Véronique Dominguez (Academia Bruylant/Université Catholique de Louvain, 2009), reprinted here with permission of the Faculty of Arts, Université Catholique de Louvain, Belgium.

I thank *Modern Drama* for permission to reprint in chapter 1 material from "Antigone's Bodies: Performing Torture," *Modern Drama* 46.3 (2003): 381–403; and *European Medieval Drama* for allowing me to use in chapter 2 passages from "Painful Processions in Late-Medieval Paris," *European Medieval Drama* 6 (2003): 65–81. Joanne Tompkins and Jelle Koopmans, respectively, edited and improved these articles.

Chapter 3 incorporates, in substantially revised form, certain ideas first developed in "Spectator Response to Images of Violence: Seeing Apollonia," *Fifteenth-Century Studies* 27 (2001): 7–20, a volume edited by Edelgard du Bruck.

Introduction

During a civil conflict in 1411, the citizens of Paris watch as a group of traitors are loaded into a cart, wooden crosses clasped in their bound hands. The cart travels its ceremonial route to the scaffold, where the prisoners are stripped and beheaded. Their heads are stuck up on spears, their bodies hung on the gallows in sacks. The leader is dismembered and each of his limbs displayed over one of the city's gates. Parisians listen to the news brought by travelers: in the surrounding countryside, the opposing faction kills, rapes, holds for ransom, starts fires, and hangs its enemies by the thumbs or feet. Devout citizens meditate upon images in their books of hours: a young man shot full of arrows, another roasted on a grill; a young woman bound to an inclined plank while her teeth are yanked out, another bound to a pillar while her breast is hacked off. From time to time, they crowd into a specially built, open-air theatre: citizens playing Roman soldiers flog three men stretched out on planks and later use the latest in theatrical slight-of-hand to roast one of them on a grill, rake him with hooks, shut him up in a furnace, and cut off his head.

Near the end of 2005, visitors to the Guggenheim Museum in New York watch for seven hours as a celebrated body artist carves her skin with a razor blade, whips herself, and shivers on a bed of ice. On another night, her bed is a metal framework placed over burning candles. Downtown, another celebrated pain artist absent from the city for nearly a decade drags the Crisco-stuffed chicken wire breasts jutting out over his black leather corset down the narrow strip of floor between two rows of chairs, close enough to grease the spectators' shoes, singing his new opera named after a medieval torture device. At the Brooklyn Academy of Music, a celebrated French actress stands without moving, her body gradually clenching with pain, for the ninety minutes it takes her to perform the presuicide monologue of a now-dead playwright. At a left-leaning off-off-Broadway venue, a New York–Afghani collaboration features stylized beating, hanging, bombing, and beheading.

About all of these performances, I wonder not only why but also why now and why then. What cultural work do these painful spectacles perform? I propose that pain is unique among sensations, not because it is inexpressible or radically unshareable, but because it creates an urgent need to communicate things to which no one is eager to listen. Knowledge of the listener's reluctance in turn produces the sufferer's reticence to speak of things that cause distress. Yet we do speak and listen—sometimes wishing we could turn away, at other times fascinated. Not only that, we stage and watch spectacles that feature the body in pain: martyrdoms, plays about torture, actual tortures in the guise of plays, self-inflicted pain presented as conceptual art. The types of pain vary, as do the types of presentation. Because pain so powerfully solicits the spectator's engagement, aestheticized physical suffering plays a vital role in creating communities of sentiment and consolidating social memory, which in turn shapes the cultural and political realities that cause spectators to respond in different ways at different times. This book investigates performances of bodily suffering: live events in the course of which a performer either simulates or actually experiences physical pain. These parameters exclude plays in which a character describes suffering that occurs offstage or in the past as well as what we would commonly consider purely emotional suffering. From a scientific standpoint, though, this distinction is meaningless: pain is an emotion. So to be more precise, this study concerns the performance of pain by means of outward physical manifestation; that is, its bodily communication.

Each chapter of *Performing Bodies in Pain* compares a particular variety of twenty-first-century suffering to similar performances of pain from the late Middle Ages. I propose that the move toward modernity during the fourteenth and fifteenth centuries entailed stresses similar to those that we encounter now, as we move through a post-modernity also fraught with uncertainty, and that the body in pain provides an especially vital focus during these transitions. I am hardly alone in suggesting that medieval cruelty is perhaps a distant mirror for contemporary cruelties. For much of the twentieth century, scholarship focused on the otherness of medieval violence. Writing *The Autumn of the Middle Ages* in 1919, Johannes Huizinga chose "The Violent Tenor of Life" as title for his first chapter.[1] As his point of departure for *The Civilizing Process*, Norbert Elias characterized knights as "wild, cruel, prone to violent outbreaks and abandoned to the joy of the moment."[2] Popular culture has taken up the medieval as a short-cut reference to brutality. When a character in *Pulp Fiction* threatens to "get medieval," writer/director Quentin Tarantino relies upon his audience to understand the equation "medieval = extremely violent," not to imagine the man singing Gregorian chant, reciting a courtly romance, or laboring with oxen and plow.³

The news media rely upon the same familiar trope. Consider these examples from the *New York Times:* Somalia is described as "a throwback to medieval times" where "heavily armed warlords rule by brute force."⁴ An analyst argues that significant portions of Africa "slid back to the medieval age...mainly because of the ravages of war."⁵ A reviewer mentions "vicious, Medieval-style wars of siege and looting and rape...in the former Yugoslavia."⁶ And as the United States armed forces invade Iraq in April 2003, a front-page article describes the Iraqi people as suffering "the most medieval of punishments at the hands of Saddam Hussein's henchmen," but mentions no medieval methods of torture: no racks, no thumbscrews, no backs broken by the wheel, no drawing and quartering. The article does mention electrical shock, though, a method perfected by twentieth-century American experts.⁷

When I initially read about Parisian traitors dismembered after execution during the Hundred Years' War, their body parts hung from the city gates, corpses remaining on the gallows for months, these scenes seemed distant and nearly unimaginable. Then at the end of March 2004, people in Fallujah burned and ripped apart the bodies of four civilians working for an American security company and hung their remains from a bridge over the Euphrates River.⁸ Staring at a picture over breakfast, I felt sick, horrified, filled with despair, shocked at how little I had comprehended on an emotional level. Still, I was not physically present at such a scene. How was it different for people who were there? And among them, how was the experience different for Americans compared to Iraqis? The corpse display in Fallujah changed the tone for Western media, which had up to that point been carefully controlled and sanitized. Journalists had been embedded in military units, putting them in the middle of the action but at the same time limiting coverage—prohibiting photographs of casualties or coffins, for one thing. The U.S. government had learned from Vietnam not to broadcast the human cost of a war that it wanted to portray as a moral imperative, the bringing of freedom to a benighted land far away. But Al Jazeera and other Arabic news organizations showed the human cost of this war all along, and if people feel that they are not getting the whole story through regular channels these days, they turn to the Internet.

Charred American corpses swaying in the breeze over the Euphrates in 2004 served as emblems of a strong resistance for some spectators. For others, they helped to justify a continued American presence or showed the always-egregious atrocity of war, yet another reason not to have engaged in this one. Photos of the bodies soon gave way to photos of torture by Americans at Abu Ghraib prison. The *Chicago Tribune* chose not to print the picture of a dog lunging at a naked prisoner that made the first page of the *New York Times*. The Chicago editor pointed out that to print such pictures would suggest "knowledge that we do not possess yet about what was happening in each case" and, furthermore, would be "seen and reacted to negatively by people all over the world, and especially in the Islamic world."[9] Some *Washington Post* readers were irate that the paper was so slow to report the Abu Ghraib scandal; others accused it of damaging the country by publishing the photos and interpreted this as more evidence of the press's animosity toward George W. Bush.[10] Then in early May 2004, Islamic fundamentalists broadcast the beheading of Nicholas Berg on the Internet. The novelty lay in the broadcast, not the execution of a civilian. *Wall Street Journal* reporter Daniel Pearl had been executed in Pakistan two years earlier. The Berg beheading's success at generating horror in the West inspired copycat executions in Haiti, Thailand, and the Netherlands. By September 2004, more than a hundred foreigners had been kidnapped in Iraq and twenty-six executed.[11] At the time, it seemed that "the gruesome video of Nick Berg...trumped the Abu Ghraib pictures in public interest and in the revulsion it inspired."[12] Abu Ghraib has perhaps won out in the long run, however, as the symbol of an American identity crisis.

Suddenly, sadomasochistic (S/M) images were not fashionably sexy, as they had been only a few years earlier; instead, their sexual component was a source of widespread consternation. The public imagination had once again reshuffled its conceptual categories. The hooded figure was posed not by fine art photographer Robert Mapplethorpe but by Pfc. Lynndie England. The picture was not gorgeously printed on high-quality paper with fine-grained emulsion for display in an art gallery but circulated digitally via e-mail before hitting the mass media. As Susan Sontag notes, the fact that the soldiers "interleaved" pictures of sexual humiliation with pictures of their own sexual activities certainly speaks to the overwhelming presence and widespread acceptance of pornography and self-documentation in popular culture.[13] Having moved from the transgressive underground to mainstream culture, S/M has now shifted further, losing its high-style naughtiness and turning glum and mundane. Yet Frank Rich points out that attempts to blame these photos on the soldiers' "steady diet of MTV and pornography" shifts blame away from the Bush administration.[14] This particular scandal seemed to play itself out as low-level soldiers were punished and plea-bargained, but information about the American use of torture in the so-called war on terror continued to grow, including evidence that the United States pursued a policy of outsourcing torture to Syria, Egypt, and Uzbekistan.[15] The abuse at Abu Ghraib was apparently no aberration.

Ignoring the voluminous and persuasive argumentation against violent coercion as a means of gaining reliable information, the government apparently felt that it had no other way to combat "stateless" terrorists and no way to combat "rogue states" such as Iraq other than invasion. In 1984, Charles Krauthammer argued that international terrorism developed after 1968 in order to exploit the media: "Since the outlaws cannot buy television time, they have to earn it through terrorist acts," and Anthony Kubiak's 1991 *Stages of Terror* inverted the relationship. Kubiak suggested that "the media do not merely need and support terrorism, they construct it mimetically as a phenomenon... because American culture as a whole needs it, desires it, is fascinated by it, and utilizes it as a central impulse in its foreign and domestic policy."[16] Media and terror are so intimately bound together at this point in global culture that arguments about cause and effect may be beside the point. In Iraq, the television network that the U.S. occupation authority set up began broadcasting in 2005 a nightly reality show called *Terrorism in the Hands of Justice*, featuring captured Iraqi "insurgents" who confess at the prompting of an offstage interrogator to acts of violence. One regular viewer said: "For the first time, we saw those who claim to be jihadists as simple $50 murderers who would do everything in the name of Islam. Our religion is too lofty, noble and humane to have such thugs and killers. I wish they would hang them now, and in the same place where they did their crimes. They should never be given any mercy." A lawyer for Human Rights Watch warns that televised confessions most often result from coercion, and some of the featured insurgents have bruises and black eyes.[17] The audience for this reality show could hardly be farther removed from those who bought $50 tickets to the documentary theatre production *Guantánamo* in New York.[18] In both cases, the war on terror creates community and at the same time provides an evening's entertainment. Questions of appropriate location and audience have opened new frontiers of ethics and etiquette: Is it appropriate to watch a beheading in school? At work? To fake a beheading as part of a political campaign or as social commentary?[19]

The speed and global reach of the media that disseminate images and reports of this contemporary violence result in significant differences from seemingly similar medieval violence. Furthermore, medieval and postmodern performances reflect contrasting conceptions of the body: in the modern (and post-modern) world, bodies have rights, one of which is freedom from pain. The body is thus a site of control; the violated body a familiar sign of injustice. Theatre continues to rely upon a dualistic picture of the suffering body as separate from consciousness, even though biomedical research is developing more nuanced models of embodied sensation. Dramatized pain typically serves as a means to get at the consciousness of the person who inhabits the body, thereby also serving as a call to action for the spectator. Whether caused by injury or by illness, bodily suffering evokes outrage. In medieval drama, by contrast, suffering creates order. The onstage suffering of Christians is itself orderly, the result of formulaic ordeals and tortures, all of which mimic Christ's Passion. What happens to pagans is less predictable, suggesting that God creates an orderly universe for believers. Pain is part of that universe. In late-medieval France, performing bodies bore the traces of the Black Death, famines, and the Hundred Years' War. Saints' cults grew in number and popularity as people turned to them for miraculous cures. Like violence, illness was a commonplace occurrence to which one needed to respond appropriately, but it was neither a punishment nor a cause for sympathy, although illness and death did call for responsible actions by survivors. Medieval saint plays include nonviolent pain only in order to feature miraculous cures: crippling gout and muteness in *Le Mystère de Saint Sébastien*, death itself in *Le Geu Saint Denis*.

Twenty-first-century evangelicals seem inclined to return to a morally uncomplicated universe with the obligation to care only about the suffering of those who have been saved. Considering wealth to be a sign of virtue certainly makes dismantling social welfare programs less problematic. Attempts in 2005 by Christian conservatives to interfere with the judiciary and block the removal of Terri Schiavo's feeding tube stressed her innocence, as if allowing her to die after fifteen years in a coma would punish her. In contrast, the prisoners whose death warrants George W. Bush signed as governor of Texas were not proven innocent, even though their guilt may in some cases have been established through a miscarriage of justice. There seem to be at least two kinds of holy war going on in the early twenty-first century: one between the predominantly Christian industrialized nations and the international Islamic movement and another between fundamentalist religion and secular (post-)humanist society. In each struggle, both sides understand the value of pain.

The questions with which I begin are deceptively simple: Why perform pain? Why watch such a performance? Why this type of pain at this particular time? I ask these questions with respect to both actual and simulated physical pain, with the caveat that pain cannot really be separated into mental and physical categories or even components. I am interested in bodily performance; that is, not verbal descriptions but actions, not pain as a theme or symbol, not representations of the body as metaphor, but actual, material bodies that show the signs of pain. Pain experience, which includes both pain and pain behavior, occurs within the realm of social relations and helps to shape those relations. Pain experience also shapes culture. Most of the performances with which I am concerned take place within the aesthetic framework of the theatre or the art gallery but are densely interwoven with other cultural performances of pain. Explicit framing devices make the art and theatre events easier to read. At the same time, though, referential transparency can obscure performative effect. For example, I discuss a play depicting torture that was initially performed within a state that regularly utilized torture. Such plays have been evaluated as mirrors of these societies or even of human nature. But what do the depiction and the practice *do*? Do they perform the same actions, or different ones? As I explore these questions, my primary focus is spectator reception. Who is watching the pain, what do they make of it, how do they arrive at an interpretation, and what does the experience of watching make of them? To what extent is pain a source of identity? Could we, at the dawn of the twenty-first century, do without suffering as a means to define ourselves both as individuals and as imagined communities?

Each chapter analyzes a particular performance that I've seen in New York since 2001 together with a comparable performance of pain from late-medieval France, taking into account the difference in these two cultures' understanding of body, spirit, and pain, and relating the performances to their historical context. I chose New York not only because it has been my base of operations during most of the time that I've spent working on this project but also as the center of the present cultural moment that I'm trying to understand. I finished the dissertation from which this book grew on September 10, 2001, and was preparing to deliver it to my committee as the planes hit the towers of the World Trade Center. That event galvanized American response to spectacular suffering, brought it unavoidably into our political and ethical foreground, and gave my project a new immediacy. All of the issues and problems were present already, but this nation has since been forced to look at things from which we had preferred to avert our eyes. As I've reevaluated my questions in the aftermath of 9/11, I've found more performances of physical pain on New York stages than I had during the late 1990s—meaning that I've had the chance to see performances of plays and by body artists that I had previously known only through documentation. I must acknowledge the narrow scope of my inquiry and stress that I don't consider New York or the United States to be any more important than other parts of the world. But they have so far been the center of my world, and I do believe that my own response as a spectator is the most solid ground from which to build. Thus I define my own location with respect to the questions that I raise, and I write from that position. I also suggest wider implications and look forward to scholarship that will expand the analysis that I undertake here.

My medieval scope is similarly narrow, although, of course, I must struggle to imaginatively locate myself within this distant culture. I chose fourteenth- and fifteenth-century France because of the relatively accessible corpus of extant saint plays from this time and place. The plays being French, I read them against as deep and localized a context as possible. Paris gets particular focus because of the city's vexed position during the Hundred Years' War, changing hands repeatedly from one French faction to another and for a number of years under English rule. The theology and medical history presented here are not all French in origin but would have been both available and influential there. I must acknowledge my debt to medieval drama scholars who specialize in archival research, and my choice of materials relies upon what they have made available in modern editions. Here again, I look forward to the work of other scholars with the requisite competence addressing the performance of pain in medieval Spain, Italy, and Germany. Unfortunately, if England did stage saint plays full of bloody suffering (and there is reason to think that this was the case), the play texts have not survived.

I must stress that this is not a narrative of historical progress, given that similar formations exist in both the late-medieval and post-modern periods. For both periods, the discussion is filled out with other aesthetic and historical examples along with the theoretical tools best suited to the particular type of performative pain, and I refer to the scientific literature on pain where it helps to elucidate the argument. The terms compassion, sympathy, empathy, and pity are notoriously slippery. I will be using each term with a precise meaning, which I discuss at greater length in the relevant chapters. To summarize briefly: I use "empathy" for the preconscious activation of a matching emotional state; that is, feeling someone's pain without making an ethical judgment about it or even necessarily being fully conscious of one's own response. This is the most inclusive form of response and is explored in chapter 1. In the post-modern period, "sympathy" means imagining the pain of another and includes the judgment that the suffering is not justified. Sympathy thus largely overlaps with "pity," crucial to the ethical framework for spectator response to pain that I adopt from Luc Boltanski's *Distant Suffering*. The medieval notion of sympathy is quite different and more concrete, tied to astrology and Galenic medicine. I restrict my use of "compassion" to its pre-modern sense of suffering together with another person, with no obligation to provide relief.

This book is organized in three sections, the first of which addresses the role of pain in the state's power over individuals. Chapter 1, "Feeling Torture," shows how the actors John Kani and Winston Ntshona use recognizable pain behavior to evoke spectators' empathic response in situations that their play *The Island* frames as torture, in order to develop an effective politics of pity. This framework depends upon the notion that one has a right to live without pain, which was inconceivable during the Middle Ages. The torments of Saint Denis in a late-medieval dramatization of his martyrdom, in contrast, encourage the private spiritual practice of compassionate vision. Contemporary cognitive science explains how empathy operates to bring individuals into a caring relation, whereas the medieval optics that provide a parallel reception theory concern themselves with the impressions formed upon the inner, spiritual senses. I argue that theatrical pain serves a vital function in producing concerted public action within post-modern culture's dispersed public spheres, and that the physical community of medieval urban culture meant that the saint play was not required to serve this purpose.

Chapter 2, "Imagining Death," also contrasts pre- and post-modern frameworks for conceptualizing spectator response; here, different notions of sympathy produce opposite strategies with respect to pain and capital punishment. The understanding of sympathy prevalent since the eighteenth century explains how we extend ourselves to imagine the pain of death—which in fact might not hurt. In deference to the public's feelings, the United States does its utmost to eliminate any signs of suffering when it puts someone to death, even as it relies upon execution to signify functional justice. The very different medieval notion of sympathy as a radical connectedness makes it desirable that everyone, even a condemned criminal or traitor, die a good death. Thus along with the pain-evoking mutilation that makes for a memorable execution, late-medieval France added the rituals of confession and contrition in order to reincorporate the condemned with the Christian community. This chapter analyzes the deaths in *Le Geu Saint Denis* and Martin McDonagh's *The Pillowman* together with the relics that they leave to continue performing in the world: the medieval play features the saint's head, which does God's work as a physical artifact without needing any internal thought process. The post-modern play leaves us a collection of pain-filled stories, the product of the condemned writer's imagination and a shadow of the playwright's oeuvre, challenging us to find an alternative catalyst for moral action.

The book's second section explores self-inflicted pain as a performance of individual power with respect to the lifeworld, taking gender into account. Two artists who perform actual rather than simulated pain within an aesthetic but not dramatic framework comprise the post-modern examples. Unable to access exact parallels for the medieval period, I triangulate between the public but not aestheticized performance of actual suffering and the visual representation of a martyr's torments. In each case, the image makes visible a crucial tension between the sacred body in pain sanctioned by the medieval church and the laity's voluntary performance of suffering. In chapter 3, "Enduring Ecstasy," I argue that the fifteenth-century miniature *The Martyrdom of Saint Apollonia,* illustrating a typical virgin-martyr scenario, activates a productive tension between the church's active disempowerment of women during the later Middle Ages and the spectacularly painful raptures of female mystics. Post-modern body artist Marina Abramović also frames her endurance rituals in mystical terms, and her early work emerged amid feminist efforts toward empowerment. Her 2005 reperformance of seminal body art actions, including her own *Lips of Thomas,* neutralizes the political force that the original performances exerted during the 1960s and 1970s. In both periods, the very ambiguity that provides an opening through which women can speak also encourages cooptation and reabsorption into hegemonic discourse.

The relation between masculinity and masochism occupies chapter 4, "Whipping Up Community." Both the fourteenth-century altarpiece *Martyrdom of Saint Sebastian and Scenes from his Life* and penitential processions of men whipping themselves appealed to God for protection from plague. The early modern imagination sexualized both the saint and the act of flagellation, and I argue against reading a modern masochism back onto the medieval phenomenon. I further argue that this construct cannot encompass Ron Athey's frankly erotic and emphatically queer performances of pain, such as his recent *Judas Cradle*. The marketing of masochism as a masculine performative during the twentieth century helped to bring his torture trilogy to widespread attention during the 1990s, but American presenters have backed away since then. Both the medieval flagellant and the post-modern pain artist perform for the sake of their community, the former as an appeal to God and the latter to help the community coalesce in defiance of persistent homophobia. But because both present a threat to the existing social order, their respective cultures overwrite their pain with less dangerous figures of masochistic masculinity.

The final section of this book comprises a single chapter that brings together threads from the first two sections. Chapter 5, "Containing Chaos," focuses on performances of chaotic violence that seem to invert and disrupt structures of power. *Le Mystère de Saint Sébastien* shows evil as an inversion of God's good creation. The hierarchy of devils issuing forth from this play's Hell mirrors the hierarchy that Jesus commands in Heaven; in a duplicate inversion, Diocletian and Sebastian are at the pinnacles of their respective hierarchies on Earth. A *sot* or fool complicates this play's structure, though, straddling the boundary between the world of the play and that of its spectators. I argue that this character, like the other grotesque elements of the saint play, serves to reaffirm order as a defense against chaotic social transformation. In the post-modern period, the extreme brutality and impossibly dark humor of Sarah Kane's *Blasted* never restore a viable order to the dramatic world that she shatters. Instead, they draw us into an experience of abjection in order to rehearse our own perseverance in the face of real-world pain and violence. Kane's plays give us tools for surviving in a world without order.

In addition to looking for similarities, I identify the important conceptual and material differences between the pre- and the post-modern. Although each chapter addresses what seems to be one type of pain, cross-historical comparison complicates the picture, as does variation within each period. Not presuming a unified audience or a single response to any performance, I argue that since pain is not a single sensation but differs between individuals, between times and cultures, and also between the types of pain that a given individual might experience, there is no reason to look for a single cultural function for performances of pain. I turn to biomedical research on pain, communication, and cognition in order to explore the ways in which we know that the performer is "in pain" and whether the pain is real or simulated. I have not made a wholehearted cognitive turn, however, and critical theory remains vital to the analysis of the relation between the current historical moment and each particular type of performative pain.

Before moving on to extended analyses of specific examples, I will present a more generalized theoretical framework for understanding performances of pain, discussing first, how pain works within the bodymind of the one who suffers, and second, how it works between people. I will begin by summarizing recent biomedical theories of pain and medieval counterparts, often but not always theological. My argument will not push this point, but I consider science and theology to be equivalent as dominant structures of belief for these two periods.

FEELING PAIN

For most of the twentieth century, the common understanding of pain hewed closely to Descartes' description three centuries earlier of the nerves as a bell rope pulled by a painful stimulus (such as fire burning the skin of the foot) and then ringing the pain "bell" in the brain. In this traditional view, pain signals damage of some sort. If no such damage is present, then a psychological problem must be creating false pain sensation. Although most dramatic deployments of pain still presume a clear cause-and-effect relation of injury to pain, scientific research began transforming popular conceptions of pain when the discovery of endorphins in the 1970s added the runner's high to the lexicon. The increasing visibility since the 1980s of chronic pain syndromes has continued this alteration, as newly emergent ailments seem to keep pace with advances in pain relief. I would go so far as to suggest a paradigm shift, barely visible in the dramatic literature that this book's first section investigates but quite important for the body art featured in its second. Current research progresses so quickly that some of what I discuss here will undoubtedly be superseded by the time of publication; however, a summary contributes to our understanding of pain's physiological as well as sociological complexity.

A major alternative to the Cartesian model of pain emerged in 1965, when Ronald Melzack and Patrick Wall formulated gate control theory: the spinal cord transmits pain signals up to the brain, but at the same time special fibers modulate the signals, as do messages that the brain sends down.[20] With injury, the type of neural transmission varies with the type of tissue damage, the circumstances of the injury, and the passage of time. Different types of nerve fiber encode and process noxious stimuli: the thin, myelinated A delta fibers and the bare, fine C fibers respond immediately to pressure, temperature, and chemical changes, both sending electrical impulses to the dorsal horn of the spinal cord. Surrounding cells augment these signals. This is immediate gate control. But the larger, myelinated A beta fibers also fire in response to noxious stimuli as well as to more benign sensations. When they do, small cells surrounding the dorsal horn then turn off the signal. Causing the A beta fibers to fire can thus mute the firing that the A delta or C fibers initiate. Massage and transcutaneous nerve stimulation (TENS) relieve pain by stimulating the A beta fibers, causing the inhibitory cells to diminish input from the others as well. The brain also sends down messages that augment or diminish the firing of cells in the dorsal horn, and psychological pain management modalities focus on these brain-down signals. Pain doesn't stop with the immediate injury, of course. As time passes, the C fibers react to chemicals including those leaking from damaged cells, cell debris broken down by enzymes, and peptides from the nerves themselves. Eventually, the processes of inflammation also bathe the C fibers with chemicals that they transmit to the spinal cells. In the case of a sudden, traumatic injury, the central nervous system blocks the sharp and immediate pain transmitted by electrical impulses from A delta and C fibers, but the C fibers later transmit chemical signals and pain does develop.[21]

More recently, Melzack and other scientists postulate a central pain matrix comprising precise portions of the brain. They base their assertions on studies using positron emission tomography (PET) and functional magnetic resonance imaging (fMRI) to observe pain-related brain activity in human subjects.[22] The science may be new, but the concept is not: Melzack points out that Descartes posited a second stage during which the soul transforms the message sent via the nerves into conscious experience. Melzack and other pain researchers are now studying this second stage of pain perception. They do not speak of a soul or nonphysical mind residing in the central portion of the brain but of a body-self neuromatrix that can actually generate pain.[23] Research into phantom limb pain is instrumental for understanding the brain's role in pain; in particular, phantom pain continues even when no signal can reach the brain because sections of the spinal cord are removed. Amputees often experience phantom limb sensations so vivid that they attempt to use the phantom—to step out of bed onto an absent foot, for example. The phantom fills a prosthesis as if it were a glove, and the phantom foot may feel wet when the artificial foot steps in a puddle. These sensations are not merely remembered but are felt on an ongoing basis. For 70 percent of amputees, the sensations include pain. Furthermore, the amputees perceive the phantom as an integral part of the body. Attempts to treat phantom limb pain began with the assumption that the cut nerve endings in the amputation stump continue to generate impulses; however, the phantom remains even when these nerves are cut, the spinal pathways severed, or the areas of the thalamus and cortex that receive the impulses removed. These measures provide only temporary pain relief. Gate-control theory proposed that spinal cord neurons produced phantom limbs by firing spontaneously after the amputation removed their normal sensory input, sending the same impulses to the cortex that the missing limb would have sent. But this explanation is also inadequate, because lower body phantoms exist even when the spinal cord is severed above the level of the spinal neurons that would produce them. In the case of one paraplegic who experienced lower body pain although his spinal cord was broken just below the neck, touching his head and neck produced activity in the part of the thalamus that normally responds to stimulation of the body below the break. One might think that these sensations exist because the somatosensory thalamus or cortex has in effect rewired itself, enabling signals to flow across previously unused synapses; however, removing the affected parts of the brain does not eliminate either the phantom limb or its pain.[24] Ongoing research is extensive and fascinating; for example, V.S. Ramachandran has successfully used mirrors to cure phantoms and related disorders.[25]

Melzack argues that more of the brain is involved than just the somatosensory system. He postulates the existence of a neuromatrix, defined as a neural network that responds to sensory stimulation and also generates a neurosignature; that is, "a characteristic pattern of impulses indicating that the body is intact and unequivocally one's own."[26] When a peripheral body part stops sending sensory input, the neuromatrix takes over and recreates it. In addition to (1) the sensory pathway through the thalamus to the somatosensory cortex, the neuromatrix includes (2) pathways through the brain stem's reticular formation to the limbic system, along with (3) the parietal lobe and other portions of the cortex involved in evaluating sensory input. Melzack includes the second pathway, which is involved with emotion and motivation, because of the affective vocabulary that amputees use to describe phantom limb sensations. The third pathway is important to self-recognition. Melzack notes that "patients who have suffered a lesion of the parietal lobe in one hemisphere have been known to push one of their own legs out of a hospital bed because they were convinced it belonged to a stranger."[27] He believes that these three systems analyze sensory signals in parallel, share information about them, and convert them into an integrated output that other parts of the brain transform into conscious perception. He does not suggest where or how that transformation occurs, but proposes that the neuromatrix imprints the output with its neurosignature.

Melzack's conception of the neuromatrix is similar to the cell assembly that Donald O. Hebb first proposed, with simultaneous sensory input creating stronger connections across the synapses between the brain cells that it activates. Hebb envisioned neural networks built up through experience. But because many people born without a limb experience a vivid phantom, Melzack argues that the neuromatrix is genetically prewired and then modified by experience: "For example, an intelligent and serious eight-year-old boy, who was born with paralyzed legs and a right arm that ends at the elbow, tells us that when he fits his elbow into a small cup so as to manipulate a lever that allows him to move his wheelchair, phantom fingers, 'like everyone else's fingers,' emerge from his elbow and grasp the edges of the cup."[28] Melzack suggests that different types of activity in the neuromatrix might be responsible for different types of phantom pain—as well as phantom seeing and hearing. The bursts of activity that compensate for loss of sensory input might produce burning pain, and powerful signals to the muscles that would move an absent or paralyzed limb might produce cramping or shooting pain. He summarizes: "The brain does more than detect and analyze inputs; it generates perceptual experience even when no external inputs occur. We do not need a body to feel a body."[29] A.D. Craig proposes that the right anterior insula maintains a metarepresentation of the physiological state of all body tissues and produces "the subjective image of the material self as a feeling (sentient) entity, that is, emotional awareness."[30] He categorizes pain, along with temperature, itch, hunger, and thirst as "homeostatic emotions" because they "reflect the survival needs of the body" and "drive behavior."[31]

Locating the origin of at least some types of pain in the brain rather than in the peripheral nervous system does not make them any less physical, of course. Whatever its mechanism, pain produces clear physical effects; in particular, it "disrupts the brain's homeostatic regulation systems, thereby producing 'stress' and initiating complex programs to reinstate homeostasis."[32] Whether initiated by physical or psychological factors, stress releases cortisol and noradrenaline (norepinephrine). Cortisol ensures the high level of glucose required for fight or flight, but prolonged cortisol release also "breaks down the protein in muscle and inhibits the ongoing replacement of calcium in bone," and it "suppresses the immune system."[33] Stress thus contributes to multiple sorts of pain syndromes, including some that are autoimmune diseases: this helps to explain why prolonged or repeated acute pain may lead to mystifying chronic pain disorders. Science no longer ties pain to its stimulus but, instead, defines it as a subjective and emotional experience. The commonly accepted definition dates from 1979: "Pain is an unpleasant sensory and emotional experience associated with actual or potential tissue damage, or described in terms of such damage."[34]

The desire for precise descriptions of pain has increased over the past thirty years along with the complexity of pain theory, the specificity and multiplicity of treatments, and the incidence of chronic pain complaints. Hospitals and pain centers now use various versions of the McGill Pain Questionnaire to quantify pain intensity and quality.[35] Melzack and Wall propose that definitions of "pain" are circular and unsatisfactory because the word "represents a *category* of experiences, signifying a multitude of different, unique experiences having different causes and characterized by different qualities varying along a number of sensory and affective dimensions."[36] For this reason, we generally define pain and pleasure through opposition to one another and by listing synonyms. The category "pain" is distinguished from "pleasure" by its aversiveness.

SHARING PAIN

For the past twenty years, theatre and performance scholars have repeatedly cited Elaine Scarry's claims that pain is a special sort of sensation because it resists objectification in language, that pain actively destroys language, and that pain is uniquely private and invisible. Although *The Body in Pain* remains invaluable as a groundbreaking analysis of torture, and I will find it useful to my own argument at certain points, it doesn't really tell us enough about pain. Scarry's authority on the relation between pain and language is Virginia Woolf's essay "On Being Ill": "English, which can express the thoughts of Hamlet and the tragedy of Lear, has no words for the shiver and the headache...The merest schoolgirl, when she falls in love, has Shakespeare and Keats to speak for her; but let a sufferer try to describe a pain in his head to a doctor and language at once runs dry."[37]

Scarry argues that physical pain "resists objectification in language" because it "has no referential content. It is not *of* or *for* anything."[38] I would object that one is not cold, hot, sleepy, or exhilarated *for* something. Like pain, these sensations all have causes but no objects. Like pain, they can insist upon one's attention in a most disruptive manner. To contend that pain destroys language entails a dualistic conception of the body and its sensations as something that must be transcended—as that which is expelled in order to define consciousness. Woolf begins her essay with the observation that "with a few exceptions...literature does its best to maintain that its concern is with the mind; that the body is a sheet of plain glass through which the soul looks straight and clear."[39] This view entails a conception of consciousness as that which is *not* physical. Pain insists on its physicality; therefore, pain is incompatible with transcendence. But language does not require transcendence, nor does consciousness. Woolf herself goes on to correct the pretense of literature: Far from being a transparent sheet of glass, "all day, all night the body intervenes" in consciousness, so that "the creature within can only gaze through the pane—smudged or rosy."[40] Just as consciousness is not isolated from the material body, pain is never merely physical; that is, it never exists in isolation from the mind.

The idea that pain cannot be communicated has an experiential basis in the fact that one can only imagine, not feel, the pain of another. Scarry says that, to the individual experiencing it, great pain is "overwhelmingly present, more emphatically real than any other human experience," and yet this experience is nearly invisible to anyone else.[41] But no sensation, emotion, or mental state can be transparently shared or fully communicated. All are nearly invisible. Yet although other varieties of sensory experience can be (and have been) used to discuss mimesis, the incommensurability of experience, and the mind/body problem, philosophers over and over again single out pain as an especially profound problem.[42] Murat Aydede and Güven Güzeldere suggest one plausible reason for philosophy's persistent focus on pain: it cannot be studied without considering subjective experience. Although the International Association for the Study of Pain defines pain in a single sentence with reference to tissue damage, a much longer qualifying note follows immediately and insists so forcefully upon the primacy of subjective experience as to give the impression of completely severing pain from any physical or physiological signs: I'm in pain if I say I am. Aydede and Güzeldere argue that pain is fundamentally different from other perceptual modalities, which can be mistaken; for example, "looking at a piece of bush in the garden and mistaking it for a cat, hearing the alarm clock and mistaking it for the telephone."[43] One difference is that we're interested in what we see, hear, or touch, rather than in the experience of perception; with pain, by contrast, our immediate concern is the pain experience rather than the object of the experience. This is of critical importance, since we cannot always identify such an object. In the case of phantom limb pain, it would seem that no such object exists although ongoing research suggests that we may soon understand the nature of the object even in this puzzling case. In the meantime, Aydede and Güzeldere identify the subjective nature of pain experience as an advantage for philosophy of mind, because "it forces the neuroscientist to pay more attention to the phenomenological information which seems to be available in introspection; it forces the neuroscientist to focus more on attempts to relate neuroscientific findings and mechanisms at the subpersonal level to what appears to be the case in pain reports at the personal level expressing subjectively accessible information." This in turn "practically forces the neuroscientist to assume that there have to be neural correlates (subpersonal mechanisms) of experience."[44] Here again, though, pain does not differ significantly from other sensations such as cold or exhilaration.

I further propose that pain seems different from other types of sensation because (1) the *other* person's pain tends to put an end to communication from the receptive end, and (2) the person in pain has a need to communicate unlike that produced by any other sensation. In the case of acute pain, the pursuit of relief temporarily disrupts normal discourse. In the case of chronic pain, the sufferer tends to become absorbed in the pain. Customary behavior patterns can be altered beyond recognition, and one feels like one has lost the other to pain. The person may still communicate, obsessively even, about the *pain*—but this is so unlike that to which one was accustomed that the person communicating no longer seems to be the same person. Upon quoting the same passage from Virginia Woolf that Scarry uses, Melzack and Wall propose that language runs dry not because words to describe pain do not exist but because one has little opportunity to use them; moreover, the words often seem absurd.[45]

One has little opportunity to use pain words not because one has little experience of pain, but because one assumes—correctly or not—that no one wants to hear them. Communication often ends because recipients cannot tolerate the messages that are being sent. I have felt helpless because I could do nothing to alleviate the suffering of a loved one and at the same time resisted imagining the sensations he endured, thereby rendering his pain incommunicable from my end rather than his. Medical anthropologist Jean Jackson says that many patients feel that they can effectively communicate about their pain for the first time when they join the community of sufferers at a chronic pain center: "In the outside world you don't want to talk about yourself, you don't want to hear about others. Here are people who are willing to listen to you."[46] Another chronic pain patient who happened to be a physician himself told Arthur Kleinman, "Pain is too much for physicians to deal with. Most of us can't tolerate listening to people in pain. We want patients who get better, or better yet if they don't they shouldn't complain."[47]

Furthermore, pain differs from other sensations precisely because of the urgency that it lends to communication. One would be hard pressed to imagine a situation in which someone felt compelled to communicate pleasure in order to put an end to the sensation. A person in pain not only asks for tangible help but also gains a measure of relief by talking. For example, Kleinman relates his experience during medical school with a young burn victim who suffered terribly during her daily debridement. In the face of her screams and pleading, he finally asked her to describe her experience. The treatment did not change, but as she began to talk about her pain during the sessions, she became more able to tolerate them and stopped fighting the medical team.[48] Didier Anzieu, also discussing burn victims, calls this a "bath of words" that replaces the damaged skin as container and map of the self.[49]

Medical anthropologists record the urgency with which chronic pain patients describe their experience, which resists objectification because of the variety and instability of sensations. A patient known as "Brian" reports a pain that he sometimes thinks is TMJ (temporomandibular joint disorder) and at other times thinks is a product of depression, which "erupts in different places in your body. It comes in my head, then I have pains in my chest, I don't know what that's all about...."⁵⁰ Although Brian cannot find an adequate expression, Byron Good notes that he is "wonderfully and frighteningly articulate."⁵¹ He experiences an urgent need to name the pain because naming would be equivalent to diagnosis and hold out the promise of relief; however, the nature of his pain syndrome makes such naming impossible. This is not because pain cannot be objectified but because his syndrome is so diverse and changeable. As a counterexample to Woolf, I offer the following description by a forty-two-year-old woman of the headaches from which she has suffered for a decade:

> My pain is a screech against an open, ripped, upside down sky. And the sky is my head, jagged and tearing, tearing, tearing. Sometimes I think it's on backwards because my teeth are in the wrong place. How can your own teeth gnash your own temple otherwise? The same way your temple is a fist all doubled up to really smash you with those steel knuckles, first icy cold, then fire hot; then flashes out in tough, ragged mandarin nails to scrape that same spot over and over. And there's a bruise—blue and purple and blood red—in the back of your eye. Your ear is being ripped off and the blood isn't blood but fire, stabbing in centimeter by centimeter down the back of your neck. And your neck fights back. It wants to be the sky so it sends the lightning back boxerlike in stiff jabs and explosion punches. Your teeth erupt and pelt you in the face; your ear bursts open and pastes itself against your eye; your eye recoils and shoots out through your temple and the blades and the whistles and the symbols [sic] and the blackboard chalk and the bombs and the jets all go off at the same time in a piercing scream. Then the rocket attached to the electric drill attached to the razors zooms down exactly on target to the temple. And a minute has passed.⁵²

This chronic-headache sufferer finds plenty of English words to describe her pain. I quote the passage in its entirety partly because it achieves its effect by accumulating images. The description is not succinct, but neither is Shakespeare or Virginia Woolf always succinct.

Those who suffer chronic pain communicate about it at great length, verbally and nonverbally. I have watched my own disappearance from the lifeworld of such a sufferer as her pain became more and more absorbing to her and distressing for me. Similarly, the breach long ago between my world and that of my father began in his pain episodes and was finalized only by death. I suggest that, for the witness, the experience of one's own disappearance from the world of the person in pain can be intolerable and often enough accounts for our readiness to shut down communication from the receptive end. But pain in art is qualitatively different from the pain in life: watching the central character in *Wit* suffer through stage-four ovarian cancer and experimental chemotherapy is radically different from witnessing the suffering of either a loved one or a stranger.[53] *Wit* allowed me to reclaim part of the pain-watching experience without having the communicative process shut down. In the theatre, the spectator remains part of the same world as the actor not only during the pain episodes, but even after death. The fact that theatrical pain is simulated is beside the point. Even if a performer experiences real pain, as is the case with the body and endurance art events that I discuss in the second section of this book, the artist creates the context and structures the event as a communicative act. But the meaning of the act depends upon the spectator and includes the spectator's assumptions about the communicative intent of the artist, the actor, the playwright, or whoever is thought to be communicating. Performance implies both intentionality and interpretation.

MEDIEVAL PAIN

These issues present even greater difficulties for medieval materials. How do we assess the performative effect of a saint play or a public execution? Do we assume that contemporary neuroscience is at last uncovering the truth about the biological mechanisms of perception and sensation, equally explanatory for long-dead spectators? I do tend to believe this, but I also think that we lose a great deal if we fail to consider how medieval people understood their world, including their bodily experience. Although medieval people had greater contact with death and with physical suffering than we do, there's no reason to think that they were less sensitive to pain or that spiritual understanding enabled them to accept it calmly. Suffering was a part of daily life, but they viewed it with horror. The miracle collections hold ample evidence that people feared surgical pain and sought the intervention of saints as an alternative; for example, praying to Apollonia, whose teeth were destroyed during her martyrdom, for relief from toothache. Although there was no very effective anesthesia, and many surgeons argued that the available soporifics were too dangerous to use, physicians sought to alleviate suffering. The analgesic properties of plants had been known and cultivated since antiquity.[54]

In her historically continuous survey of pain from the Hippocratic corpus to the present, Roselyne Rey credits the influence of Stoics rather than Christianity for what appears to be "silence or disregard for pain" in the Middle Ages, since Stoic philosophy considered moral virtue to be the greatest good and thus devalued the body. Rey notes that in antiquity, pain was considered not a signal but a disorder, with no positive value.⁵⁵ Both Ancient Egypt and Mesopotamia attributed pain to invading demons or other supernatural forces. The notion that there might be natural causes begins with the Hippocratic physicians in the fifth century BCE, as do the theories of elements and humors that remained central to medicine through the Renaissance. Democritus substituted for demonic agents a notion of irregularly shaped atoms with hooks painfully stimulating the small atoms of the soul in a particular part of the body. Plato postulated that the noxious atoms were instead sharp triangles poking into the veins to disturb the mortal soul in the liver and heart or even to disrupt the immortal soul's rational operations in the cerebrum. Like Plato, Aristotle considered both pain and pleasure to be passions of the soul, but Aristotle acknowledged the link between these passions and the sense of touch. Blood and the heart were central to his conception of mind and sensation, with waves of pain and pleasure traveling along the blood vessels to the heart. Hot blood or a soft heart could cause pain. Like Aristotle, Galen believed that external objects leave impressions upon the body's soft stuff and that excessive stimulation produces pain, but he shifted the locus of control and perception to nerves and brain.⁵⁶ These ideas contributed to medieval theories of sensation and cognition, which chapter 1 discusses at greater length.

Galen elaborated the notion that an imbalance of humors was responsible for the pain associated with illness, and his second-century texts formed the foundation for medieval medicine. Both the Hippocratic corpus and Galen addressed the fact that the site of pain sensation can be quite distant from the site of injury. Galen developed the notion of sympathy to explain how a malady or pain in one organ can spread to another even though no nerves or vessels connect the two locations, such as the head and liver, reproductive organs and vocal apparatus, or stomach and many other organs or areas. Although by the seventeenth century scientists were criticizing this as a failure of rational thought or a species of occultism, neither the phenomenon nor the ideas disappeared.⁵⁷ Chapter 2 treats sympathy and its transformations at greater length.

Scholastic physicians discussed pain not directly but in the context of disease and treatments. They classified types of pain and argued about the classifications, using as a basis Avicenna's eleventh-century categorization of pain into fifteen categories—many of them corresponding to those in use by the McGill Pain Questionnaire. In general, they divided pains into those caused by trauma and those resulting from humoral imbalances, and descriptions of illness indicate that they considered pain to be a problem in and of itself, not merely a diagnostic sign.⁵⁸ Medieval medicine relied upon study and rational debate rather than upon experiment. There was no dissection until the sixteenth century. Galen had vivisected animals, but this practice disappeared until the eighteenth century. The reported vivisection of live criminals by Herophilus (ca. 330–260 BCE) and Erasistratus (304–245 BCE) of Alexandria was not resumed.[59] Given the limited effectiveness of herbs and the soporifics available for surgery, people resorted to the intervention of saints. Given our growing understanding of pain as a bodymind phenomenon and the impact of psychological treatment modalities, we should not denigrate approaches to pain borne of medical ignorance and superstition. On the other hand, we should not romanticize the holistic herbal approach, the "innocence" of pre-Enlightenment civilization. Nor should we assume that medieval conceptions of pain were uniform and static. The late-medieval culture of pain with which this study is concerned follows upon the decimation of Europe by the first onslaught of the Black Death between approximately 1347 and 1350. The fact that doctors trained in scholastic medicine were helpless in the face of the plague undermined their authority and helped to pave the way for change: all sorts of practitioners sold remedies, and in order to compete, physicians began to incorporate these things—including alchemy and magic—into their practice. They also stepped up efforts to control such nonacademic practitioners as midwives, surgeons, and apothecaries. The Black Death transformed medieval medicine as physicians began to reject the ancient authorities and the universities began to favor the teaching of practice over a strictly theoretical education.[60]

One might be tempted here to move from this notion of the plague experience as a positive force for change into a metaphorical conflation of plague and theatre, in the manner of Artaud, which slides all too easily into a stereotype of plague everywhere and always, witch trials, trial by ordeal, the Inquisition, boiling oil. Some of these phenomena will indeed appear within these chapters; others will not, because they belong earlier or later than the saint plays that provide my dramatic focus. And rather than covering all available material, I choose to delve into a few sources and to embed them in a rich and deep context. I believe that these examples are emblematic of a particular slice of time and particularly appropriate for comparison to our own performances and their milieu. As medieval Europeans understood very well, "symbols are matters of relationships which must in some way be publicly recognized and remembered—they are not absolutes, but function entirely within social life."[61] Late-medieval social life wove commemoration of martyrdom together with private torture and public execution. To my twenty-first-century eyes, these spectacles seem to function within coherent symbolic systems; my world, to be anything but coherent. Yet this perception owes more to my immersion in the contemporary world than to the coherence of the past. A subsidiary aim of my project is, indeed, to break apart the uniform and unified Middle Ages as a simple cultural signifier or easily viewable mirror for the modern world. Even scholars, if they do not specialize in the period, far too often conceive of a medieval world in terms not that far removed from the opening scenes of *Monty Python and the Holy Grail*, which collapses roughly six centuries of pain together indiscriminately: identifying the year as 932 AD, the image of a body raised up on a wheel leads into a sketch about plague; during combat, King Arthur cuts off the limbs of a black knight one by one; and a procession of monks solemnly hitting themselves in the face with boards leads into a witch trial. I certainly don't criticize this film for historical inaccuracy, but in using the Middle Ages as a lens with which to examine the world in which we are enmeshed, it behooves us to be specific about *which* Middle Ages.[62]

1. Feeling Torture ∽

Plate 1 Photograph of John Kani and Winston Ntshona in *The Island* at the Brooklyn Academy of Music, April 2003. © Richard Termine. Courtesy: BAM Archives.

The play begins with a loud siren and a spotlight on the central area of the empty stage, then a blackout. The lights come back up on John Kani and Winston Ntshona digging and digging, then occasionally pushing an (invisible) wheelbarrow across the stage to dump the contents where the other man digs. The actors show the effort required to raise the wheelbarrow with a grunt, planting the feet wide, gritting the teeth, clenching the jaw, lifting with the whole body, walking bent over. After fifteen minutes of this, they show relief at the removal of (invisible) manacles by rubbing their wrists. Kani holds and turns his ankle, then gingerly touches his leg. Ntshona touches his eye, crawls on his hands and knees, and shakes stiff fingers just in front of the eye. Kani unzips his pants, pretends to urinate into his hands, and attempts to wash Ntshona's eye. As they begin at last to talk, Ntshona wipes his eyes repeatedly,

one after the other, and moves his eyebrows up and down. There has been no story yet other than what spectators can infer from the actors' mime.
—*The Island*[1]

Four Parisian tradesmen playing Roman soldiers seize three of their peers, in role as Christian evangelists. Ordered to strip off their clothing, the Christians meekly obey. The soldiers take up rods dipped in red paint and beat the actor playing Saint Denis, patron saint of France, throwing insults at him as the red paint transfers the marks of their blows to his body. Denis tells those watching to suffer their own ills without complaining, because pain in this world leads to joy in the next. The soldiers beat his companions as well and then try increasingly severe punishments, all to no avail: they clap the saints in irons and throw them into prison, stretch each man out on an inclined plank for more flagellation and then concentrate on Denis, grilling him over flames, throwing him to ravening beasts, roasting him in a furnace, and finally resorting to crucifixion. The saint calmly asks God to protect him and continues to proselytize for his faith, unscathed.
—*Le Geu Saint Denis*[2]

Plate 2 Flagellation of Saints Denis, Rustique, and Eleuthere from the *Légende de Saint Denis: Reproduction des Miniatures du Manuscrit Original Présenté en 1317 au Roi Philippe le Long*, ed. Henry Martin (Paris: Champion, 1908).

This chapter develops models for spectator response to post-modern plays that stage torture and medieval dramatizations of tormented martyrs, asking what they might reveal about the relation between the individual and the community. Relying on each period's ideas about mind and sensation, I argue for using different ethical and emotional frameworks to view pre-modern and post-modern pain: post-modern theatre stages pain to raise human rights issues. Spectators respond with empathy, ideally precipitating what Luc Boltanski calls a politics of pity that has the potential to produce social change. In contrast, medieval theatre stages pain as a component of affective spirituality, and spectators respond with compassion—in the pre-modern sense of cosuffering. In both periods, spectacular pain elicits an obligation, but the nature of that obligation differs. Thus the post-modern martyr play inspires outrage and public action, whereas the medieval saint play nourishes private spiritual practices, just the opposite of what one might expect given the popular conception of modernity as the rise of the individual out of a communal, unified culture in the Middle Ages. I propose that one type of cultural structure requires the opposite type of cultural representation: it is precisely the individualism of modern (and post-modern) culture that needs empathy as a tool to produce concerted political action. In late-medieval culture, Christians were obligated to suffer compassionately in private. The critical difference between the cognitive sciences of the two periods supports this notion: our understanding of empathic response is relational, human to human, whereas theirs was a matter of divine impressions upon the inner spiritual sense.

South African actors John Kani and Winston Ntshona, shown in plate 1, created *The Island* in collaboration with playwright Athol Fugard in 1973 and restaged it in 1999 with the assistance of Peter Brook. Their revival tour included performances in Paris and London. By the time they reached the Brooklyn Academy of Music in 2003, both actors were sixty years old and Kani had become artistic director of Johannesburg's Market Theatre. At the end of the digging scene that opens this chapter, the play text describes a performance of pain that had grown somewhat blurry in 2003: "*They stop digging and come together, standing side by side as they are handcuffed together and shackled at the ankles. Another whistle. They start to run...John mumbling a prayer, Winston muttering a rhythm for their three-legged run.*"[3] I remember a local Chicago production that I saw in 1976 and use that to imagine what Kani and Ntshona would have been like as younger actors: the ordeal through which they put themselves, the skill with which they maintained the wrist and ankle contact while running in place, the way they received imagined blows from their invisible guard—the hardest of them landing on Winston's eye and John's ankle, the eventual removal of the shackles, being searched, finally lurching into their cell. Now interruptions to the run looked more like tripping than reactions to being hit, and vocal virtuosity replaced the physical virtuosity that shaped the play's opening pantomime thirty years ago. One reviewer observed that the actors' mimicry of "the sounds of the shovels plunging into the sand, the wheels of the barrows creaking and the irritating whine of hovering flies" produced an effect of "music, eerie, rhythmic and somehow gorgeous."[4]

We recognize pain by reading its physical manifestations, and actors use these to communicate. Kani's ankle rubbing is a simple gesture, easy to read; Ntshona's facial actions, more complex but also legible. According to one study, pain produces four typical facial movements: "brow-lowering, orbit tightening, levator contraction and eye closure."[5] Another study found that subjects were very successful at masking pain. When they attempted to do this, the only expression that researchers could detect was a decrease in blinking and a tightening of the eyelids. Those who faked pain also blinked less often, however, suggesting that infrequent blinking might have less to do with pain than with the cognitive activity involved in pretending (or trying to follow the instruction to pretend). The increased incidence of lip pull during faking indicates the social complexity of pain behavior. The action is more characteristic of smiling than of pain, and may have been related to embarrassment or amusement. The fakers used all the same indications as those who were really in pain, but intensified some of the signs.[6] The extent to which pain behaviors such as these and pain experience itself are culturally specific falls outside the proper scope of this study, which centers on performances of pain as cultural work. As Melzack and Wall point out, though, the pain process does not begin with the stimulation of pain receptors; rather, "stimulation produces neural signals that enter an active nervous system that (in the adult organism) is already the substrate of past experience, culture, anticipation, anxiety, and so forth."[7] Even if the facial expression of pain is innate behavior, its *meaning* is not independent of culture. Alternatively, if the nonverbal expression of pain and other emotions is learned behavior, most of the learning takes place subconsciously, and variations are subtle. Communication works smoothly as long as performance and reception take place within shared discourse communities, meaning that all participants have a common set of verbal and nonverbal behavioral conventions. We read pain behavior against convention to find a potential meaning. We then test that meaning against the context to see if it works. We often make mistakes, of course, when meanings are ambiguous or when we engage with members of other discourse communities who play by different rules. Chronic pain provides particularly good examples of the way pain behavior functions as a language, because its physical markers are often not readily apparent and patients must learn to display or to hide them as required.[8] Although the absence of intelligible pain signals conforms to the conventions established in certain situations—a grimace or any other pain behavior would be out of place in most ballet performances, for example—such absence fails to conform to the standards of the medical profession, who must rely upon behavior for diagnosis.

If I lower my brow, narrow my eyes, raise my cheeks, and then after several seconds close my eyes, you very likely perceive me to be bravely enduring pain to which I must finally surrender. If I step on something sharp and pull my foot away, you perceive a reflexive withdrawal from a painful stimulus. If I walk on broken glass with my brow lowered and eyes narrowed, you perceive me to be undergoing a painful ordeal. If I walk on broken glass with a neutral countenance, you perceive me to have in some way mastered my pain: perhaps I control my facial expression or transcend the sensation. If I grimace involuntarily, then I do not *perform* pain (in the sense in which I am using the word) because I don't intentionally mean anything by my grimace—providing, of course, that you perceive my grimace to be involuntary. If you believe that I grimaced on purpose, then you mistakenly read an intentional meaning into my behavior and perceive it as a performance although I do not. If someone puts me on a platform and causes me to grimace by poking me with a sharp stick, then you attribute an intention to the person causing my grimace. If I grimace in the course of a play in which I act the part of someone poked with a sharp stick, then perhaps you perceive my character's involuntary grimace and attribute an intention to the character who poked her, as well as attributing other intentions to various persons whom you consider to have produced the interaction. These persons most likely include the playwright and quite possibly the director. Whether you attribute any intention to me other than to embody the character depends upon your conception of acting.

Within the dramatic structure of *The Island*, the actors' easily readable performances of pain not only create a bond between their characters and situate them within a hostile environment, but also create solidarity between the characters and the spectators. The primary focus of the story line is the relationship between the two men, which comes to crisis when John's ten-year sentence is reduced so that only three months remain, whereas Winston will serve out a life sentence. They work through John's jubilation, Winston's resentment, their anger at the injustice of the situation, and their helplessness. Finally, portions of Sophocles' *Antigone*, which they have been rehearsing and arguing over, are inserted as a play within the play. John speaks Creon's lines but never quite takes on his character. When Winston speaks as Antigone, the parallels between her situation and his own are unmistakable, and for the final lines of the play he speaks for himself although he uses the character's words:

> [*Tearing off his wig and confronting the audience as Winston, not Antigone.*]
> Gods of our Fathers! My Land! My Home!
> Time waits no longer. I go now to my living death, because I honoured those things to which honour belongs. (77)

Performances of *The Island* actualize the remembering that John promises to Winston in the text: although many Antigones remained in effect buried alive at Robben Island, they were not unheard and unmourned.

For spectators in—or knowledgeable about—South Africa in the mid-1970s, the title alone would identify the play's locale, because Robben Island was its only island prison, and so many political prisoners were held there. For spectators seeing it in other locations or at other times, advance information makes the prison location explicit. Yet the script itself remains ambiguous well into the scene in which John tries to clean Winston's eye. Winston's anger builds during this episode until he begins to yell for the guard. John tries to quiet Winston even while ministering to his injury. Then the roles reverse: Winston notices blood on John's ear and tends to it. Only after they have aided one another and begun to clean themselves do they describe the scene that we have just watched, so that we fully understand what they had been forced to do: each man was digging a hole in the beach, then filling in the other man's hole. Antigone's bold, defiant burial of her brother has been turned into torture: the task is the opposite of self-directed, and each man's sand buries the labor of his fellow prisoner. But it does not bury their solidarity.

This use of pain to construct empathic bonds is common, and the creators of theatrical events count on spectators to understand and share the actors' emotions, including their simulated pain; in other words, to respond with empathy. The word "empathy" was coined early in the twentieth century to translate *Einfühlung*, which means "feeling into" and was used in nineteenth-century German aesthetics to explain how we derive pleasure from projecting ourselves emotionally into inanimate objects.[9] Martha Nussbaum defines empathy as the "imaginative reconstruction of another person's experience, *without any particular evaluation of that experience.*"[10] Although she considers empathy to be a conscious imaginative effort that can exclude not only judgment but also shared affect,[11] experimental neuroscience uses the term to mean the preconscious activation of a matching emotional state. In order to accommodate both concepts, I will refer to the first as *imaginative empathy* or *empathic imagination* and use the term empathy *tout court* for the basic response that may not include conscious effort. In either case, empathy does not imply a moral stance but can and often does serve as the foundation for moral and ethical judgments and actions. Acknowledging that many scholars use quite a different definition of empathy, with a moral stance as its essence, I have chosen to adopt Nussbaum's morally neutral definition because it maps well to the scientific term.

In empathic response, perceiving another's emotion activates the same emotional state in oneself. In 1999, researchers at the University of Toronto identified the neurons activated by pinpricks to a subject's hand and observed the same neurons firing when the subject watched the experimenter's fingers being pricked.[12] Research has proceeded apace and already offers a rich picture of the neurological mechanism involved, although many of these ideas will undoubtedly be superseded by the time this book is published. Using a perception-action model of the brain, Stephanie Preston and Frans de Waal proposed in 2002 that empathy works by activating the perceiver's representations of the emotional state, which in turn "*automatically primes or generates the associated autonomic and somatic response, unless inhibited.*"[13] The "representation" in this sense of the word is a typical pattern of neural activation, the physical correlative of an image or other representation in the abstract sense with which we commonly use the word. The perceiver's relationship with the object perceived crucially affects the response, suggesting that subject-object similarity is vital to activating representations of emotional states and thus to empathy, but that familiarity can supplant similarity.[14]

Tania Singer proposed in 2004 that empathic response to pain involves all of the components of pain minus the sensory input. Assuming that couples are likely to feel empathy for one another, her study used functional magnetic resonance imaging (fMRI) to study the brain activity of sixteen women while applying an electric shock to either their hands or their partners' hands, in random order. The woman could see her own hand and her partner's, together with cues indicating whether she or her partner would receive the shock and whether its intensity would be low (painless) or high (painful). She could not see her partner's face or other visual emotional cues. The researchers compared the fMRI results with psychological empathy scales and found a positive correlation. The results further suggest that the areas activated by empathic pain are activated in anticipation of pain as well.[15] There is a danger that the studies so far are influenced by data analysis methods that exaggerate the commonality, however. In a 2007 study of the neural areas responding to pain observation in comparison to pain experience, India Morrison and Paul Downing eliminated averaging and spatial smoothing of data and found that the two conditions activated adjacent but distinct areas with an overlap for some but not all subjects.[16]

Although ongoing developments will continue to refine the models, research to date supports the notion that some portions of the brain's pain matrix are functional; others, affective and subjective. To give a somewhat simplified example, a blow to my shoulder activates portions of my brain associated with a reflexive withdrawal along with other portions that enable me to feel both that the blow hurt and that it happened to me. Seeing or even imagining a blow to the shoulder of someone with whom I am emotionally involved activates only the affective portion of the pain matrix. This is not to say that empathic response has no sensory component, as an extreme example illustrates: Ninety percent of Sarah Chesterman's skin is completely lacking sensation. Yet she finds watching horror movies nearly unbearable. She cannot feel a burn to her own leg, recognizes it only by seeing it; however, she has a deep physical response to the sight of another person's injury, including visceral sensation and a change to her heart rate and breathing. As Jill Bennett puts it, "Lacking skin sensation as the first line of defense, she finds that the image goes straight to the core—or heart—of her in a quite literal sense."[17] Chesterman says, "When people watch [thrillers or horror] films they squirm. I think that the physical act of squirming is one of feeling one's own body, it is an act of distancing the sensual experience being depicted—a way of feeling your own body and sending messages to the brain."[18]

The creators of *The Island* embed incidents that evoke spectators' empathic pain response and reactive squirm within narrative contexts likely to draw them closer to the suffering character. Exceptions to this common use of pain are so striking that they illustrate its normative quality; for example, a torture scene that serves as prelude to the bloodbath in Martin McDonagh's *The Lieutenant of Inishmore* readies the audience but never delivers the anticipated squirm.[19] The play introduces Padraic, a psychopathic terrorist lieutenant, to the stage in the act of torturing a drug dealer who is suspended from the ceiling by an ankle. Padraic taunts him with a knife, asking which nipple he should slice off. But the scene is interrupted by news more urgent to Padraic—that his cat is dead. Even before this transition, the hilarious dialogue short-circuits one's tendency to empathically experience the threatened nipple slicing. McDonagh toys with the squirm but blocks it, thereby creating an obstacle to the spectator's imaginative empathy with either the torturer or his victim (who does not reappear in the play). Although the dialogue in *The Island* is often quite funny, the laughs do not begin until after the performance of physical pain has ended. In this latter case, both the pain and the laughter encourage the spectator's engagement with the characters, and the laughter also prevents the pain and suffering from becoming the play's central source of pleasure.

If the modern discourse of individual human rights eroded pain's teleological meaning, the development of effective anesthesia beginning in the nineteenth century produced not only the expectation that one can live free of pain, but that to do so is a right; therefore, to inflict suffering upon another person violates that person's rights. Since the mid-twentieth century, to represent or even to look at suffering creates ethical anxiety. Luc Boltanski argues that encountering suffering face-to-face obligates one to provide reasonable assistance; that is, an action to alleviate suffering that does not put one at risk. Only those with specialized roles, such as firefighters and police, must risk their lives in order to save others. For anyone else, one's relationship to the sufferer delineates one's level of obligation. One would be expected to save one's child, for example, or perhaps even one's neighbor. Other people may undertake heroic rescues, but they have no moral obligation to do so.[20] Distance introduces additional ethical precepts. If one sees suffering at a distance, Boltanski argues, the principle of reasonable sacrifice does not require one to drop everything and go to help. Two forms of action are available: paying or saying. Because giving money does not on its own form a group among the donors, this form of action may be pity but does not constitute a politics.

Boltanski calls public speech the "least unacceptable" response to suffering at a distance, because it maintains integrity for the witness and differentiates ethical spectatorship from spurious viewing. Not just any type of speech will do, however—and I would extend this notion of speech to other sorts of communicative performances, including theatre. Boltanski notes that a strictly factual description of a hanging, for instance, "would be considered out of place, 'indecent' or 'inhuman.'" Factual description requires one to view the suffering objectively; that is, to describe the sufferer and his pain as an object, creating an asymmetrical relation that "distributes the humanity of the different partners unequally" with mastery "distributed entirely on the side of the subject who is describing."[21] Three types of speech are available, according to Boltanski: *denunciation*, which imagines and accuses a persecutor of the unfortunate; *sentiment*, which imagines a benefactor to whom urgent appeals can be directed on behalf of the unfortunate; and the *aesthetic*, which translates the suffering into the sublime—quite literally sublimating it.

Torture itself operates in the realm of public speech, as Elaine Scarry argues so convincingly. Ideally (from the torturer's point of view), the victim's recantation or confession affirms that the torturer's version of reality is true. In this sense, says Scarry, the torturer aims to appropriate the victim's voice. Even without such "true" speech, the victim's scream, grimace, or other sign of pain serves as an alternative form of speech acknowledging the superior power of the torturer. But anyone who gives voice to the victim, who gives an accurate account of the pain, can project the image of the sufferer's subjective experience out into the world.[22] To stage the body in pain is to bring the victim's suffering into public as an aesthetic topic, in Boltanski's sense, and potentially as denunciation or sentiment. Yet when put into practice, any theatrical aesthetics of atrocity runs up against audience expectations shaped not only by mass culture but also by various ethical and critical systems. I would suggest that, to a large extent, post–World War II anxiety about representations of suffering turns on the question of whether such representations become too fully aesthetic, turning atrocity into a source of pleasure while forgetting the material suffering of those who are thus represented. Although some propose that art should effectively accuse or urgently appeal, Boltanski discusses the shortcomings of both these types of speech at length.[23]

A closer examination of the conditions under which *The Island* was created and then revived can help to elucidate the interaction of performance text with social context and the resulting politics of pity. Although the play was created in South Africa under apartheid, it was first performed during a tour of Europe and America and performed in South Africa only after the tour. Kani and Ntshona developed the play as a companion piece to *Sizwe Banzi Is Dead*, after performances of that play in Port Elizabeth generated an invitation to tour.[24] Inspired by Polish director Jerzy Grotowski to create with and from the actors of the Serpent Theatre, playwright Athol Fugard came up with generative tasks for the actors and scripted the play, leaving room for further improvisation within performances.[25] Early in the rehearsal process, Kani and Ntshona were working outdoors on a blanket that they repeatedly folded in half. When they ended up with enough space for only their feet, they were reminded of Robben Island. The *Antigone* story came into it later, when they reached an impasse because they were so emotionally involved with the material. Even the choice of story has connections to the actors' personal experience. Kani's first role with the Serpent Theatre in 1965 had been Haemon in Sophocles' *Antigone*. He replaced the actor Norman Ntshinga (a company founder), who was accused of supporting the outlawed African National Congress and sent to Robben Island. Much of the play's prison material comes from Ntshinga's experience: he did, in fact, perform a version of *Antigone* for fellow prisoners while Kani was playing his role outside.[26] When Ntshinga was released after two years, he carried stories to Kani and Ntshona. Other information came from company member Welcome Duru, who had returned from Robben Island in 1966. Duru described the transport of prisoners to the Island and the work teams,[27] for example, and Ntshinga told of his work *span* (team) being beaten as they ran back to their cells, then tending to one another's wounds—experiences that made their way into the opening scene of *The Island*.[28] The use of senseless but exhausting labor as torture (being given a bucket and told to empty the sea, or being told to uproot a tree)[29] and the prisoners' devices for maintaining morale (giving a parodic "weather report and news bulletin" or telling stories in a cinematic form) also came from Ntshinga's stories,[30] as did the difficulty of taking leave when a prisoner was released. Ntshinga's young cellmate told him, "you'll forget us.... But don't worry, we'll never forget you."[31] In South Africa, before the Soweto uprisings, as social freedoms were being eliminated in order to preserve apartheid, *The Island* turned Antigone's burial of her brother into an insidious torture. But buried alive in prison, Winston conveyed the message: Remember me. I can still speak.

The tour had an undeniable impact on the lives and careers of Kani and Ntshona. The fact that they had to be registered as "household employees" of Fugard in order to travel outside the country or even to Fugard's home in South Africa was widely reported during the tour and helped to raise British and American awareness of pass laws—as did the subject of *Sizwe Banzi*, of course.[32] During the tour they were careful to represent themselves as artists, not only insisting upon the right to an identity that their country's pass laws denied them but also mindful that news reports would be reprinted in South Africa. The actors shared a Tony award for Best Actor and returned to South Africa with international acclaim that could not eliminate the restrictions to which they were subjected, although it made those restrictions harder to enforce. They could tour and they could visit Fugard, but then they returned to life in what Ntshona called "a nightmare."[33] Kani and Ntshona could "play" Antigone's situation in South Africa as long as they were careful to code it as a play. But the actors were arrested when their improvisation during performances allowed contemporary political references to peep out from under the play's "cultural cloak." They spent fifteen days in solitary confinement for derogatory references to the Transkei region's acceptance of independence, which they saw as acquiescing to apartheid. During a discussion between the actors and the African Activist Association at UCLA during the tour, an interlocutor faulted the play for not particularizing the background of the prisoners. Kani explained that if they called the play *Robben Island* or made any explicit reference to the penal colony, "you would have read in the *New York Times* one paragraph of what happened to us. And you would only march from UCLA down to the mayor's office and tomorrow you would be back in your nice comfortable seat and that's the end of it. And this is the way the outside world ever participates in the struggle in Africa."[34] Their subsequent arrest was indeed reported in the *New York Times*, and the New York theatre community demonstrated for their release at the South African Consulate.[35] Given the earlier incarceration of actors Ntshinga and Duru at Robben Island, it seems safe to assume that their enhanced status brought Kani and Ntshona some protection.

One can also assume that the boycotts and marches staged by people in the "outside world" (who might spend some of their time in nice comfortable theatre seats) made some contribution toward the ending of apartheid. Although I was already well aware of the situation in South Africa when I first saw *The Island* (along with *Sizwe Banzi*) in 1976, I did learn more from watching these plays—the characters certainly did not seem like "separate human beings from the moon" presented as entertainment only, the accusation made at UCLA. My experience as a spectator led me to political action. Just as importantly, my empathic response to the spectacle of suffering and these actors' virtuosity persisted in memory, helping me remember that I *don't* stand outside, continuing to influence my engagement in the world. In Boltanski's terms, *The Island* nourished the imagination of spectators and precipitated their commitment, thus contributing to a *politics* of pity.[36]

Yet Kani's comment at UCLA points up a vexing problem: well-meaning observers can all too easily imagine themselves to be separate from and superior to those who would build a society by hurting other people. For "developed" nations that disclaim torture and cruel punishment (whatever the true situation may be), during the twentieth century the practices became evidence for classifying other societies as "underdeveloped."[37] For example, when John Conroy set out to find out "how an ordinary person becomes a torturer,...what happens to torture victims,...why torturers are rarely punished, and...how torturing societies justify their acts,"[38] many people asked him whether he planned to visit "nations well-known for their use of torture."[39] They implied that "torture was something done in some backward civilization by the barely human and certainly ignorant."[40] His study focuses on three recent cases, none of them in "backward" civilizations: one occurred in Northern Ireland, another in Israel, and a third in Chicago. Judicial torture was in fact a European colonial import that the Dutch brought to South Africa in 1652, believing that it was necessary in order to produce confession. At first they tortured both Europeans and natives, eventually restricting its application to the indigenous population. The practice was abolished in South Africa with the English conquest in 1797 (and was abolished in Holland a year later). When South Africa became independent in 1961, torture did not return *quite* immediately, but it was clearly in use by 1964. Edward Peters describes independent South Africa under apartheid as "the extreme of colonialism, an independent colonial state with a dominant population of colonizers who re-introduced a practice that had, in the law and in general report, ended during an earlier stage of colonization."[41] Furthermore, the use of torture by the South African government was thoroughly interwoven with its concern to protect foreign investment, and the associated anti-Communist rhetoric served to reassure investors and government officials in the United States and Europe.

Any delusion of ethical distance and superiority that might have been available to American spectators during the 1975 tour of *The Island* had grown shaky for the 2003 revival tour, concurrent not only with the U.S. invasion of Iraq but also with hundreds of people being held incommunicado at Guantánamo and other locations. The play still showed two prisoners in solidarity, resisting wrongful authority, but the reception context for *The Island* with respect to British and American spectators changed in 2003 from what it was in 1975: then, the wrongful regime was apartheid South Africa; now, the wrongful regime was the Bush administration. This is not exactly an inversion. Most of the play's spectators in 1975 were likely to have been politically liberal, with a negative affective relation to the recent Nixon regime, the Vietnam War, and American complicity with South Africa. Since the performance that I saw in 2003, revelations about abuse of prisoners at Abu Ghraib and in Afghanistan, along with extraordinary rendition of suspected terrorists, have produced an even bigger change in Americans' frame of reference, further narrowing the gap between our government's practices and those that inspired *The Island*. The revival displayed Ntshona and Kani as hero-survivors of apartheid, reminding me not only of past indignation but that a politics of pity can be effective.

To precipitate the type of commitment to a cause that Boltanski calls a *politics* of pity, the spectacle of suffering must enter the public sphere. Jürgen Habermas defined this as a space of impartial rational debate and tied it to the development of cheap, widely distributed print journalism in the eighteenth century—a debatable but influential view that I will revisit near the end of this chapter.[42] In the post-modern world, mass migration combines with electronic mass media to produce what Arjun Appadurai calls "diasporic public spheres" within which the imagination provides "a space of contestation."[43] Appadurai distinguishes fantasy, private and divorced from action, from imagination, which has become in recent decades "a staging ground for action, and not only for escape."[44] Rather than promoting impartial debate, the mass media encourage a collective imagination or "community of sentiment"; that is, "a group that begins to imagine and feel things together."[45] Although the theatrical and other performative events at the center of this study are not mass media and thus provide some continuity of comparison with their pre-modern counterparts, we cannot forget that they function within a mass-mediated world. We've seen the interweaving of newspaper coverage with both tours of *The Island*, not only bringing audiences to the theatre but also maintaining their involvement in the issues that the play addresses, including intervention on behalf of the actors when they returned to South Africa in the 1970s. Word of mouth may bring us to the theatre for a particular event, but live performance is inextricably bound up with film, television, the Internet, cell phones, podcasts, Twitter, and whatever other media are emerging as I write.

The first tour of *The Island* contributed to the sort of coordinated emotional commitment necessary to constitute a politics of pity and thus made a contribution, however eventual and partial that may have been, to the end of apartheid. Lacking such an explicit and clearly localized target, the revival tour presented an opportunity to remember and reassess, but it contributed to the community of sentiment forming in opposition to official policies and interrogation practices that contradict both our laws and our self-image. The United States entered into an intensified period of anxiety during the second term of George W. Bush's presidency. Many of us wanted to believe in the rule of law but felt unable to trust our government. The popular media provided powerful indications that what we really believe in is the heroically moral maverick: both Supreme Court Justice Antonin Scalia and former president Bill Clinton invoked Jack Bauer of the television series *24* in public policy discussions,[46] and the lawyers who designed our controversial interrogation protocol cited Bauer more often than the Constitution.[47] The two themes of *24* that stand out most strongly for me, though, are whether we can trust those in charge and whether we as individuals can effectively balance out the moral demands that urge us to act. From within the community of sentiment nurtured by *The Island*, then, *24* could—somewhat surprisingly—reinforce opposition to so-called harsh interrogation. One would imagine little overlap between this community and those who seriously wished for real-life Jack Bauers to wage Bush's war on terror,[48] although I suppose that might be a tenable libertarian position. Empathic response to performative pain contributes to forming communities of sentiment but does not dictate their contours. Thus a particular social context will put any given performance to its own uses, as the two tours of *The Island* illustrate. We should, therefore, expect our own response to a saint play to differ substantially from that of its first spectators.

* * *

We must struggle to imagine ourselves as Parisians watching scenes of torment from *Le Geu Saint Denis*. I'll have more to say about the play as a whole in the next chapter; for now, let's just concentrate on its spectacular suffering. Having apprehended Saint Denis and his two companions in the dangerous act of converting Parisians to Christianity, the Roman provost Fescennin and his henchmen carry out a standard series of torments. To begin with, they order the three Christians to strip and then beat them with bloody rods ("*de courroies sanglantes*," ca. 515), making the injury visible to spectators. They beat Denis alone for more than twenty lines, and then his companions for another five. Denis draws an explicit parallel to the scourging of Christ: "Sweet Jesus Christ, I give you thanks for your willingness to have the traces of your holy Passion inscribed upon my body" (518–21).[49] He then switches from prayer to direct address ("*Cy die au peuple*"), ensuring that the audience understands the lesson: "Good folk, don't be sad if you see me tormented because through earthly pain comes eternal gladness. Take strength and courage in your hearts, and suffer all pains in great joy" (522–27).[50] After a brief interlude during which the saints are clapped in irons and thrown into prison, the flagellation resumes. As illustrated by plate 2, the four *tirans* stretch each saint on an inclined plank called a *selete* or *cheval* and joke about the pain they inflict, while the provost insists that his sergeants must hit harder because the Christians do nothing but laugh (660).[51] This beating continues for thirty lines, after which Denis is placed on a grill over a bed of fire (663–88), thrown to savage beasts that haven't eaten for a week (689–714), put into a hot furnace (718–49), and finally crucified (750–95). In each case, he goes willingly to the torment, asks God to protect him, and remains unharmed.

Le Geu Saint Denis is the fifth of six saint plays in manuscript 1131 of the Library of Saint Geneviève in Paris.[52] These plays could be presented as a cycle or independently, and each has two possible endings: one that finishes with a traditional *Te Deum* and an alternative ending that links it to the next play. They primarily relate the legends of the first Christian martyrs, and they all accentuate the role of Saint Denis.[53] The late-fourteenth- or early-fifteenth-century text is written in literary language, based on francien but containing many forms of regional dialect used in northern France, and there are many geographical allusions to the Parisian region.[54] The manuscript also contains a *Mystère de la Passion* composed during the fourteenth century, and the fact that such a varied collection of mystery plays is found in a single manuscript has encouraged historians to view it as the repertoire of a confraternity.[55] There may well have been performances both before and after the manuscript was copied. In any event, *Le Geu Saint Denis* would quite likely have been performed in Paris at some point before the end of the fifteenth century, most likely after Charles VII regained control of the city in 1437. Evidence suggests that dramatic productions were rare in Paris during the Hundred Years' War and related civil unrest, which I discuss at greater length when I return to this play in the following chapter.

Graham Runnalls imagines the performance taking place in a small theatre in the round, with spectators and actors in close proximity, mansions (which the play calls *logeis*) mixed in among the audience scaffolds. A confraternity might have produced an intimate indoor staging as part of its annual festivities. Whatever their other activities, each confraternity held an annual banquet, in most cases on the feast day of its patron saint. All members were required to attend, and they elected officers, dined, distributed alms to the poor, and engaged in various entertainments. These indoor banquets provided one vital staging ground for late-medieval saint plays, the other being city-wide performances in purpose-built outdoor theatres. Whereas entire communities came together to stage mystery plays in the provinces, Charles VI chartered the *Confrérie de la Passion* in 1402 to produce them in Paris.[56] We cannot know for certain which form of staging was used for *Le Geu Saint Denis*, whether the arrangement of *logeis* was circular, or exactly how the audience was situated with respect to the action, but we can speak with some confidence of action moving between the defined *logeis* and the neutral playing space here called the *champ* or *jeu*, more commonly known to theatre historians as the *platea*. The play thus shares many features with French saint plays in general, the violent torment of the saint chief among them.

Bloody special effects were common in the medieval theatre. The producers of the Admont Passion Play dipped various apparatus in red paint: whips and rods that left bloody marks during the flagellation, a sponge to ooze red down Christ's face when the crown of thorns was pressed into his scalp, and more sponges wrapping the club used to break the thieves' legs.[57] At Modane in 1580, a father-and-son team of artisans both named Thomas Mellurin agreed to provide a dagger from which blood would "issue forth in the accustomed manner" when used to strike a death blow to the breast. They also provided a suit of pigskins for Christ, painted with his wounds and the marks left by flogging; and for two Jesuits, "two dummy bodies to rip up or saw through the middle, from which shall come out entrails and blood."[58] Dummies were widely used, capable of spilling both guts and bones as Saint Barnabas or being flayed as Saint Bartholemew for the Bourges *Acts of the Apostles* and pulled apart by horses as Saint Ypolite for a French Saint Lawrence play.[59]

In modern and post-modern theatre, actors' performances of pain typically create a bond between their characters and situate them within a hostile environment, and they also create solidarity between the characters and the spectators. While this isn't *entirely* different from the bloody special effects popular in the medieval theatre, I suggest that spectator response was quite different from the politics of pity that I discussed earlier. In modern usage, compassion not only includes empathy or pity but also entails an obligation to alleviate suffering. Prior to the eighteenth century, however, compassion meant only to suffer together with another person.[60] For clarity's sake, I will use the term "compassion" only in this medieval sense of cosuffering. The difference between modern pity and medieval compassion stands out most clearly if we consider not the martyr but rather the poor or the disabled. Medieval entertainments made no bones about their suffering, nor did medieval philosophy or theology. Hans-Jurgen Diller observes that medieval religious depictions of the fate of the damned were intended to induce *Schadenfreude*, a response of which we are now ashamed but they were not.[61] Along the same lines, medieval drama uses sinners and the disabled as objects for either miracles or derision. Plays about Saint Martin, for example, include a blind beggar and a cripple who fail in their attempt to avoid miraculous cures by the saint's relics. A version by Andrieu de la Vigne extracts this episode and turns it into a farce to be performed after the main saint play.[62] This would not seem to be an effect of representation, since real disability provided similar diversion. In 1425, for example, Parisians dressed four blind men in armor and paraded them through the streets with a drummer and a banner showing a pig in order to advertise the next day's entertainment: the men were given clubs and led into an enclosed area together with a pig. If they succeeded in killing the pig, it would be theirs—presumably to butcher and eat. Naturally they hit one another more often than the pig, "so that if they had not been wearing armour they would certainly have killed each other."[63] The potential provision of pig flesh satisfied Christian society's obligation to aid the disabled and disadvantaged, for which alms sufficed. Imaginative cosuffering was not required.

Both the saint and his suffering were anything but ordinary. Denis clearly does feel the blows that the audience sees inflicted, because he reiterates the beneficial effects of pain. But he does not suffer from the other torments—all of which were, interestingly enough, outmoded forms of public punishment with which audiences would have been familiar only through iconography and theatre. Fourteenth- and fifteenth-century Parisians were unlikely to have seen anyone grilled, thrown to wild animals, baked in an oven, or crucified.[64] Elizabeth Lalou notes that one might expect spectators to respond differently to outmoded tortures than to those still familiar and legal. Most salient, in her opinion, is the fact that torments and executions were opportunities for stage tricks and were appreciated as such.[65] I do not wish to contest this point or to diminish its importance; however, an appreciation of special effects does not obliterate other responses to the incident being staged. The torments in *Le Geu Saint Denis* are common to saint plays in general, to the vitae that are their source, and to late-medieval devotional imagery. As early as Hrotsvit's tenth-century dramas, obstinate Christian virgins were beaten, boiled in cauldrons, hung up to be raked with flesh hooks, and roasted in furnaces.[66] The Host was subjected to much the same series in the Croxton *Play of the Sacrament* and the *Mistere de la Sainte Hostie*. These torments replicate the Passion of Christ and provide a route to compassion. Clifford Davidson and Véronique Plesch both argue that the suffering in Passion plays was intended to draw the spectator into the scene, to produce a visceral and emotional engagement with the Passion while watching, and furthermore to provide a memorable image for later contemplation.[67] Plesch argues that scenes of torment became longer (in lines) and larger (in number of actors) over the course of the late Middle Ages not because they appealed to the debased tastes of the crowd, as some have assumed, but because they are meaningful.[68] She further asserts that this development aimed to produce during meditation "an almost sensory identification with the holy figure," being thus "intensely private" rather than communal.[69]

The concept of spiritually useful pain was new in this period. Medieval theology began with two basic conceptions of pain, taking *impassivity*, or the ability to tolerate pain, from the Stoics. Early Christian martyrs introduced the idea that God enabled them to transcend pain entirely; that is, to be *impassible*. Thomas Aquinas refined this concept in the thirteenth century: saints were exempt from physical suffering, like Adam and Eve before the Fall and like blessed souls in Heaven, but unlike normal living humans.[70] Then in the later Middle Ages, ordinary Christians began to imitate Christ's suffering as a means of individual salvation and thus to cultivate *compassionate vision* as a component of affective spirituality. Both the Virgin Mary and Saint Francis served as models for this mode of response.[71] The martyr might be impassible, but the spectator suffered. That was the point of contemplating devotional images or watching dramatic performances. Compassionate suffering would in turn provoke the free choice to perform the Seven Corporal Acts of Mercy and was to be in fact joyful, because it would result in freedom from the eternal suffering occasioned by the Fall.[72] For the medieval Christian, compassion did not entail an obligation to alleviate the suffering of others; instead, it constituted an obligation to suffer with Christ and the saints.

Spiritual guidebooks advocated a sort of imaginative exercise startlingly similar to the technique of substitution familiar to any modern Method actor: when meditating on the Passion, one was to imagine familiar people in the roles of Christ and other Passion players, in order to fully enter into the experience.[73] A twelfth-century treatise recommended "that the meditator place himself as though actually present at the events, forming detailed pictures through the faculty of the imagination."[74] As Mitchell Merback puts it, devotional imagery "furnished a literalized space for the imagination's deployment."[75] In the participatory spirituality of the late Middle Ages, the performance of a mystery play was closely related to other visual experiences such as the elevation of the host, meditative viewing of relics and sacred images, and contemplation of memory images, all of which "allowed for bodily participation in the divine,"[76] as Suzannah Biernoff argues. In addition to the immediate experience of public viewing, the theatrical suffering at the center of late-medieval saint plays persisted in the form of memory images that remained available for imaginative contemplation. Late-medieval optical theory provides us with a medieval counterpart to the cognitive neuroscience that we've used to analyze contemporary performative pain. Aristotle's comparison (in *De Anima*, 450a 25) of memory to the wax in which a signet ring leaves an impression remained popular throughout the Middle Ages, and it underpins Aquinas's understanding that the eye becomes "like" that which it sees, just as the wax conforms to the ring. For Aquinas, sight produces a *spiritual* change, whereas other senses involve *material* change. But he considers the spiritual to be physical and fully embodied.[77]

Late-medieval theories of vision were not entirely in accord, but some common features make it possible to sort out how people were likely to understand the experience of looking and remembering. I don't mean to suggest that the average Parisian read optical theory, but rather that these ideas were part of the general paradigm underlying late-medieval theology and shaping spectacle, just as biomedical theory shapes our own. In the thirteenth century, both Robert Grosseteste and Roger Bacon combined Aristotle's conception of intromission with the extramission theorized by Plato and Galen. As Biernoff explains, the theory of intromission postulates that all material objects send out sensible species that make an impression on the substance of the eye and of the brain. The "species" is the object's power, which Grosseteste also calls "similitude." The eye emits its own species, which he thought of as rays of light.[78] For Bacon, sight operates in a manner similar to the other senses: there always has to be a medium to transmit the sensation produced by external objects. For touch, the medium is flesh; for sight, the eye. Both are permeable membranes or bodily borders. In both cases, there is distance between the perceiver and the object. The eye is a receptive medium at the apex of a visual pyramid that originates at the object, but it also reaches out, in effect touching and exploring the object. Galen thought that "in the presence of light, the air between the eye and its object is infused with pneuma," resulting in sight. The air is thus sensitive, just as the eye or nerves are. Biernoff likens vision to "an invisible [but not immaterial] connective tissue between the observer's body and that of the object."[79] Vision also entails pain because it changes "sensitive humours and membranes of the eyes."[80] Bacon writes that the anterior glacialis "must be somewhat thick, in order that it may experience a feeling from the impressions [species] that is a kind of pain. For we observe that strong lights and colour narrow vision and injure it, and inflict pain.... Therefore vision always experiences a feeling that is a kind of pain."[81] For the late-medieval spectator, images are material; vision, a *passio*; and the line between pleasure and pain, indistinct.[82]

Bacon defines two kinds of sight, "outer (carnal or corporeal) and inner (spiritual or intellectual)." The outer senses belong to the realm of the flesh, meaning that sensation is not a trustworthy source of knowledge. Medieval science paid little attention to the wrinkly cortex, focusing instead on the chambers inside the cranium that housed the "marrow-like substance" of the brain. Bacon thought of the five internal senses as "bodily organs" residing in these chambers: from front to back, the common sense and imagination in the first chamber, cogitation in the middle, and estimation and memory in the third. Each sense organ receives its particular species and passes it to the common sense, which collects sensations but also differentiates them. The common sense is too slippery to retain species, but they pass next to the imagination, which stores impressions. Estimation and memory in the rear chamber parallel the common sense and imagination but "are attuned to the 'insensible' nature of sensible objects," meaning "innate qualities" or "complexions" that the senses in the first chamber do not apprehend because they "are not reducible to the sensory contents of sight, hearing, touch, taste or smell" but that produce emotions in the sensitive soul (or instinctual responses in animals). Estimation collects these complexions, and the memory stores them.[83]

To summarize Bacon's optics, the thing perceived is physically present in (at least) two places: in the external world and in the receptive medium, whether that be air, skin, eye, chamber of the brain, or a combination of these. Biernoff ties this to incarnational theology and the Eucharist: Jesus is the species of God, and the Host is the species of Jesus/God. This is why it can be broken into pieces and yet he is fully present in each.[84] Aquinas says that memory images "'dwell within' us as 'traces of actual sensations...just as sensations arouse appetitive impulses [emotions] whilst the sensed objects are present, so do images when these are absent.' Psychological states, then, are not subjective responses to a thing or a situation, but originate in the objects themselves."[85] For the medieval spectator watching a Passion play or gazing upon an image of the crucifixion, Jesus was physically present in the eye or in the brain; the same would be true for the depiction of a tormented saint; and the same would be true when the spectator later recalled that image to mind. Inner vision constitutes inner presence.

This understanding of the brain as plastic, malleable, and impressionable does bear a surprising degree of similarity to the current biomedical understanding, but the medieval Christian would expect to retain Christ or the saint as a living presence in the memory chamber. And that would be enough—there was no moral imperative for outward action in response to what one watched. To a modern sensibility, this might appear callous. Indeed, medieval enjoyment of spectacular suffering once led to the modern judgment that medieval people were either less sensitive or were inured to pain. But this doesn't mean that they were constitutionally lacking in empathy. I would propose that medieval Europe simply did not need theatre to create bonds through empathy, because daily life occurred face-to-face in a dense mesh of relationship. People carried out most of their activities in the streets and squares rather than inside their dark and crowded houses. Thus they largely lived in public space, immersed in a kind of immediate community that most of us would find hard to imagine. Not that medieval Paris, by far the largest city of its day, was a place where everyone knew everyone else. A certain degree of urban freedom existed, as Simone Roux describes it, even the possibility of moving to a new part of the city for a fresh start "uninjured or unencumbered by a bad reputation, family ties, or anything else that had become insupportable."[86] Having done so, though, it was vital to establish a social network. The written evidence consistently shows a distrust of isolated individuals.[87]

The late-medieval cities of Europe were enclosed by walls, with population on the increase again after general declines of up to 40 percent due to plague and adverse climate during the middle of the fourteenth century. Medieval cities offered immigrants both skilled and unskilled work, charity to help them through emergencies, and a rich cultural life. Country dwellers learned about life in the city through a chain of face-to-face contact, often knew of people who were living there already.[88] Although by this time the trades were diffused across the city, certain groups lived in concentrated areas: recent immigrants usually on the outskirts together with other people from their natal villages; high-status foreigners such as wealthy merchants in part of the central area; smelly or noisy trades away from the center; and controversial or politically powerful groups in enclaves but intermingled with other trades. In most but not all cities, the rich and poor gradually segregated during the later Middle Ages, with the former in the city center and the latter at its edges.[89]

These cities had begun in the twelfth century as markets with local customers, selling both agricultural products from the surrounding area and goods that professional merchants brought from farther away. The urban elites started as landowners who profited from the crops grown on their estates and then, as they became engaged in manufacturing, also began to seek more distant markets for their goods.[90] The guild system developed largely to provide quality control.[91] There was no clear distinction between merchants and artisans, because the merchant guilds included anyone who sold a significant quantity of goods, whether locally or through export. Although no person could belong to more than one guild at a time, people did change membership as circumstances required. The degree to which guild mastership or even membership was inherited varied by city and across time, but the artisan class was generally endogamous and the individual guilds exogamous. A guild master directed the work of journeymen, skilled laborers who got their training on the job or through apprenticeship and were then hired by the day or week. There was a large pool of young men in the cities, both journeymen and apprentices, with intermittent employment and very little power.[92]

The guilds typically formed fraternities for the social and charitable activities of their membership, but the relationship might develop in the reverse direction as well; that is, a religious or charitable fraternity might become associated with an occupational guild due to its connection to the church in the parish where the guild members lived. Fraternities generally outnumbered guilds, and banquet expenditures exceeded charity.[93] In Robert L.A. Clark's apt summary,

> The ritual and theatre of urban confraternities were dynamic forms which allowed for the systematic processing of experience and its articulation into symbolic systems of meaning, and the analysis of their fundamental structures will show that both ultimately served as vehicles for the self-definition and social promotion of the groups in question. Through the manipulation of these symbolic structures, they promoted their socio-ideological values, reconciled these values when they were in conflict, and ordered their world.[94]

Whether they were staged indoors or out, then, theatrical performances were part of an intensely public life.

Yet saint plays encourage a turning inward to private devotional practices, in contrast to our antitorture plays that foster a politics of pity. I'd like to suggest that the difference results from the different configuration of the medieval public sphere. Carol Symes argues that all of the conditions that Habermas lists as prerequisites for the emergence of a public sphere were present in medieval communities: "'early finance and trade capitalism,…long-distance trade,…horizontal economic dependencies' that disrupted traditional hierarchies, and the ways that 'the great trade cities became at the same time centers for the traffic in news,' opening up a 'new sector of communications.'"[95] As for media, medieval public culture included preaching and pamphleteering along with ritualized public behaviors. Kingship and other explicit power structures were performative enterprises that depended upon the public to participate and accept conventions. The only thing missing is the commercial news media that followed upon print culture, and Symes points out that this no longer seems clearly to be a deficit given the extent to which power manipulates the mass media.[96]

In the diffuse public spheres of post-modern global culture, we need empathy as a tool to foster communities of sentiment and produce concerted political action. Medieval urban culture had physical community—not a village in which everyone knew all members, but still a web of relationships in which everyone was enmeshed. The confraternity itself was at base a mutual aide society and operated within a Christian framework.

The difference between *Le Geu Saint Denis* and *The Island* is the sort of commitment that they nourish. The post-modern martyr play inspires outrage and public action, whereas the medieval saint play nourishes private spiritual practices. The critical difference between post-modern cognitive neuroscience and the late-medieval optics of compassionate vision supports this notion: our understanding of empathic response is relational, human to human, whereas theirs was a matter of divine impressions upon the inner spiritual sense.

2. Imagining Death ✧

Billy Crudup pulls on a black hood and kneels on the floor. Jeff Goldblum points a gun at his head and starts a countdown, but he pulls the trigger halfway to zero. Crudup falls over sideways. A wastebasket sits on the table center stage, lighter fluid flaming up inside it, ready to immolate the thick sheaf of papers that Zeljko Ivanek clutches on the other side of the room: the stories that have led to the martyrdom of Crudup's character, Katurian K. Katurian.

—*The Pillowman*[1]

Plate 3 Saint Denis picks up his head, with two angels to guide him, while Larcie watches, from *Légende de Saint Denis*.

> In the mansion that represents Heaven, the actor playing Jesus watches from behind his gilded mask the action in the main playing space: Saint Denis prays, then the sergeants chop at the saints' necks. Dummy heads roll, Rustique and Eleuthere fall to the ground, but Denis stoops down to pick up his own head. Angels lead him forward singing "Gloria tibi domine," then place him under a blanket and leave the playing area.
>
> —*Le Geu Saint Denis*[2]

This chapter examines the role of imagined pain in performances of sanctioned killing by the state, both on stage and off. Central to my comparison are differing notions of sympathy, now understood as an extension of the imagination but in the Middle Ages as a radical connectedness. This difference has implications for actual execution in each period, with the gallows rituals of late-medieval France providing reintegration for the community and the opaque American death chamber doing its best to efface the humanity of the condemned. Both the premodern and the post-modern state stage-manage their executions carefully as a mechanism for social control; however, the fact that they must kill always reveals their failure of control. The spectacle of suffering presents a danger to the state because, as Foucault points out, authorities cannot control spectator reception, and executions have often enough caused people to glorify the condemned.[3] Theatrical events typically exploit the same dynamic here as with torture, placing simulated execution within a dramatic framework that highlights the weakness and even the wrongful nature of the regime that puts people to death. Each of the plays at the center of this chapter presents a morally upright person facing execution, and each death produces a relic that continues to work in the world: for *Le Geu Saint Denis*, the saint's head; for *The Pillowman*, the manuscript that the protagonist dies in order to preserve. I will argue that the nature of the relic differs because the pre-modern and post-modern conceptions of physical body and interiority differ.

Both *Le Geu Saint Denis* and the public executions described by an anonymous Parisian between 1405 and 1449 show virtuous characters acting in the best interests of rightful authority regardless of temporary shifts in power and even when faced with death.[4] The two texts are roughly contemporaneous, with the *Parisian Journal* perhaps a bit earlier, and both put death on display in order to encourage reconciliation. I'd like to suggest a connection to the medieval notion of sympathy that Galen's scientific schema of humors, together with astrology, helped to shape: that is, as a kind of natural resonance not only between people but also between human beings and celestial bodies, organs and organisms, maladies and their cures, and animate and inanimate entities.[5] Certainly, many people still believe in such resonances although Western medicine does not, but they are less likely to speak of them as sympathies and are unlikely to put much credence in remedies such as the "powder of sympathy," which was supposed to heal wounds when it was "applied to a handkerchief or garment stained with blood from the wound, or to the weapon with which the wound was inflicted."[6] Medieval science understood the pneuma permeating the air and serving as a medium for vision to also enter the body and be transformed into vital and animal spirits. Based upon his dissection of pigs and apes, Galen thought of the ganglionated chain of nerves running along the spinal column and reaching into the viscera as a complex system of pathways along which the animal spirits traveled from organ to organ, establishing physiological sympathy between organs; hence, this chain became known as the sympathetic nervous system.[7]

Late-medieval France provided ample opportunities for death to restore balance, and a review of some salient events will help to ground my discussion for the reader not familiar with this history. The Hundred Years' War with England began in 1337 over contested territories that are now part of France but had been English fiefs, complicated by claims to the French succession: Edward III of England claimed the throne through his Capetian mother when Charles IV died in 1328 without male heirs, but the French crowned Philip of Valois as Philip VI. There were long periods without any active fighting, as each country dealt with other problems including the Black Death, and it was during a period of truce with England that civil struggles began between the Burgundian and Armagnac factions for control of France. Rather than appointing a regent when Philip's grandson Charles V died in 1380, the four remaining princes "of the blood"—that is, in a direct line of descent from Louis IX—had Charles VI crowned and consecrated at age twelve with themselves as his educators and advisors. He assumed full powers in 1388 but suffered his first of many debilitating attacks of madness in 1392. During the remaining thirty years of his reign, his uncles engaged in a prolonged struggle for control of the government. In contrast to the more or less stable allegiances in other parts of France, Paris switched hands repeatedly: first the Duke of Burgundy controlled the city, then the Armagnac faction who supported the Duke of Orléans, then the Burgundians again. High points include 1407, when the Duke of Burgundy had the Duke of Orléans murdered; 1418, when the Dauphin fled from Paris, and the Burgundians drove the Armagnacs out; and 1419, when the latter group had the Duke of Burgundy killed on his way to a meeting with the Dauphin. His successor turned to the English for support, and Charles VI signed the Treaty of Troyes in 1420. Among other provisions, it declared the Dauphin (Charles VII) illegitimate and gave the crown to Henry V of England, who had reignited the war in 1415 and seemed at this point to be winning. When both he and Charles VI died in 1422, the Duke of Bedford took control of Paris as regent for the infant Henry VI. The route of the English began at Orléans under Joan of Arc's leadership in 1429 and continued after her capture and death. Within a year after the Burgundians recognized Charles VII as king in 1435, French troops drove the English from Paris and then from the remaining regions by 1453. Charles VII remained alienated from his nation's leading city as he consolidated his rule and built a unified French nation.[8]

Pieter Spierenburg argues that public execution was vital to establishing absolute monarchy and then faded away as the modern nation-state grew more secure.[9] Pain's role in legal processes underwent significant change during the late-medieval and early-modern periods. Trial by ordeal had ended early in the thirteenth century, and the time for truly gruesome public executions was yet to come with the witch trials and wars of religion in the sixteenth century.[10] During the fourteenth and fifteenth centuries, torture took place behind closed doors, theoretically applied only in order to elicit the confession that itself became valid only after being written down, read out in court, and affirmed by the accused. The increasingly professional judicial system kept trials out of public view as well.[11] Spectacular suffering was now reserved for sentencing and execution, sharing recognizable forms all over Europe as Esther Cohen points out. Thieves were hung and murderers beheaded; heretics, witches, and sodomites were burned; traitors, drowned; counterfeiters, boiled; and those women who were not burned were buried alive. Those in power arranged the spectacles and called upon crowds to witness and thereby legitimate their exercise of power.[12]

In order for this system of justice to be effective, the public had to feel involved and adequately avenged. By granting confession and absolution of the repentant criminal, the church played a key role in casting the spectator as a participant in the execution of justice.[13] Until the late fourteenth century, criminals had been denied confession and shriving. The bodies were left to hang on the gallows for months or even years, then cut down but left to decay on the ground below. The criminal was thus excluded from the Christian community even in the afterlife. Then religious ceremonies of penitence changed the character of the spectacle, and by the end of the century, execution had become a ritual of expulsion followed by reincorporation.

Confession and absolution rehumanized the criminal and reintegrated him into the community, serving as both salvation for the criminal and spectacular evidence of God's grace and power.[14] According to Mitchell Merback, an execution could serve either as a "living *exemplum* of despair" if the condemned refused to confess and show remorse or as an example of the "good death" if he made his peace with God and prayed for forgiveness.[15] There was a widespread preoccupation with dying well, and one's fate after death was thought to hinge on it. Saint Catherine of Siena guided the nobleman Nicholas Tuldo through his death, catching his head when it was cut off, and many devotees turned to Saint Barbara, "patroness of the good death and protector against sudden and unprepared demise."[16] As a public ceremony, the execution restored balance for the community—in effect, the good death of a properly repentant murderer could cancel out the necessarily unprepared death of the person murdered.[17]

In Paris, elaborate processions to the gallows often followed in reverse the royal entry's path along the rue Saint Denis.[18] Both Henry V and the infant Henry VI made use of this performative ritual in Paris, as did the Capetian and Valois kings. Dressed to make their identity and station apparent (as were those going to their execution), a procession of citizens greeted the king outside the city. Together, they entered the city through the Saint Denis gate, where a pageant welcomed the king, and then moved to an entertainment organized by the Hôtel de Ville at the Ponceau Fountain. Next, the Confraternity of the Passion presented a pantomime or tableau vivant in front of the Hospital of the Trinity. The procession then passed through the Painters' Gate, where political harmony was the theme. As the king progressed through the commercial center of Paris, he encountered guild pageants at stations including the Hospital of Saint Catherine, the Church of the Sepulcher, the Great Butchery of Paris, and the Châtelet (where the *basoche*, the law clerks' guild, took charge of the presentation).[19] Like a royal entry, an execution is a rite of passage. Both king and criminal are liminal; that is, between states, separated from society under a previous identity, but not yet reintegrated as that which they will become.[20] Whereas the king is ceremonially recognized as such during the royal entry, the criminal is divested of all insignia of his social identity. Stripping, whipping, and even mutilation all contribute to performative shame and loss of identity.[21] Cohen says that the typical criminal procession in fifteenth-century Paris began at the prison, often moved to the site of the crime, and from there to the Place de Grève (for the beheading of a nobleman) or to a gibbet outside the city walls (for a commoner's hanging). Prisoners were usually pulled in a cart or dragged on a hurdle rather than moving under their own power, and the procession included acts of contrition and public recantation. The nobleman's head ended up on display at the gibbet, and his limbs might be displayed at the city gates[22]—the *Parisian Journal* features all of these.

The book can be divided into three periods, and the nature of the deaths characterizing each period reveals the *Journal's* implicit polemic. First, from the *Journal's* start in 1407 until the death of Charles VI, ritualized executions and other forms of processional suffering contribute to social order, while Armagnac rebels commit disorderly mayhem. During the second phase, from 1420 to 1436, English rule brings some stability to Paris, but the proper order of things is disrupted and the executions often enough botched. Like many subsequent analysts, the Bourgeois blames French infighting for English successes. Third, Paris is left to fend for itself during the gradual return to peace, and ceremony disappears—perhaps because the French nobility are no longer being executed; instead, English prisoners are drowned and beggars, thieves, and murders put to death. The *Journal* shows the Parisians supporting each ruler in succession, creating an overall portrait of citizens who simply desire the orderly rule of law without unbearable taxation. Some have speculated that the Bourgeois wrote the *Journal* in retrospect, to excuse his earlier support of the Anglo-Burgundian faction, and it could certainly serve this purpose. Their typical characteristics changing with each successive government, the *Journal's* executions justify Parisian acquiescence to sixteen years of English rule and at the same time establish steadfast loyalty to France.

Consider two exemplary executions during the *Journal's* early phase, with the city under Burgundian control. First, on 7 October 1409, Jean de Montaigu, Grand Master of the King's household, was arrested by the Provost of Paris, Pierre des Essarts. Implicated as an Armagnac partisan, he was

> put into a cart, wearing his own colours: an outer coat of red and white, hood the same, one stocking red and the other white, and gilt spurs. His hands were tied in front of him, holding a wooden cross. He was perched up in the cart like this and taken with two trumpeters before him to the Halles. There they cut his head off and afterwards his body was taken to the Paris gallows and hung up as high as it would go, in its shirt and hose and gilt spurs. (31)

His body remained on the gallows for nearly three years (69). Second, two years after the execution of de Montaigu and a good many others, Colinet du Puiseulx "sold" the bridge to St. Cloud to the Armagnac confederates. After the Burgundian faction retook that town, 12 November 1411,

> [Puiseulx] and six others were brought to the Halles in Paris; he was on a plank higher up in the cart than the rest, with a wooden cross in his hands, dressed as he had been when captured, as a priest. He was taken on to the scaffold like this, stripped naked, and beheaded, he and five of the others. The sixth was hanged, as he was not one of their evil confederacy. This Colinet, the false traitor, was dismembered, his four limbs hung up one over each of the chief gates of Paris, his body on the gallows in a sack, and their heads stuck up on six spears in the Halles, like false traitors that they were. (59–60)

These executions are typical for the early portion of the *Journal*. The traitors are of the noble class and have betrayed King Charles VI and the Duke of Burgundy. The means of conveyance, the contrite pose, the clothing as a sign of identity (real or assumed), the punishment, and the disposition of the corpse are all formulaic.

Contrasting with the ceremonious execution of noble traitors by the Burgundian rulers of Paris, reports of Armagnac mayhem in the countryside are sprinkled through this portion of the *Journal*. In the villages around Saint-Denis in 1411, for example, "they hanged people up by the thumbs or the feet, they killed or took for ransom, they raped women, and started fires" (55). Peace between the factions in August 1413 brought the Armagnacs into power in Paris and a temporary end to the executions. The bodies of those executed as traitors were taken down and buried in consecrated ground, to the consternation of the Bourgeois (80–81). The so-called peace also brought oppression, and the Bourgeois justifies riots in 1418 by describing an Armagnac plot to drown all the women of Paris in sacks. Those "confederates" not slaughtered by the mob were driven from Paris (112–19, 125–30). The Bourgeois' final assessment is that the rioters "martyred more people than the ancient enemies of Christianity did, ... But their cruelty was not comparable, God knows, to that of the confederates, and that is why the people rose up against them" (125–26). The Bourgeois repeatedly compares the Armagnacs in particular, but also the English, to Saracens and to tyrants such as Diocletian. Yet he casts no aspersions on the Dauphin, who escaped with his Armagnac supporters, leaving the ground clear for reconciliation after his return as King Charles VII in 1437.

With the end of peace, the *Journal* cites Armagnac atrocities outside Paris as explicit justification for Burgundy to negotiate with the English (149–50); for example, the Bourgeois greets the English conquest of Meaux in 1422 with relief because that town's Armagnac tyrant, the Bastard of Vauru, was "a crueller man than ever Nero or anyone else was" (174). In 1420, this tyrant captured a young working man, tortured him, and demanded an unreasonable ransom from the man's pregnant wife. When she arrived late with the money, de Vauru "pitilessly drowned or hanged" several other peasants in front of the exhausted woman, took her money, and only then revealed that he had already hanged her husband. Annoyed by her outburst of grief, the tyrant had her beaten and then bound to the elm tree where nearly a hundred earlier victims hung, "all her clothes cut off short so that she was naked as far as her navel, an inhuman thing to do!" As corpses stirred in the breeze, "the feet of those hanging lower down brushed against her head," and night fell:

> When she thought about the dreadful place where she was, so terrifying to human nature, she began to grieve and sob all over again, saying, "Oh God, will this awful suffering never stop?" She shouted so loud and so long that the people in the city could hear her plainly, but none of them would have dared to go and get her away; they would have been killed. In all this pain and crying, the pains of childbirth took her, partly because of her anguished shouting, partly because of the cold wind which attacked her on all sides. Her pains came faster and faster; she shrieked so loud that the wolves which used to go there for corpses heard her; they went straight to the noise she was making and attacked her, especially her poor naked belly—they opened it with their cruel teeth, pulled out the child in pieces and tore the rest of her body to bits. (174–75)

The unpredictability of events, along with the victim's innocence and the emphasis on her suffering, sharply distinguishes the disorderly violence of the Armagnac faction from the ritualized executions carried out by the Burgundians. In addition, the relation between the nobility and the common people who witness their exercise of power could hardly be more different. One type of killing seems to create order; the other, to destroy it.

During the Duke of Bedford's regency, Paris appears subject to a kind of hybrid violence, with executions that adhere to the established ceremonial form but also disrupt it. In 1428, for example, when "an esquire called Sauvage de Fremainville was captured…He was quickly bound and put on a horse, hatless, his hands and feet tied" (221). The Regent ordered an immediate hanging "without hearing his defence—they were very much afraid he would be rescued, for he was of very great lineage." The prisoner is not properly attired, has no trial, and is not allowed to confess. Moreover, both he and the executioner suffer additional pain that is not part of the punishment itself. Accompanying the prisoner and the Provost of Paris was "one Pierre Baillé, originally a shoemaker's boy in Paris, then tipstaff, then Receiver of Paris, and now Grand Treasurer of Maine."

> This Pierre Baillé, when Le Sauvage wanted to make his confession, refused to let him live so long but made him climb the ladder at once and climbed two or three steps up after him, shouting at him. Le Sauvage did not reply to his liking, so this Pierre gave him a great blow with a stick and gave the hangman five or six too, because he was talking to him about his soul's salvation. The hangman, seeing Baillé's ill will, was afraid he might do something worse to him, and so, being frightened, hurried more than he ought to have done and hanged Le Sauvage; but because of his haste the rope broke or came undone and the condemned man fell and broke his back and one leg. Yet he had to climb up again, suffering as he was, and was hanged and strangled. (221–22)

Unseemly haste combined with the *arriviste* Baillé's bad temper to botch this execution, illustrating the dangers of a disrupted social hierarchy.

The *Journal* shows ordinary Parisians suffering at all times, but they are worse off when neither the Duke of Burgundy nor the English are in Paris to protect them. During most of the English period, the Bourgeois focuses on the progress of the war and on hardships due both to natural disasters and to being cut off from the French countryside. As though the English troops had behaved well up to this point, the *Journal* describes their depredations in the villages around Paris only immediately before the troops of King Charles (no longer referred to as the Dauphin) retake the city in 1436. After France regains Paris, ceremony disappears—perhaps because the nobility are no longer being executed. English prisoners brought from Pontoise present a "sad spectacle" in 1441 as they are led out of Paris, "coupled together two and two with very strong rope, just like hounds being led out to the hunt, and their captors riding tall horses which went very fast. The prisoners had no hoods, all bareheaded, each wearing some wretched rag, most often without shoes and hose—everything, in fact, had been taken from them but their underpants" (345). The prisoners who cannot pay their ransom are drowned "with no more compunction than if they had been dogs" (346). After this, political treachery disappears from the text as well, and the Bourgeois mentions the executions only of ragtag criminals at the margins of society. Those who were formerly the "Armagnac confederates" are now the rightful French rulers, and they execute rightfully; however, the public ritual described thirty years earlier is now absent from the text.

Even when the means of death conformed to a clear symbolic code, the execution was a complex performative act. Cohen points out that its secular and spiritual messages often conflicted, and Merback identifies three competing narratives—one constructed by secular authorities, another by the people, and a third by the church.[23] Chroniclers stress the importance of spectators—many of them—as an active component of the events. Public reaction ranged from tears to bloodthirsty shouts and was anticipated by the authorities who designed an execution—but not always correctly. Last-minute reprieves and popular rescues were possible, adding a degree of suspense, and an unmarried man at the gallows could be spared death by a woman willing to marry him.[24]

Nor was the performance itself always orderly. Jody Enders points out that the executed prisoner sometimes refused to play his role and that the spectators were upon occasion "forced to invent their own pathos when the victim failed to provide it."[25] She cites the execution of Pierre des Essarts, the Provost who had earlier arrested Jean de Montaigu and was then implicated in the Armagnac conspiracy of 1413. After several months' imprisonment,

> On 1st July 1413 the Provost was dragged on a hurdle from the Palais to the Heaumerie or thereabouts and then made to sit on a bench in a cart, holding a wooden cross in his hand. He wore a black slashed outer coat furred with marten skins, white hose and black slippers on his feet. Thus he was taken to the Halles and his head was cut off and stuck up a good three feet higher than the others. (73)

This much of the description conforms to the formula that was typical for this period. The ending is mostly orderly as well:

> When he realized that he had got to die, he knelt down in front of the executioner, kissed a little silver figure that the executioner had round his neck, and forgave him his death very kindly.... Thus was Pierre des Essarts beheaded and his body was taken to the gallows and hanged as high up as it would go. (74)

Given these portions of the text, one can easily see two forces at work. First, the secular authorities, who may have used torture to produce a confession of guilt, impose the punishment. Theirs is the power to inflict pain and to expel the traitor. Even before that, they had the power to decide that he *was* a traitor. In this case, they have labeled as such the man in charge of Parisian security. Second, the church has the power to produce a confession of sin during the execution spectacle and thus to reintegrate the traitor. He still dies but returns to the Christian community, which is not clearly separable from the polity.

A third voice, that of the prisoner, is not always present in the records or in the analyses. Des Essarts is an exception. The text interposes a remarkable coup between his formulaic pardon of the executioner and his death: "He asked all the lords that his deeds should not be proclaimed till after he was dead; this they agreed to" (74). The display of a prisoner's crimes was a preeminent component of the punishment ritual. That des Essarts retained an unusual power even in death is shown by this ability to exact concessions from those who executed him. Des Essarts was not fully shamed. Indeed, his very shamelessness is what I have thus far left out of the description. Like the secular authorities, which condemn, and the clerical, which absolve, des Essarts anticipates the response of spectators: "The astonishing thing was that he did nothing but laugh all the time from the moment he was tied to the hurdle till his death, just as he used to do in the time of his greatest majesty." The spectators, in turn, seem to carry out their customary performance with little regard for the event they see: "Most people thought his brain had turned, for everyone watching him was crying bitterly, weeping more miserably than you ever heard tell of for any man's death. And he laughed, he alone. He imagined that the people would prevent his death" (74). Indeed, the Bourgeois has earlier mentioned that the Parisians loved des Essarts "because he defended the city so well" (52), and that "no Provost for a century past had been so well loved both by the King and by the people" (70). The people here—as throughout the *Journal*—behave as they should, whereas both the powerful prisoner and the lords who have sentenced him go against form.

Enders assumes that the spectators wept because they identified and commiserated with des Essarts. But some of them must have known, as did the Bourgeois, that the Provost "intended to betray the town and deliver it into the hands of its enemies, to commit very great and dreadful murders, and to rob and pillage the good inhabitants of the good town of Paris who loved him so loyally" (74). Spectators might well have wept bitterly because they were betrayed by one in whom they had placed their trust—who had been, even worse, in charge of justice. They might have wept at the spectacle of a man whom they had loved refusing to repent and being, therefore, denied a good death. Some might have cried to have been left more vulnerable to English attack by the execution of this Frenchman who had defended their city so well.

Spectators might also have felt reassured by playing their part in the ritual, even though the prisoner refused to play his. The execution ritual simultaneously erases and reinforces social differentiation, just as ceremonial inversions both mock and support the given social order. The "spectators" at a public execution perform for one another, for the criminal, and for the authorities. Some might have wept because they were expected to, regardless of their personal sympathies. Their performance created a world regardless of the feelings of individual spectator/participants. During a period when Paris was violently divided, the proper performance of the crowd at des Essarts' execution enhanced the appearance of unity. Perhaps at some moments the crowd was able to perform unity in the strict sense of performativity—that is, to bring it into being. I propose that it did so in the long run, in spite of the many violent reversals throughout this period. The various forms of suffering and the political crises of the fourteenth and fifteenth centuries produced a desire and a clearly visible need for a government that was both secure and just. One result was progress toward absolute monarchy. As Charles VII pulled France back together, those who might have in the past served as competition or as checks—the church, the nobility, and the cities—were willing to have their power subsumed under that of the ever-more-sacred monarchy.[26]

As a ritual of expulsion, the execution confirms the boundaries of the community. When confession is added, the ritual also emphasizes integration and redemption, but it does not erase the expulsion; rather, it excludes *and* reintegrates the criminal, and the community can imagine itself as both bounded and unified. In the end, reincorporating the excluded criminal within the Christian community makes marginality and dissent less tenable for the community in secular terms as well.

As represented on the medieval stage, execution also brings the past into the present and thus confirms the continuity of the Christian community across time. Because most saint plays feature at least one beheading, medieval producers had ample opportunity to develop the requisite special effects. The play of Saint George performed at Turin in 1429 required eleven severed heads and a complete body of the saint, along with many other items related to dummy bodies; in Majorca, one dummy filled with straw substituted for Saint Crispin and another for Saint Crispinian; the Bourges *Acts of the Apostles* needed two severed heads and "a well (*puys*) to throw the dead bodies into," also requiring Saint Paul's head to "bounce three times, and from each bounce will spring up a fountain from which will flow milk, blood, and water."[27] The manuscript is not forthcoming with the mechanics of this last scene, but there is no reason to think that the Bourges producers didn't manage to make it happen.

Following upon the severe torments that martyrs survive with equanimity, decapitation symbolically severs the connection between soul and body—although the soul is not understood to reside in the head, the face is the clearest sign of identity. Yet the martyr's decapitation is a reward rather than an ending: he or she goes straight to Heaven without any time in Purgatory. Their very deaths keep saints present and active in the world. As Patrick Geary notes, "in the West, the preferred medium through which God used his saints was their bodies. Their corpses were seen as the *pignora*, literally, the security deposits left by the saints upon their deaths as guarantees of their continuing interest in the earthly community."[28] Saints maintained an ongoing and reciprocal relationship with the Christians who cared for their relics. Monastic communities mediated between the living and the dead by praying to the saints on behalf of the local population and by performing the ritual veneration of relics needed to maintain the saint's patronage and protection. When the relationship between the religious and the lay communities was disturbed, the monks used ritual humiliation of the saints' relics to punish not only the lay community but also the saints for allowing the situation to arise.[29]

The head of Saint Denis was a particularly important relic. As the first Bishop of Paris, he converted the Gauls to Christianity during the third century and was martyred by Roman civil authorities. Late-medieval France endowed this Denis with aspects of two additional historical figures as the result of a *Life of Saint Denis* written in 835 by Abbot Hilduin of the abbey Saint-Denis, which lies just outside Paris. Hilduin attributed to Saint Denis certain mystical and theological texts actually written by Denis the pseudo-Areopagite in sixth-century Syria. More directly relevant to this play, Hilduin also believed that this was the same Denis as the Bishop of Athens mentioned in the Acts of the Apostles, XVII:32–34, martyred during the first century under Domitian.[30] Dynastic crises tended to produce new versions of the saint's life that shored up both the abbey Saint-Denis and the monarchy, including a new *Life and Works* written at Saint-Denis around 1223–33 and Yves de Saint-Denis's version of 1317, the source for some of this book's illustrations. The conflation of figures was maintained officially until 1722 in spite of all evidence to the contrary.[31] French kings had visions "proving" that Saint Denis was their guardian. He protected the king's body from harm of any sort, whether wounds or illness, protected his soul as well, was with him at his death, and by the late Middle Ages helped him to escape not only Hell but also Purgatory.[32]

In *Le Geu Saint Denis*, after the saint picks up his head and sings God's praises, his angel escorts conceal him under a blanket and return to Paradise. Spectators were expected to understand that these angels have taken his body to Etrée, where the following play features the construction of a church.[33] But in the 1317 version of his life, Denis carries his head to the village of Catulliacum and gives it to a woman named Catulla, who places the saint's body in a tomb near her home. The name of the village is eventually changed to Saint-Denis, and the abbey is located there.[34] That different treatments of the legend deposit the relics differently is hardly surprising. Although the abbey Saint-Denis had the corpse of the third-century Bishop Denis of Paris, crusaders brought what Colette Beaune nicely terms "competing bits of skeleton" to France after the conquest of Constantinople in 1204. When the body of Bishop Denis of Corinth arrived in Rome, Pope Innocent III hedged his bets: just in case the Denis who converted Gaul was *not* the apostle converted by Paul, he made sure that both bodies were safely lodged at the abbey Saint-Denis. But the Cistercian abbey of Longport, in competition with Saint-Denis for royal favor, had a head retrieved from Byzantium that was alleged to belong to Denis the Areopagite. Notre-Dame also entered the fray around 1350 with the claim to have the top of Denis's skull. Saint-Denis objected "that every version of the story of Saint Denis said that the saint had been decapitated; none claimed that the top of his skull had been removed."[35] The dispute accelerated to the point that it was tried before the Parlement of Paris in 1410, and partisans of the various relics staged rival processions and forbade their competitors from preaching. Charles VI and his brother Louis, Duke of Orléans, supported the monks of Saint-Denis. Given that Denis is the patron saint of France and that his communion with Jesus and *post mortem* carrying of his own head are the two moments of his life most often illustrated, I think we have to understand them as especially important to the French public imagination—at least historically. Denis has direct contact with Jesus. Although foreigners might cut off his head, he can pick that head right up again. The close ties between Saint Denis and the French crown make the metaphor obvious.

Le Geu Saint Denis presents two vertical hierarchies that mirror one another, the world ruled by Roman emperor Domitian comprising an antiworld that duplicates but inverts the proper order of God's creation. The play's structure conforms to Jelle Koopmans' observation that medieval religious drama stages a conflict between good and evil, made visible in the quotidian world as an opposition between all that conforms to the social norm and is, therefore, good, because it accords with God's will, and that which escapes this norm and is, therefore, *not* good but its opposite.[36] Jesus himself appears on stage first in the company of three angels to administer communion for Denis and his evangelical companions in jail before their execution (839–91) and once again when he dispatches two angels to take Denis' body to Etrée (1005–9). Saints Rustique and Eleuthere have little independent identity within the play. They shadow Denis, both amplifying his presence by putting three bodies on stage instead of one and also helping to create a hierarchical continuum, from Jesus to the nation's patron saint, down to the companions whom he supervises, on to the bourgeois converts within the dramatic frame, and from them to the late-medieval spectator. As Brigitte Cazelles asserts, saints were "not so much models to be imitated as they were exceptions to be admired."[37] Their closeness to God entails distance from normal humanity, an intermediate position that makes them available as intercessors. The Parisian bourgeoisie form the base layer of the play's spiritual hierarchy, free—like their counterparts in the audience—to choose between good and evil. Through onstage conversion, Lisbie and Larcie move up from this group of undifferentiated Parisian pagans to join the martyrs in death, and one assumes that Catulle secretly converted to Christianity at some point in the past.

At this play's spiritual nadir, the emperor Domitian directs the actions of Parisian provost Fescennin and his henchmen. The medieval staging practice of simultaneous setting gives to God's world and the pagan antiworld a powerful visual impact beyond what the text conveys. By itself, this play requires three distinct locations: Heaven, from which Jesus dispatches the angels; Rome, from which Domitian directs the persecutions; and Paris, to which Pope Clement sends Denis on his evangelical mission. Other plays in this cycle of early martyrs require Damascus and Athens. Hell was very likely present although no devils figure in this play, because they do take an active part in the cycle's immediately preceding *Martyrdom of Saint Peter and Saint Paul*. Didascaliae clearly indicate that Paradise is elevated, and a direction at line 130 for Lysbie to descend suggests an elevated Paris as well. We can reasonably imagine all of what the text calls *logeis* as raised and decorated seating areas where actors waited while other scenes played out in the neutral space. Runnalls thinks that the action in prison, the inn, or the home of Catulle might be played in the neutral space (*champ* or *jeu*).[38] This is certainly where the martyrs are tormented and beheaded. Through most of the play, then, Domitian and his minions rule the physical playing space, with Jesus or his angels making a few incursions, but Denis is always its spiritual center.

The inverse mirroring of good and evil carries through at the level of dialogue as well. When Denis preaches that "our God is the true God, and true man, and old and new" (113–14), his Parisian listeners ridicule what they perceive as a contradiction, suggesting that "when he goes out, he has an old cloak and a new robe" (121–22) or that "he has often gone to bathe in the fountain of youth" (130–31). Denis responds with a sermon on God the creator and incarnate savior (141–71). Like the other Parisians, "*le plus noble bourgois*." Lisbie starts out incredulous and challenges Denis to explain why many gods are worshiped if only a single God exists. Unlike the others, however, he listens and gradually accepts what he is told. Lisbie's final question, how this singular God can have three natures, is a request for clarification rather than a counterargument. After Lisbie's baptism, alarmed fellow citizens go after Denis as a mob with knives drawn but then flee in terror when they find that they don't dare to harm him (135–342).

Meeting the Roman provost Fescennin and his sergeants on their way to put an end to Christian proselytizing in Paris, these pagan citizens repeat blasphemous (and surely amusing) *reductiae* of the saint's preaching:

> Sir, he preaches one God in Paris, who makes all the hills and dales. He goes on horseback without horses. He makes and unmakes all at once. He lives, he dies; he sweats, he shivers. He cries, he laughs; he watches and sleeps. He is young and old; weak and strong. He makes a cock into a hen. He practices black magic. I don't know what else this could be. (388–405)[39]

Upon arrival in Paris, the Romans behead Lisbie because his wife Larcie denounces him (461–85). But the saint turns the profane world upside down as well. When the sergeants bring Denis and his companions before Fescennin, Denis turns all comments and questions into opportunities to interject the word of God. When a sergeant, for example, calls him an evil old man and threatens to send him—undoubtedly transported by blows—to "Pierrelate," Denis replies: "Jesus Christ, who for us was taken to Pilate, save you gentlemen!" (413–17).[40] I'll revisit the function of this pervasive verbal inversion in chapter 5.

Later in the play, having watched the three saints calmly prepare for death in prison and receive communion from Jesus, Larcie also converts to Christianity (839–912). Plate 3 shows her watching the saints' execution, after which she calls the sergeants "bad tyrants, bad pagans" and demands to know why they kill Christians, "who have a good religion, true and whole," whereas theirs is "bad and vain, false, disloyal, and damnable" (1042–46).[41] In response, they chop off her head. Then, frightened by the angelic hymns, the sergeants flee. Larcie obeys (without instruction) the true Christian authority after her conversion, in contrast to her preconversion complicity with a transient secular authority—a fine example for Parisians in a time of repeatedly shifting allegiances. Lisbie and Larcie show their audience what constitutes a good death.

As antimodels for behavior, the play provides Roman sergeants bearing typically alimentary names: Menjumatin (morning-eater), Humebrouet (soup-slurper), Hapelopin (gobbet-snatcher), and Masquebignet (fritter-face).[42] Gluttony gets the best of them when they're supposed to be dumping the saints' bodies into the river. They fight over the tart that Catulle offers them, spur one another on in an extended drinking bout, then climb onto the table to sleep off the meal—giving her servants the chance to safely bury Rustique and Eleuthere (1089–164). This episode's inverse complement follows, in a sort of epilogue featuring two saints whom Denis had earlier sent off to preach in Meaux: Senctin and Anthonin stop at an inn on their way to Rome, where they have been tasked to deliver an account of Denis's acts and his martyrdom, and they show no interest in the sumptuous feast they are offered. Senctin pays the innkeeper handsomely to take care of Anthonin, who has fallen ill, and then travels on alone. The greedy man allows Anthonin to die, steals his belongings, and throws his body into a refuse pit (1234–1323). Here Jesus intervenes once again, sending the angel Michiel to turn Senctin back so that he can restore Anthonin to life by the power of Saint Denis (1324–94). The dishonest innkeeper is frightened, repents of his wrongdoing, returns Anthonin's gold, and converts (1395–1474).

The play is surprisingly conciliatory: the guilty are not punished, unlike the father of Saint Barbara, who is struck by lightning after he beheads his daughter; the soldiers killed when the wheel with which they were torturing Saint Catherine explodes; or the tormentors of Sapientia's daughters in Hrotsvit's play, who are killed by the bursting pot of oil and exploding furnace. After denouncing her husband and causing his death, Larcie converts and receives a proper Christian decapitation. Even the sergeants remain unharmed after they torment and behead Saint Denis. They merely flee the holy spectacle in distress, then get drunk and lose the bodies that they were charged to dump into the Seine. The absence of punishment is clearly a feature of the drama itself rather than the underlying narrative: the 1317 life of Saint Denis ends with the Emperor Domitian assassinated after proclaiming himself a god. Thieves strip his corpse, which is then thrown to the dogs.[43] Crucially, *only* the Roman authorities inflict harm in the course of this play. When the Parisians attack Denis, they find themselves impotent—perhaps implying that the French enjoyed God's protection even before they converted. As Beaune points out, the late-medieval French thought of themselves as having replaced the Hebrews as God's Chosen People: they "believed their country was the best and most ardently faithful of all Christian kingdoms.... From it sprang saints, not heroes."[44]

Taken as a whole, this six-play cycle supports the central importance of a whole and unified Paris. The cycle ends with *Les Miracles de Sainte*

Geneviève, celebrating the city's patron saint. Of this play's fourteen separate episodes, the longest shows Geneviève securing divine protection for her city, under attack by the Huns. The martyrs of the manuscript's earlier plays all return to the stage and support her efforts with prayers and praise. In another episode highlighting the importance of Paris, Saint Geneviève provides the lime required for the church that commemorates Saint Denis at Etrée and a miraculous wine jug to keep the stonemasons happy while they build it.[45] Staging Paris as a valuable and indisputably French city, the performance of *Le Geu Saint Denis* and its companion plays provided an opportunity to perform reconciliation and, by means of performance, create a unified France. If, as Koopmans suggests, mysteries were performed in order to "cajole" God,[46] perhaps performances of *Le Geu Saint Denis* exhorted him to let Paris heal its wounds. Those who were involved in the Hundred Years' War conceived of it as being fought to restore justice. Victory was given by God and served as a sign that the cause was just, whereas defeat showed God's *temporary* displeasure with social disorder and sinfulness.[47] The performance of *Le Geu Saint Denis* demonstrated to God that France was indeed the most Christian of nations, forgiving and unified, and deserving of his grace.

In a world infused with pneuma and with God, the relic is a visible reminder of his presence and involvement. God is not directly perceived or accessed but instead glimpsed through the lives of holy men and women and reached through them as well, alive or dead. Instead of this radical connectedness, *The Pillowman* gives us a radical separation: a man alone facing his judges, who are his accusers and executioners as well, unsure not only of the rules but even of the charges, taking responsibility for his imagination. The pain that he imagines and that we watch makes us care about him. The jarring and unjustified death, though, makes us wish for ways to connect that don't depend upon suffering.

* * *

The Pillowman's climactic execution features no pain behavior to speak of. Like most executions acted out on stage, it's over quickly, understood in terms of what has gone before and often enough also what comes after it. Watching Crudup die as McDonagh's character Katurian K. Katurian is about shock and finality, not pain. We see a similar effect in the recent American/Afghani collaboration *Beyond the Mirror* as it stages beheadings and a hanging in silhouette behind a screen: heads drop forward one after another, seeming to vanish as a pole is drawn across at neck level; later, a head drops suddenly to the side, suggesting a neck broken at the end of a rope.[48] *Beyond the Mirror* moves quickly through successive regimes in Afghanistan—the Soviet occupation, the mujahadeen, the Taliban, the United States chasing after Osama bin Laden—each of which kills Afghanis one way or another. The executions gain their effect through clean abruptness: A shot and a fall, a jerk and a head drop, and suddenly we see an actor as "dead"—a perceptual slap, built up to but never quite prepared for. Execution makes an effective final punctuation for plays ranging from *Machinal* in 1928 to the *Dead Man Walking School Project*, ongoing since 2005, and it ends each vignette in Stephen Sondheim's musical *Assassins*, first staged in 1991 and revived in 2004.[49] Whether the death on display is overtly painful or not, it easily evokes pain—in the eye of the beholder, as it were.

We perceive violent death as painful because we tend to equate pain and death, but we may be quite mistaken. When shot in the chest in 1981, former actor and then-president Ronald Reagan didn't even know that he was wounded. He said, "I had never been shot before except in the movies. Then you always act as though it hurts. Now I know that does not always happen."[50] Investigating the surprising fact that even the most dire injuries sometimes cause no immediate pain, although pain does develop later, Patrick Wall begins with the example of a Swiss army officer who sustained multiple fractures in a skiing accident but felt only shame as he supervised his rescue from the crevasse in which he was wedged. The pain began forty-five minutes later, as he lay in a helicopter on the way to the hospital. Wall notes that, of the Allied troops wounded on the Anzio beachhead in 1944, 70 percent of those admitted to a certain hospital said that they were not in pain. The stress and excitement of the battlefield do not provide an adequate explanation, as he learned by interviewing amputees. Of the seventy-three who lost limbs in a wide variety of situations—some of them in traffic accidents or while asleep—during the 1973 Yom Kippur War, all but a few reported experiencing no pain at the time of injury; instead, they used neutral words such as "bang" or "thump" to describe the sensations. And outside the context of war, 37 percent of the 138 patients that Wall and Ronald Melzack interviewed in a Montreal emergency room said that they felt no pain when they were injured.[51]

As Wall came to understand it, our brains produce pain as a potential for action. He proposes that the brain analyzes sensory input not to determine what has happened but to determine what action is appropriate. The action need not be carried out: brain imaging studies show that when subjects endure a painful stimulus without moving at all but later are able to describe the pain that they experienced, the most active areas of their brain are those involved in motor planning (not actual motor movement).[52] Pain also activates the part of the brain involved in attention, helping to explain why distraction can provide relief. Wall says that the purpose of attention is to put together those sensory inputs that are relevant to carrying out a single action, and that we pay attention to only one thing at a time—multitasking is actually quick switching.[53] Pain is a plan of action to avoid a stimulus that could produce injury or death. Being killed, the epitome of passive subjection, puts an absolute end to avoidance or any other action.

We cannot know what it feels like to die; however, we do know what it feels like to hurt, and we extend ourselves imaginatively, drawing upon our store of embodied experiences, to share the pain of an actor, of an effigy, of a corpse. Here I adopt Martha Nussbaum's definition of "sympathy" as "a painful emotion occasioned by the awareness of another person's undeserved misfortune," necessarily involving the spectator's judgment that the suffering should not occur.[54] Adam Smith introduced the understanding of sympathy as an imaginative exercise and a moral faculty in the eighteenth century: "Though our brother is on the rack... our sense will never inform us of what he suffers.... By the imagination we place ourselves in his situation, we conceive ourselves enduring all the same torments, we enter as it were into his body, and become in some measure the same person with him."[55] Sympathetic imagination has become for us a matter of course. For example, the recent production of McDonagh's *The Lieutenant of Inishmore* featured the sawing off of heads and general dismemberment of corpses throughout the second act, the beautiful shale floor of the set running with blood. Not only are the "sufferers" dead within the dramatic narrative of this play, but they are clearly dummies. Spectators cringed at the brutality, but they also laughed heartily at the jokey dialogue, at the difficult labor of cutting through a limb or a neck, and at the gruesome ordinariness of the scene as it is staged.[56] Both the blood and the mutilation evoked pain even though no one was hurting.

This situation more closely resembles medieval execution than it does contemporary capital punishment. As Austin Sarat notes, contemporary executions ideally are painless, medicalized, and hidden.[57] The methods currently available in the United States are, in descending order of popularity, injection, electrocution, gas, hanging, and firing squad. Means of execution go out of fashion as supposedly more humane (less painful) technologies develop. The search for painless ways to kill began in the late eighteenth century, as Western Europe and America increasingly punished with incarceration rather than pain.[58] Sarat points out that the state seeks painless methods of killing in order to distinguish lawful execution from the crimes that it punishes and also to make sure that the condemned cannot "become an object of pity and, in so doing, appropriate the status of the victim."[59] When convicted, wealthy criminals in the United States may serve long prison terms but are not executed. For the notorious, execution runs the danger of creating a hero. The federal jury rejected the death penalty for Zacarias Moussaoui in May 2006, sentencing him to life in prison.[60] The following December, the execution of Saddam Hussein in Iraq provided new fodder for Shiite-Sunni division and frustration for the United States, both exacerbated when someone leaked a cell phone video of the hanging.[61] During arraignment at Guantánamo Bay in June 2008, Khalid Shaikh Mohammed proclaimed his wish for martyrdom, and others of the detainees accused of planning the 9/11 attacks followed suit.[62]

Technology serves to distance the killing, to mask the state's agency, and to "hierarchize the relationship between the state and those whose lives it takes."[63] The courts that address challenges to capital punishment obsessively try to read the signs of pain on the body of the executed, but what really obsesses them is the suffering of witnesses—both those present at executions and those who imagine them. The search for a painless way to kill is motivated by a desire to prevent *witnesses* from suffering.[64] As Dwight Conquergood points out with respect to lethal injection, "Putting the prisoner to sleep before killing him or her...keeps up the appearance of decency, protects the witnesses from messy scenes, and masks the violence of state killing with a humane medical procedure."[65] The state relies upon our imaginative equation of death with pain even as it hides the controlled and sanctioned violence of capital punishment from view. Most Americans never witness such events in person. The media shrink from showing actual death but maintain our grisly fascination with representations of suffering that, as Susan Sontag puts it, produce not only "the satisfaction of being able to look at the image without flinching" but also "the pleasure of flinching."[66]

Both medieval French and contemporary American executions are staged to shore up the state's control, but they differ in important ways. In addition to the act of killing, multiple components of the medieval execution ritual (such as stripping the prisoner of identity and status before death, then mutilating and displaying the corpse afterward) reminded the spectators that the condemned could be any one of them. Rather than expelling and then reincorporating the contrite criminal, traitor, or heretic on the gallows, modern executions dehumanize and expel the condemned in order to exonerate the state. Medicalized and hidden procedures erase the pain and death of a criminal who is already outside the community, always-already stripped of status. Arguing that "contemporary execution rituals work their magic and derive their efficacy from the effusive power of the effigy," Conquergood writes:

> Because a jury will never vote to kill a human being, the fundamental task of the prosecutor is to turn the accused into an effigy composed of his or her worst parts and bad deeds. Before they are strip-searched and strapped down to the execution gurney, the condemned must first be stripped of all human complexity and reduced to human waste, the worst of the worst. These waste parts are then crafted onto prefabricated figures: stereotypes of the violent criminal, cold-blooded killer, animal, beast, brute, predator, fiend, monster.[67]

With the condemned effectively dehumanized, arguments in favor of the death penalty focus not upon punishment but upon the survivors' need for closure.

In the face of real or theatrical execution during any historical era, it remains open for the spectator to identify the state killing as wrong. The botched execution provides the readiest ammunition for such accusations, as we saw when the Bourgeois for implicitly polemical effect described late-medieval botching as an exception. Spectacular suffering occurs in contemporary American executions only as a result of accidents or resistance by the condemned. Conquergood points out that the most important form of agency remaining to condemned prisoners is the ability to fight back and destroy the illusion of painless killing; for example, Gary Graham resisted and protested his innocence all the way to the Texas execution chamber in 2000. He had to be forcibly removed from his cell, and he protested, "they're killing me tonight, they're murdering me tonight" even as the poison made its way into his system.[68] Even when the prisoner does not fight back, accidents "knock down the ritual frame and expose the gruesome reality of actually putting a human being to death."[69] Conquergood details a multitude of possible technical failures: for the electric chair, bad connections or too much voltage; for lethal injection, hard-to-find veins; for hanging, faulty calculations of the rope-to-weight ratio required to hang a person without ripping off the head or leaving the body to dangle and slowly strangle.

Even without accident or incompetence, execution can look painful; for example, the gas chamber fell out of favor because it proved too hard to prevent common reactions such as thrashing, convulsing, and foaming at the mouth. Whether the condemned experiences pain during the execution or is already unconscious when the reaction occurs is moot: the spectators *see* suffering. Electrocution loosens the sphincters and causes the eyes to bulge out—even worse, the condemned caught on fire more than once in Florida, leading Justice Leander J. Shaw, Jr. to contrast the electric chair unfavorably with what he considers a painless death by guillotine. He appended photographs of a botched electrocution to his dissenting opinion, arguing that electrocution is not only painful but also mutilates and disgraces the victim, whereas the guillotine is objectionable only because of its violence and the bloody spectacle that it produces.[70] Timothy Kaufman-Osborn likens killing a woman to a botched execution. Although the "occasional state-sponsored killing of a woman materializes and so reinforces the liberal ideal of equality before the law," the female body is "conventionally coded as docile, as nonpredatory, as in need of masculine protection." Killing a woman thus highlights the brutality of capital punishment, regardless of the fact that the woman is herself a killer and clearly does not correspond to the conventional image.[71]

The Pillowman's stark and brutal execution bridges the gap between the medicalized "death cure" and the kind of executions that Americans tend to think of as occurring in other parts of the world. Violent death is hardly rare on stage, ubiquitous in McDonagh's plays. *The Pillowman* is unusual, however, in framing the death of the protagonist as a lawful execution in a totalitarian state where the police are authorized to execute a criminal as soon as they are convinced of his guilt. The state depicted in this play is repressive, arbitrary, and unpredictable—that's all we know about it, and both of its police representatives seem to be sociopaths. At the play's start, Katurian doesn't know why he has been arrested, except that it's connected to his stories. He assumes that the authorities have found a political message and scrambles to prove that none was intended.

Interrogation by the mercurial Lieutenant Tupolski (Goldblum) soon establishes that the stories link Katurian and his mentally deficient brother Michal (Michael Stuhlbarg) to a series of macabre child murders. They go over a few of the plots, including "The Little Apple Men": a girl tricks her abusive father into eating little apple men containing razor blades but then chokes to death on her own blood when the surviving apple men climb down her throat seeking vengeance.[72] Katurian has published only one of the hundreds of stories he has written, and Tupolski makes him read this one aloud: in "The Tale of the Town on the River," the Pied Piper of Hamelin responds to a little boy's act of kindness by hacking off his toes—a reciprocal kindness that prevents the boy from joining the procession of children dancing after the piper to their death (21–22). Katurian has read all of the stories to his brother, though, and comes to believe that Michal blithely murdered two children to test out how "far-fetched" they were. Michal readily tells Katurian how difficult it was to make the apple men, conceal the razor blades, and then force them down the girl's throat when she refused to eat them. He says that he was surprised at how much blood the little boy lost when he cut off his toes (48–49). The stories "ain't all that far-fetched," he decides (50).

Tupolski and Ariel (Ivanek) fear that a missing girl's fate mimics "The Little Jesus," in which parents satisfy their daughter's desire to be Jesus by crucifying and then burying her alive (67–72). This is the "ticking bomb" scenario that motivates their harsh interrogation tactics. Ariel beats Katurian on stage in full view of the audience, tortures him offstage with electric shock as we watch his brother Michal's reaction, and pretends to torture Michal offstage as we watch Katurian. As with *The Island*, the creators of this theatrical event count on spectators to understand and share the actors' emotions, including their simulated pain; in other words, to respond with empathy. That Michal's offstage screams provoke Katurian's first outburst of anger and resistance, whereas Katurian's leave Michal largely untroubled, goes far to establish the physical and moral character of the brothers, the one motivated by concern for his brother; the other, fatally lacking empathy—or so it seems for much of the play. Even though injustice reverberates throughout the dialogue, the execution functions not to raise questions of justice but as a motivating force in transforming the individual writer's relation to his own mental life. In contrast to *Le Geu Saint Denis*, *The Pillowman* puts Katurian's inner life center stage from the very beginning as he tries to behave properly in a situation that he doesn't understand. He doesn't debate with himself but spills his guts at every opportunity as he struggles to comprehend the relation between his stories and his arrest. He goes through a gradual conversion, starting as a prisoner willing to give up all beliefs and values in order to preserve his life and ending as a writer willing to sacrifice his life to preserve his stories.

Katurian takes responsibility, but justice remains private: coming to believe in his brother's guilt, he suffocates Michal with a pillow in the jail cell that they share. By this point, the stories are more important to him than Michal and more important than his own life. To ensure that his stories survive, he confesses to killing Michal, to killing his own parents, and to the murders that he and the detectives believe Michal committed, and he attaches the relevant stories as exhibits to his confession. The ploy appears to fail when the policemen discover that Katurian has not actually killed any children (hence the blazing wastebasket when he is shot). But in a final twist, the stories have converted Ariel, who preserves the manuscript. Through the stories, then, Katurian remains present and active in the world. For a post-modern, post-Christian spectator, the writer's imaginative creations take the place of the saint's relics. Significantly, the "Little Jesus" of Katurian's story does not rise again on the third day because the blind man who passes by her grave doesn't hear her clawing at the coffin as she runs out of air.

Katurian narrates this story in an interlude after killing Michal, as a quartet of actors play it in pantomime. Earlier he takes his own part in "The Writer and the Writer's Brother," his fictionalized version of the chain of abuse that produced his morbid imagination and Michal's brain damage: in his story, their parents abuse Michal from the age of eight, and Katurian hears this happening without fully understanding. When he reaches fourteen, the parents reveal that they've been faking the sounds of torture in order to stimulate his creative genius. Years later, though, the successful author returns to his childhood home and discovers his brother's skeleton together with a story better than any that he's ever produced. The writer burns his brother's story. But Katurian immediately corrects this version with the truth, still acting out his part: at fourteen, he found his brain-damaged brother alive and smothered their parents with a pillow (31–35). McDonagh creates a dramatic world within which pain breeds more pain, and one might well read *The Pillowman* as an allegorical exploration of his own imaginative output, with Katurian's abusive parents standing in for the horrifically entertaining Irish culture that he earlier dramatized in *The Cripple of Inishman, The Beauty Queen of Leenane,* and *The Lieutenant of Inishmore.*[73] Indeed, childhood abuse links Katurian to Ariel, who has smothered his own pederast father with a pillow (82), the implicit explanation for his excessive pursuit of vengeance against child abusers and last-minute rescue of the stories. The play's central issue is how the imagination is shaped and how it, in turn, shapes the material world. Michal hates "The Writer and the Writer's Brother" and doesn't fully accept Katurian's explanation that the tortured boy is the real writer, and the storyteller is the writer's brother (58–59). Michal prefers life to art, particularly because it's his own life at stake.

The eponymous story "The Pillowman" is a fable about suffering and responsibility. When misery brings a person to suicide, a man made of pillows takes the person back to die instead at the point in childhood when all the suffering began. He makes the death look like an accident, so that survivors don't have to deal with the emotions that suicide would engender. This lifelong task brings the Pillowman to despair, though, and he convinces the pillowboy that he once was to immolate himself. As he burns, he hears "the screams of the hundred thousand children he'd helped to commit suicide coming back to life and going on to lead the cold, wretched lives that were destined to them because he hadn't been around to prevent them, right on up to the screams of their sad self-inflicted deaths, which this time, of course, would be conducted entirely alone" (47). Katurian recites this story for Michal in their jail cell during the last moments that he believes in his innocence. He later adds a posthumous footnote to "The Writer and the Writer's Brother," rising and pulling the hood off his bullet-shattered head to tell us about the child Michal turning down the Pillowman's services in order to keep his brother's stories in the world. One might understand that, because it was his brother's pain that shaped the writer's imagination, the suffering boy's bodily experience is the real author of the stories. Because Ariel then douses the flames rather than burn the manuscript, and Michal has reappeared to speak his lines in this final story, one might be tempted to conclude that good stories justify the pain. But McDonagh doesn't quite let himself off the hook or comfort the spectator: this is a Michal as imagined by Katurian, a final self-serving rationalization by the writer.

To read this play solely in the context of the playwright's biography or writerly concerns is inadequate to the subject of this book, of course. In everything but its political and legal structure, *The Pillowman* seems to be set in contemporary England or the United States. Contextual filters for its Broadway audience in 2005 included the continued American occupation of Iraq, the ongoing but overshadowed action in Afghanistan, and controversy over the death penalty in the United States. Some spectators may well have seen the webcast decapitation of Nicholas Berg in May 2004 and found it part of their frame of reference when watching McDonagh's plays a year or two later. I had the inverse experience: feeling compelled to watch the video while writing this chapter, I thought of *The Pillowman* as Berg knelt in front of his hooded captors, and *The Lieutenant of Inishmore* came to mind after they pulled him over sideways and I watched the executioner sawing away at a prone body, finally holding up a head for the camera.[74] I was dumbfounded and then, afterward, very sad to have watched a death and at the same time not quite able to believe that I had done so—no pleasure of flinching for me in this instance. Even as sanctioned state killing occurs behind closed doors in the United States, beheadings broadcast on the Internet and charred bodies hanging from a bridge in Fallujah provide the Western public with evidence that Islamic militants and the so-called insurgents in Iraq are different, more brutal, less "human." When the British police shot a suspected suicide bomber in the London tube, and he turned out to be an Egypt-born electrician on his way to work, the Western press did not characterize their action as an execution even though the result was the same.

The distinction revolves around that between terrorism per se and state terrorism, and public performances negotiate their way around the divide. Frank Rich attributes the success of the *Assassins* revival in 2004, compared to the original production's lukewarm reception in 1991, to Americans' new sense of vulnerability after 9/11.[75] He notes that the would-be assassin Samuel Byck, who tried to hijack a jetliner in 1974 in order to drop it on Richard Nixon in the White House, seemed like a joke at the time of the first production and all too familiar at the time of the revival, as did the religious zealotry motivating a number of the other assassins. *Assassins* does entertain a sort of conspiracy theory, but it is strictly nonsynchronous: the musical shows a series of cranks acting in isolation but inspired by those who had gone before them, culminating with an appearance by John Wilkes Booth in the Texas Book Depository, actively inciting Lee Harvey Oswald to kill President Kennedy. These crimes and capital punishments gave audiences in New York an unusual opportunity to watch executions within a dramatic framework that didn't question the morality of the killing. I suspect that Frank Rich, for one, might have been less comfortable in 2004 with a play that featured the unproblematic execution of failed Islamic suicide bombers.

The Pillowman's Katurian dies for his imagination, more dangerous to the state than the murders that his brother commits—or so he thinks. In the real world, imagination is what the state must grapple with when it kills, because we extend ourselves in sympathy to imagine the pain of death. Even as it seeks to efface suffering and dehumanize the condemned, though, the execution itself works upon the imagination. Noting that "rituals incarnate and make visible abstract principles and inchoate concepts—such as 'Justice,'" Conquergood argues that "executions anchor belief in the criminal justice system, dramatizing in an especially vivid way that 'something is being done,' that the system is in control, order has been restored."[76] Because death penalty discourse revolves around justice in post-modern America, the execution ritual is constructed carefully to exonerate the state even while bolstering its authority. The medieval state, in contrast, used the suffering and contrition of the execution ritual to reintegrate the condemned within the Christian community. Ideally, this good death restored sympathy by putting the world back in balance. The *Parisian Journal* describes more than forty years of public execution in such a way as to exonerate the citizens of Paris. In contemporary America, the execution shores up the tenuous authority of the state with an image of justice; in late-medieval France, with an image of social cohesion.

This difference in register carries through to the nature of the relics that deaths produce. Katurian's manuscript acts upon the imagination, which provides a means of connection between otherwise self-contained individuals. The play that contains this relic also acts upon an imagination that it renders problematic, dependent upon suffering for its power to reach us. We care about what's inside the head, whereas the medieval audience for *Le Geu Saint Denis* granted power to the head itself. The saint play focuses upon events, behaviors, and signs. Much of the dialogue describes the action, and the rest is primarily argument or prayer. Similarly, the Bourgeois describes weeping and the violence of regime change but not the thoughts of the citizenry (including his own). Neither of these late-medieval texts delves into what we would understand as the inner life of its characters, some of whom do change but without expressing the sorts of conflicting thoughts or doubts that modern psychology might expect to motivate such change. The saint play's conversions are instantaneous: Lisbie engages in debate with Denis, but not with himself; Larcie is a silent pagan one moment and an avowed Christian the next. We need to be careful in drawing any conclusions about medieval psychology from a narrative convention; however, unless we entirely reject the notion that textual practices both reflect and help to shape mental structures, we can at the very least infer that medieval culture gave a different place to interiority.[77]

The head of Saint Denis reminds spectators that the saint remains literally present and active in the world, an intermediary through whom they can appeal to God. Performances of *Le Geu Saint Denis* might well constitute just such an appeal, thus affecting a divine as well as a human audience and providing quite material benefits for the city that stages it. Performances of *The Pillowman* put our isolation and moral ambivalence on stage for our uncertain contemplation.

3. Enduring Ecstasy

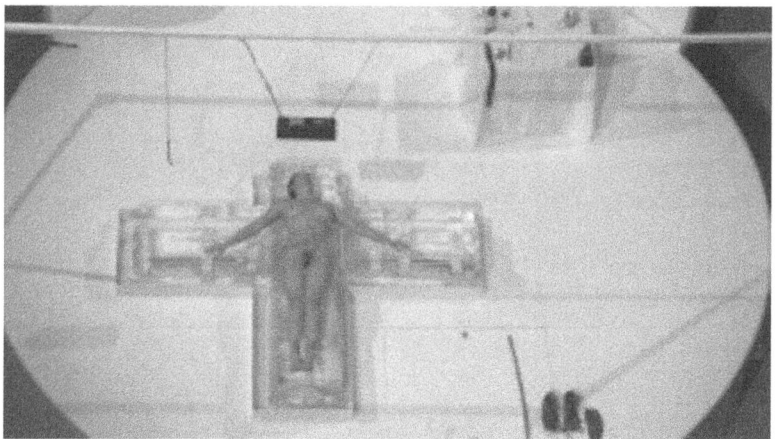

Plate 4 Film still of Marina Abramović performing *Lips of Thomas* at the Solomon R. Guggenheim Museum, New York, November 14, 2005, from the film *Seven Easy Pieces*, dir. Babette Mangolte. © Marina Abramović. Courtesy: Sean Kelly Gallery, New York.

When I arrive at the Guggenheim Museum, Marina Abramović is using a razor blade to cut the first line of a five-pointed star on her stomach. The place is packed. Abramović, naked, is installed on a round platform in the middle of the rotunda. Spectators fill the floor in front of her and line the first few spirals of the museum's ramp, with a scattering higher up. I assume that those on the floor have come to see Abramović reperform her 1975 body art action *The Lips of Thomas*, but some others must have been caught on their descent from the museum's concurrent Russia! exhibit. Abramović blots the cut with a white cloth. Slipping her feet into boots that wait nearby, putting on a military cap and picking up a heavy wooden staff, she stands and cries, her belly heaving, tears streaming down her cheeks as she listens to a Russian folk song. She lies down on blocks of ice arranged in the shape of a cross, her body shaking; then kneels on the floor and whips herself; finally sits at the table, slowly eats a spoonful of

78 Performing Bodies in Pain

honey, and takes a sip of red wine. Abramović repeats these actions, varying the sequence, until midnight. A metronome ticks away. She seems to be pacing herself. The printed program describes what had taken place in 1975: at a gallery in Innsbruck, she ate a kilo of honey, drank a liter of red wine, broke the wine glass with her right hand, used a shard to cut the star on her stomach, whipped herself until she no longer felt pain, and then lay down on the ice. Spectators finally removed the ice, ending the piece thirty minutes after it began.

—*Seven Easy Pieces*[1]

Plate 5   Jean Fouquet (ca. 1415/20-1481), *The Martyrdom of St. Apollonia* from *Le Livre d'Heures d'Etienne Chevalier: The Suffrage of the Saints*, MS 71, fol 39. Photo: R. G. Ojeda, Musée Condé, Chantilly, France. Photo Credit: Réunion des Musées Nationaux/Art Resource, NY.

Two men pull taut the ropes binding a young woman to an inclined plank and another pulls her golden hair, while a fourth man yanks out her teeth with pliers nearly as long as her body. A devil peers over the shoulder of the hair puller, whispering words of encouragement in his ear. Two of her tormentors look at her, but the other two turn their gaze outward, inviting the vicarious participation of spectators distributed according to their engagement with the spectacle: seated on and under the scaffolds, even climbing a pole to get a better view. Costumed actors and musicians mix in with them, waiting in their mansions among the audience scaffolds. The fool turns his back on the action, one hand on his nearly bare bottom, its skimpy and semi-transparent covering seeming to hold a load of feces.
—*The Martyrdom of Saint Apollonia*[2]

In this chapter, I examine the loophole through which women using pain as a means to alter consciousness create a way to speak within regimes that would silence them. They articulate a spiritual rationale, but their performances also function within a gendered system of communication, and their meaning exceeds the performer's conception even as it fails in productive ways. I will argue that, in M.M. Bakhtin's terminology, the female body in pain is "dialogical." That body's double voices say opposing things, but neither voice is given the final word and they do not resolve into a dialectical synthesis.[3] As the conventional object of art rather than its creative subject, women found new opportunities for expression in the first wave of conceptual art performances in the 1970s. Systematically ignored, trivialized, and silenced, female artists sought to develop a new language of the body—often enough, the body in pain. Three decades later, body artist Marina Abramović's commodity value continues to rise in the art market as she re-presents examples of this political art within a spiritual framework that highlights a sharing of energy and mystical merging of artist and spectator. Late-medieval religious women faced even greater obstacles to speech, and they also turned to suffering. Jean Fouquet's miniature of *The Martyrdom of Saint Apollonia* makes visible a tension between the ascetic withdrawal of the anchoress and the mystic's ecstasy—a tension central to the female saint play watched and remembered by late-medieval French audiences and also to the virgin-martyr narrative at the base of these cultural products. On one level, Apollonia presents an emblem of the closed, sealed body recommended by the church. At the opposite extreme, she evokes the ecstatic, speaking, crying, and self-torturing female mystic whom the church increasingly suppressed during the fourteenth and fifteenth centuries. In order to more fully explain the cultural work of these medieval female bodies in pain, I'll also reach back a couple of centuries and north to the Low Countries, where ecstasy blossomed among beguine mystics during the thirteenth century.

Faced with the challenge of expression within a repressive cultural economy, some women perform outside the realm of rational discourse. I would suggest that we take seriously the self-reported experience of mystics even as we analyze the cultural construction of their spiritual explanations. Although neuroscience is still far from having a clear picture of the mechanism involved, hypnosis research presents convincing evidence that trance states differ from normal consciousness. Positing a need to alter consciousness in all cultures at all times, Jerome Kroll and Bernard Bachrach compare variations in rules and methods with variations in cuisine: one must eat, but the food can differ enormously. They argue that the capacity to experience altered states varies between individuals and can be developed.[4] Ariel Glucklich summarizes the mechanics of the process:

> The more irritation one applies to the body in the form of pain, the less output the central nervous system generates from the areas that regulate the signals on which a sense of self relies. Modulated pain weakens the individual's feeling of being a discrete agent; it makes the "body-self" transparent and facilitates the emergence of a new identity. Metaphorically, pain creates an embodied "absence" and makes way for a new and greater "presence."[5]

Mystics empty themselves through pain and prepare the way for a new birth. What they discover in passing through that emptiness is generally what they set out to find—in other words, determined by their belief system. The medieval mystic understood herself to transcend the carnal by being raptured away to another, higher realm. Her vision was both corporeal and spiritual, a merging with God. Abramović, in contrast, has a post-Christian understanding of this experience inflected by Buddhism: she transcends the objectifying gaze through a shared vision that effaces the boundaries of the self, merging with the other in the present moment.

For more than thirty years, Abramović has used her body to manifest sources of conflict and suffering, and spectators invest these cultural traces with unpredictable personal significance. Even if her performance of *The Lips of Thomas* in 2005 had exactly duplicated the actions of her 1975 version, response would have differed because the setting, cultural milieu, and the spectators themselves were so different. *Seven Easy Pieces*, dedicated to Susan Sontag and curated by Jennifer Blessing, provided a most unusual opportunity to encounter this kind of work in the flesh and not only to compare the fleshly experience to what one might have imagined, but also to compare this performance with the original events. Taking inspiration from the work of other artists is not new for Abramović. As a young woman in Yugoslavia, she heard that Chris Burden had been arrested after being crucified on a Volkswagen that was driven around Los Angeles. In fact, Burden's *Trans-fixed* (1972) was much less dramatic: after a doctor affixed him to the car with nails, a few friends pushed it out of the garage, took the picture, and pushed it back in. Yet regardless of the discrepancies, the story that Abramović heard influenced the challenges that she set herself during the mid-1970s and sparked her desire to reperform the performances of other artists.[6] A conversation with Susan Sontag in 2002 began the process of bringing this long-dormant desire to fruition.

In addition to *The Lips of Thomas,* Abramović performed versions of Bruce Naumann's *Body Pressure* (1974), Vito Acconci's *Seedbed* (1972), VALIE EXPORT's *Action Pants: Genital Panic* (1969), Gina Pane's *The Conditioning* (1973), and Joseph Beuys's *How to Explain Pictures to a Dead Hare* (1965). The museum provided a program with the name of each night's piece, a statement by the originating artist, the original performance location and date of each event, and its duration. Abramović's versions all lasted from 5:00 p.m. until midnight. Aside from the half hour that I spent (with some guilty feelings) in the museum café, I stayed with Abramović until midnight for *The Lips of Thomas.* I was curious to discover what would change for me, and for the artist, over the course of seven hours. As the night went on, each variety of action took on a different valence: the wine and honey seemed to nurture and soothe her; the flagellation, to purge. In contrast, lying on the ice—as shown in plate 4—remained a purely passive ordeal. Abramović eventually stopped jerking around and crying out as she lay down on it, but by 8:00 she continued to shiver as she sat at the table after lying on the ice, her body trying hard to warm up. After whipping herself, to which she reacted vocally throughout the event, she looked intent, energized, powerful. Many turned away from the flagellation, which seemed much like an athletic feat to me. I watched the cutting action unmoved, but the space became very quiet at those points, no movement, little whispering. On the third cut, someone called out, "you don't have to do it again." Obviously others were more disturbed by it than I.

I had a strong desire to read Abramović's affect, but there were few legible markers. Her face remained impassive as she cut her stomach, in sharp contrast to her weeping during what I would call the "Young Communist" segment, which was not part of the 1975 action: in addition to wearing the cap and boots, which evoked her Eastern Bloc upbringing, several times she opened out the cloth with which she blotted the cuts on her stomach and tied it to the staff, waving it as a flag.[7] These accessories and the music suggested an association between her tears and the pain of memory, clearly marking Abramović's crossover from the visual art world into a performance genre more closely allied with theatre. The entire week-long event at the Guggenheim smacked of theatre, a fact that met with distaste from some conceptual art stalwarts. In a letter to the *New York Times*, conceptual artist and sculptor Tom Marioni objected that Abramović thus became an actress, not an artist.[8] Clearly, this distinction remains important to Marioni and to Chris Burden, who would not cooperate with the project. But Abramović herself has been pointedly blurring this line for fifteen years. She has said that she and other performance artists considered the theatre their enemy in the 1970s, "a fake, a staged experience." By the mid-1990s, however, she was giving audiences "both a stage-play and a performance."[9]

Abramović began reperforming *The Lips of Thomas* in European and American theatres and opera houses in 1993 as part of a work called *Biography*, which used a recorded autobiographical narrative to contextualize the brief reenactment of many of her early art actions.[10] The elements of *The Lips of Thomas* that she chose to include in that piece, the star-cutting and the flagellation, referred not only to her personal history but also to an opposition between God and the state upon which she focused in telling that history: her mother was an atheist and partisan, her father a communist, and both parents participated in Yugoslavia's Communist Revolution. Interestingly enough, her maternal grandfather was a Patriarch of the Orthodox Church, making her childhood a mixture of military discipline at home and religious life with her grandmother.[11] By reinscribing these symbols with the details of Abramović's own life story, *Biography* made them both concrete and mutable. The Guggenheim version replaced this narrative with costume, props, and the song "Slavic Souls" sung in Russian with a photocopied translation available at the entrance desk. The actions thus hovered between theatre and antitheatrical body art. In contrast to some of her early actions, there was no question of the artist losing control. And like the proscenium stage configuration that separated Abramović from her audience when she performed *Biography*, security precautions at the museum eliminated the ready access to the performer's body that was integral to her gallery settings in the 1970s. There was no possibility for spectators to end the action and no apparent danger to provoke that sort of intervention.[12]

The notion that the sharing of extreme bodily experiences could circumvent cultural boundaries had great currency during the first flowering of body art in the 1960s and 1970s, when these so-called seven easy pieces were first performed. To mention only the most prominent figures in theatrical theory, Antonin Artaud's conception that a "theatre of cruelty" could act directly upon the repressed unconscious, like a physical agent, influenced the visual arts as strongly as it did the theatre,[13] and Jerzy Grotowski thought that it was possible to strip away the accretions of culture through a *via negativa* that would enable the actor to make a "total gift of himself." Grotowski proposed that attempting "to incarnate myth, putting on its ill-fitting skin" could bring us to "an experience of common human truth"—provided that the confrontation and stripping away are brutal enough.[14] For like-minded artists and audiences, a psychic nakedness produced through confrontation with the human body in extremis appeared to be the only form of deep contact possible in the modern world.

Many early body artists wanted to perform another culture into being. Like their contemporaries in other fields, they were optimistic about the power of a changed language to change perceptions and, furthermore, understood alterations in the perceived world to be substantive and lasting changes. Surely, some of the spectators who saw *The Lips of Thomas* in 1975 were familiar with Abramović's earlier Rhythm series, from which she required rescue more than once, and with other actions she had performed that same year: *Art Must Be Beautiful. Artist Must Be Beautiful* (she brushed her hair simultaneously with a metal brush and metal comb until her face and hair were damaged); *Role Exchange* (she exchanged places for four hours with an Amsterdam prostitute); *Freeing the Voice* (she lay on the floor with her head tilted back and screamed for three hours, stopping when she lost her voice); *Freeing the Memory* (she free-associated until no more words came to her); and *Freeing the Body* (she wrapped her head in a black scarf and moved to a drumbeat for eight hours, stopping only when she collapsed).[15] Given the feminist orientation of the first two actions and the theme of a painful liberation from constraints and social conditioning in the other three, spectators in 1975 might reasonably have read *The Lips of Thomas* as a ritual escape from a repressive culture. The Christian references in the flagellation and the cross of ice are obvious, and knowledgeable spectators might recognize the honey and wine as elements of Eastern Rite Catholic ritual or read the star as the symbol of international Communism.[16]

Although I consider *Art Must Be Beautiful. Artist Must Be Beautiful* and *Role Exchange* to be the only explicitly feminist actions of Abramović's entire career, a feminist interpretation of any body art action by a woman would not have been unlikely at the time. The 1960s had seen protofeminist performances such as Yoko Ono's *Cut Piece* (1964) and Shigeko

Kubota's *Vagina Painting* (1965), for which the artist squatted to paint with a brush strapped to her underpants—a witty rejoinder to the critical discourse generated around Jackson Pollock's action paintings in the 1950s and Yves Klein's use of nude female models as "living brushes" in 1960.[17] Feminist artists of the 1960s and 1970s repeatedly articulated the need to be recognized as "speaking subjects." Perhaps the best-known formulation is Carolee Schneemann's: "I was allowed to be an image but not an image-maker creating her own self-image."[18] For *Interior Scroll* (1975 and 1977), her most explicit feminist statement and one of her most widely known actions, Schneemann unwound out of her vagina a scroll from which she read a text that began "I met a happy man / a structuralist filmmaker" and ended "Oh No he said we think of you / as a dancer."[19]

By the time Abramović performed the first version of *The Lips of Thomas*, French feminism was grappling with "phallogocentrism"—that is, the problem posed for every woman by a language system that requires her to say "I," but at the same time reserves the "I" position for men. In order to operate in the symbolic realm (in other words, to speak), a woman must imagine herself to be male *or* imagine herself as men imagine her. Hélène Cixous proposed resistance by means of *écriture féminine*: "Woman must write her self: must write about women and bring women to writing, from which they have been driven away as violently as from their bodies."[20] Luce Irigaray's related solution was *parler femme*—that is, to speak in such a way as to reproduce the doubleness of women's position within language systems and the fluidity of their libidinal energies.[21] VALIE EXPORT presented female body writing in concrete terms with *Eros/ion* (1971): she rolled naked over broken glass, a sheet of glass, and paper for approximately ten minutes,[22] framing her action in terms of transformation: "Pane of glass means: transparency. Broken glass means: lesions, cuts. Does the same material evoke the same meaning? To change the state of the material means to change the meaning of the material."[23] Roswitha Mueller sees a shift in context for "glass," which is present as shards and as a sheet. The context within which the body communicates also shifts, as a result of its interaction with the glass: "The body as bearer of self-inflicted signs creates another meaning out of its wounded state."[24] In other words, the wounds are transformed into signs when EXPORT rolls onto the paper. And this was Gina Pane's explicit project during the 1970s, to develop a body language that would communicate through the "wound which became sign."[25] Pane said that "man's language no longer corresponded to his needs and attitudes" and that by returning to "primitive elements" such as "milk, fire, blood, and suffering," she could "restore a vocabulary which can be universally understood."[26]

For a spectator who was receptive to such work, to really *feel* something, to be shocked into a different sort of awareness and to be thereby differently sensitized to her own lifeworld might have been enough. Rational access to the event was not always essential. Such a spectator could be reasonably satisfied by a heightened sense of immersion in the present moment, interpret pain as a guarantor of authenticity and take it as a synecdoche for experience. Well into the 1980s, some feminist performance theorists understood the claim to speak directly with the body, thereby speaking *outside* of language, to be an inherent virtue of women's performance art.[27]

Yet even with these bodily performatives, the context sometimes carried legible meaning in addition to its phenomenal impact. In their original context, many body art events performed an explicit social critique that Abramović's 2005 reperformance often obscured. Pane lay on a iron framework over burning candles for the thirty-minute *The Conditioning*, for example, as the first part of a triptych called *Self-Portrait(s)*. She followed this with *Contraction*, making cuts around her fingernails with a razor blade but concealing her action from the audience, instead projecting images of women applying nail polish and then turning the camera on the faces of female spectators. Finally, for *Rejection*, Pane repeatedly gargled and spit out milk that mixed with blood from a cut in her mouth.[28] Pane's actions made visible the potential pain and self-violation that social conformity entails for women in particular, even as she claimed her body as material to use as she might wish, in pain or in pleasure. Abramović's reperformance of *The Conditioning* reasserted the artist's claim to her body and its sensation, but without the same social comment. The duration further changed this action, transforming Pane's controlled production of concise visual images into an ongoing endurance event, turning Abramović into a latter-day Saint Lawrence grilled to bring about a spiritual transformation for her audience. This spiritual bent was further developed by the following night's restaging of *How to Explain Pictures to a Dead Hare*, the artist's head covered in honey and gold leaf, whispering to the eponymous rabbit. The program explained at length the symbolism of each element and their interaction, all revolving around thought processes and the limitations of rationality. Much like Abramović, the originating artist Beuys described his technique as an attempt "to seek out the energy points in the human power field, rather than demanding specific knowledge or reactions on the part of the public."[29]

Radical claims for the transformational power of phenomenological shifts met with increasing skepticism after the 1970s, and the critical response to *Seven Easy Pieces* was measured, if celebratory. The event offered an opportunity to make sense of the 1970s, to reassess those ideas and ourselves. We may no longer be able to believe in the revolutionary power of extreme art, but we can recognize a need for contact and emotional intensity in a time of distress, frustration, and despair. Abramović solicits her audience's emotional engagement by offering up her pain, and each night's event was a test of endurance for spectators as well as for the artist. Each person had to decide when to leave, whether to stay through the boredom and the pain of standing for hours or sitting, back unsupported, on the floor. When the time was up for *The Lips of Thomas,* and the guards began trying to empty the museum, the still sizable audience applauded for perhaps ten minutes. I talked to other people who felt, as I did, that we owed it to her to stay. In fact, since the late 1990s she has defined the exchange of energy with her audience as her primary interest,[30] and for long intervals between actions she simply gazed out at us.

Abramović has grown increasingly focused on her subliminal interaction with spectators since *Expansion in Space* (1977), the first event for which she and her then-partner Ulay had a large audience. They ran and slammed their naked bodies into two moveable columns in a parking garage, and the energy that she felt coming from the public made Marina able to continue for thirty minutes after the columns stopped moving and Ulay left.[31] During *Nightsea Crossing* (1983), she experienced her first altered state as she and Ulay sat in silence facing one another across a table. Her perception changed so that she saw everything behind as well as in front of her, at times could smell "the intrinsic scent" of every individual person present. The attempt not to blink created "gaps between thinking" that finally led to a total transformation of perception:

> Ulay completely disappeared in front of me. I saw only blue, but the most intense clear blue in the shape of his body. When I saw this I thought now I have to blink because I don't like spooky things. So I blinked, but the blue didn't change. I just kind of relaxed and stayed with the blue. That's when I had my first complete out-of-body experience. After two or three minutes of sitting motionless you start feeling the body. Then after one hour, two hours, you have muscles and such tension that if you don't move in a second, I'm going to faint. And then when you say to yourself so what if I just faint, something clicks in your mind and there's no pain anymore. You have to go through such a door of pain to liberate that energy, and people don't get that far into that space to confront such pain.[32]

Abramović is describing the use of pain to enter a trance state, which in turn alleviates the pain to some extent. Neuroscience supports the notion that the trance state has a measurable impact upon pain experience. Because those experiencing ritually induced trance states can't sit still for scientific measurements of brain activity, as Judith Becker points out, the evidence comes primarily from hypnosis research.[33] Between 1992 and 2006, for example, Marie-Elisabeth Faymonville, Mélanie Boly, and Steven Laureys used hypnosis in combination with local anesthesia to control pain in more than 3,300 surgical procedures. Although no precise definition exists, there is general agreement that hypnosis includes absorption, "the tendency to become fully involved in a perceptual, imaginative or ideational experience"; dissociation, "the mental separation of components of behavior that would ordinarily be processed together," often including a feeling that one's actions are not voluntary; and suggestibility, "an enhanced tendency to comply with hypnotic instructions" due to "suspension of critical judgment because of the intense absorption of the hypnotic state."[34] This same team used fMRI to record the activity of neurons by a painful stimulus. In a normally alert state, the pain activated what is often termed the pain matrix; that is, the "bilateral thalamus, primary somatosensory cortices, insula and MCC [mid-cingulate cortex]." Under hypnosis, however, the stimulus activated only the "primary somatosensory cortex"[35]—the only portion *not* activated in empathic response to pain. Wolfgang H.R. Miltner and Thomas Weiss found that both hypnosis and distraction decreased the brain's electrical response to pain and also reduced subjective reports of pain intensity. They note that other experiments with highly susceptible subjects suggest that hypnosis works "based on a breakdown of neural communication between neural structures involved in the processing of pain."[36]

During the 1970s and 1980s, Abramović sought out trance techniques and experimented with endurance events, seeking to understand and deepen her own experience. Then after she and Ulay separated following *The Lovers/Great Wall Walk* (1988), Abramović began making objects that she considers catalysts for the audience. Dissatisfied with the "voyeuristic attitude" of spectators, she "created objects which enable the audience to have certain experiences."[37] For a 1995–96 installation at the Museum of Fine Art of the Canton of Thurgau, originally a Carthusian monastery, she covered the floor of the vault with marble sand and placed four tall chairs facing the wall. Abramović wanted visitors to sit in the chairs for a considerable length of time, to be still and just look at the wall without their feet touching the floor. There were also four ladders, reaching up to the small windows of the vault. These were intended as "symbols of various levels of physical, human, or spiritual development." The first was normal and could be easily climbed. The second had knives as rungs. The third was glowing metal, and the fourth was ice. She wanted the audience to understand that "if you can climb all four of these ladders, you have reached a higher state, both metaphorically and in reality." Although she did not expect anyone to actually climb, she wanted to show that "there are different ways of reaching a certain spiritual state. The fact that, in our cultural sphere, we cannot climb these ladders doesn't mean that no-one else can."[38] More recently, Abramović taught week-long workshops that "train future artists not to see with their eyes alone, but with their entire bodies."[39] The curriculum bears a strong resemblance to certain paratheatrical events led by Grotowski's former actors in which I took part during the late 1970s. She told Hans Ulrich Obrist that she designs her performances, like her sculptural objects, to create for the spectators "some kind of mental gap so that they can't explain it rationally. They will look for tricks, and when they can't find the trick... their knowledge... will have to collapse" and "they will have a completely different way of seeing things."[40]

I can't say that the performance caused my knowledge to collapse, but Abramović's aim helps to explain the obscurity of her title, *The Lips of Thomas*. I have never come across an explanation or even a discussion, and the museum's publicist told me that Marina prefers for the audience to make its own meaning. I initially put the title together with the sacrificial imagery and thought of the biblical Doubting Thomas, who finds proof of the resurrection in touching the lips of Christ's wound. Yet I later came to suspect that she had in mind a different Thomas; that is, Saint Thomas Aquinas, whose *Summa Theologica* addresses the question whether God should be praised with the lips. After noting all the scriptural arguments for and against verbal devotions, Aquinas answers that we praise God with our lips to arouse our own devotion and that of other people, but that "it profits one nothing to praise with the lips if one praise not with the heart."[41] Read in this context, Abramović's wordless *Lips of Thomas* pulls her heart back and forth between her family's incompatible Christian and Communist devotional practices—yet this biographical reading does not encapsulate the performance, nor were many spectators likely to arrive at this interpretation. *The Lips of Thomas* positions her body and its sensations, pain most particularly, at the center of a mystified circle, available for perception but defying rational comprehension.

Spectators for the 2005 reperformance were quite likely to place it in context with *The House with the Ocean View* (2002), for which Abramović lived and fasted for twelve days in a three-box set mounted on the wall of the Sean Kelly Gallery.[42] Newly residing in New York, the artist conceived of that living installation "as a gift to the city about living in the moment in difficult times and in peace."[43] Ladders leaned against each box, but their rungs were butcher knives, sharp edge up to emphasize her self-incarceration. People visited, many again and again, many staying for hours to watch her drink water, shower, use the toilet, sit, stand, and lie down. They watched her grow thinner, weep, sing softly, gaze at the spectators.[44] For me, the most important moment of *The House with the Ocean View* had been Abramović standing at the edge of her box set, above the sharp edge of a knife, swaying slightly, holding my gaze, tears in her eyes and mine. I couldn't leave the gallery until it closed that evening. I didn't want to leave her alone (she remained there all night). I felt responsible to her. Abramović explained that she cried so much because people "project their own sadness onto me and I reflect it back. And I cry out in the saddest way, so they are free."[45] She said that people were "like drunks," coming to make a visual connection with her for twenty minutes each day when the gallery opened before going to work. Because many of these visitors later told her that they had no particular connection to the art world, she concluded that she filled a craving to be looked at in an intimate way.

The installation was then rebuilt the following August for an episode of *Sex in the City*, with an actress standing in for Marina: Carrie Bradshaw (Sarah Jessica Parker) visits the installation with friends and dismissively comments that taking showers, sitting alone, and starving yourself is how all single women in New York spend Friday nights. Then she returns alone and has a more thoughtful response. This appropriation amplified recognition by the mainstream media, turning Abramović into an art star by the time the 2005 project got underway. Well-funded, presented by a major museum, with ample press coverage, *Seven Easy Pieces* was the place to see and be seen that November. The audience was always interesting; for me, never more so than during the first evening when the French artist Orlan, whose work is so similar but at the same time diametrically opposed to that of Abramović and other artists who acknowledge and work with pain, strolled the ramps in conversation with a companion, her surgically refigured face and half-black, half-white pompadour making her as much of a spectacle as Abramović's reperformance of *Body Pressure*.

When I returned to the Guggenheim for the final evening of *Seven Easy Pieces*, a new work entitled *Entering the Other Side* (2005), the first thing I saw was a huge blue velvet and satin tent covering the stage, and I wondered whether the artist was inside. Walking past its stripes, some with a reddish tint, I wondered if it was supposed to evoke the American flag. Then halfway up the first ramp, I saw Abramović at its peak and thought of Winnie in Beckett's *Happy Days*. This seemed like a surprisingly topical conclusion to the series, to have a woman buried to her waist in American patriotism. As the evening went on, though, I decided that these associations were mine alone—which didn't diminish my enjoyment of them. An hour or so into the event, I walked up to the third-level ramp and looked down on her, realizing for the first time that the artist's gigantic blue dress duplicated the inside shape of the Guggenheim and the stripes, its ramps. Abramović's only action was to gaze at her audience, changing the position of her arms, perching on a hidden support or standing, twisting at the waist, never in any visible pain; in fact, the movements were clearly designed to make this less of an ordeal than the previous night's actions.

I stayed for a bit less than three hours of this event, engaged for much of the time in a stimulating conversation with artist Jane Philbrick. She had also seen *The Lips of Thomas* and found it distressing to see a female artist reinscribe what she perceived as the stereotype of the objectified victim. Our conversation about the place in Western culture of naked women in pain helped to reveal for me the late-medieval virgin martyr lurking behind this entire weeklong event.

* * *

Jean Fouquet's miniature of the *Martyrdom of Saint Apollonia* (ca. 1452–60), a popular example of theatre in the round for theatre history texts, lines up nicely with *Seven Easy Pieces*. The Guggenheim's spiral ramps echo the miniature's circular scaffolds, as shown in plate 5; Abramović's seven ordeals, the martyr's predeath torment at its focal point. Some scholars think that Fouquet illustrated an actual performance of a now-lost saint play, although others argue that he merely employed representational conventions that we now consider theatrical.[46] Interestingly enough, *none* of the special effects that Peter Meredith and John Tailby describe are used to stage the gory torment of a virgin martyr, although the property lists for Barcelona's *Corpus Christi* procession in 1424 include platters with the emblems of many, such as two breasts for Saint Agatha, the two eyes of Saint Lucy, a torture horse for Eulalia, flames for Cecilia, a wheel for Catherine, along with halos for these and many more. Apollonia gets only a halo.[47] We do know that such torments were staged, though, and regardless of its provenance I will let Fouquet's miniature stand in for an image lingering in the memory of a late-medieval spectator after gazing upon a virgin martyr center stage. Apollonia's story is typical; this image, very much a product of the miniature's historical moment.

Jocelyn Wogan-Browne identifies the essential elements of a virgin-martyr narrative as a young and beautiful virgin, wealthy, Christian, and running afoul of a powerful pagan male—an emperor, a judge, or her father—who wants to arrange a marriage. When she insists upon remaining chaste,

> The virgin is threatened, then incarcerated, stripped naked, publicly flogged, lacerated, burnt and boiled, and dismembered in some way,... Her conduct during all this remains impeccable, her ability to reason unimpaired, and, to the frustration of the tyrant, her bearing and her arguments frequently convert his attendant soldiery and populace whom he then has to martyr as well. Finally, when the virgin and God have displayed enough of God's supreme rule over the world, she concludes her passion by going to formal execution by beheading.[48]

Fouquet shows the dismemberment phase of this standard torment series.

All versions of Apollonia's martyrdom from a third-century account by Bishop Dionysius of Alexandria through the thirteenth-century *Golden Legend* entail swift and violent tooth-breaking by a pagan mob followed by the saint's voluntary leap into the fire with which they threatened to burn her. Leslie Abend Callahan argues that both a late fourteenth-century *Passio* and Fouquet's miniature transformed this death into a slow and cruel torture during the late Middle Ages, "an apparent shift in focus from the narration of events to the highlighting of one moment of physical pain and torment."[49] The image of Apollonia is not unusually violent, of course. The book of hours that Fouquet illustrated for Etienne Chevalier also includes the inverted crucifixion of Saint Peter, the x-shaped crucifixion of Saint Andrew, and the stoning of Saint Lawrence—all of these martyrs male, one must note. The other female is Saint Catherine, but he does not show her in torment.

Feminist scholarship has tended to overlook the preponderance of male martyrs in the dramatic corpus. During the 1980s and 1990s in particular, quite laudable feminist attempts to extend theories about the objectified female body to medieval evidence inadvertently suggested that virgin martyrs were the only ones suffering at center stage. This was hardly the case. Sadly, we don't have reliable statistics about plays and performances in medieval France—and here I join the oft-repeated appeal for archival research on the model of Records of Early English Drama (REED).[50] The productions catalogued by Petit de Julleville do give some hard data, though.[51] From 1290 until 1604, he lists ninety-six plays celebrating male saints and thirty-six female, with an overlap in two cases (Berthe and Pepin; Lazarus, Magdelaine, and Martha). Only three of these performances took place earlier than the fifteenth century, thirteen more before 1448, and ten after 1550, placing the great majority (ninety) between 1450 and 1549. At all times, the male saints outnumber the female. During the hundred years of heaviest activity, he lists sixty-seven male saint plays and twenty-five female. Saint Barbara is the most popular female saint, with twelve representations; Catherine, a close second with nine. The male saints show more variety, with seven John the Baptists and five each of Sebastian, Nicholas, and Jacques. Saint Denis appears only once, at 1520 in Amboise. Only three of the productions took place in Paris: a Saint George play in 1422 and Crespin and Crespinen in 1443 and again in 1458. One would, of course, prefer not to rely upon a compendium from 1880, and we shouldn't imagine that Petit de Julleville's list is either accurate or comprehensive. But the list of manuscript and early print editions of saint plays that Graham Runnalls compiled corroborates the pattern: of fourteen print and twenty-seven manuscript sources, we find eight female saints (which includes three of Barbara) and thirty-two male.[52]

Sarah Kay points out that medieval Europeans adapted hundreds of saints' lives from Latin into Romance vernacular languages, but they did not indiscriminately popularize all saints. Mary of Egypt, who carried on a "lurid sex-life prior to her repentance" was popular, as were martyrs, especially virgin martyrs. Kay notes the potential in these vitae for "a kind of pious pornography." She says, "It is difficult not to be complicitous with the prurient sadism of these tales as we read them today."[53] This widely considered position presumes that spectators imagine themselves occupying the gender positions available within the pictured scenario and thus understands Apollonia's ideal viewer to be male, a surrogate for the man who commissioned the miniature. Although I will argue for a more complicated and richer model for spectator response, the powerful male gaze makes a good starting point—it helps to explain Philbrick's dismay at watching Abramović's naked suffering.

Brigitte Cazelles suggests that the miniature's composition positions the spectator within an imagined half-circle that mirrors the half-circle within the picture. She argues that, although Apollonia is at the center of the picture and the spectator is assumed to occupy the corresponding center of its mirror image, this composition would *not* cause Chevalier (or his surrogates) to identify with Apollonia as victim.[54] Cazelles argues that the composition interpellates viewers as voyeurs or even as persecutors of the saint—that is, the work draws them into those particular subject positions by "hailing" them in a way that they recognize and to which they respond without thinking.[55] In the miniature, then, Apollonia's body calls upon its viewer to imagine pulling ropes or yanking teeth, or at least to enjoy watching others do so. Chevalier was a wealthy and powerful man who served Charles VII as Treasurer, and one might thus conclude that meditating upon such an image would increase his enjoyment of power over others, including but not limited to beautiful young women.

Yet the image positions its ideal spectator opposite a throne that is empty because the emperor has left it and stands at Apollonia's left shoulder, pointing at her teeth—embedded in the action that he authorizes, in other words, the epitome of wrongful rule. Chevalier and others likely to have access to the book—men and women of his own social circle—are not interpellated as potential occupants of the throne but as witnesses to its emptiness. Given what France had endured over the course of the Hundred Years' War, the miniature would seem to convey the urgency of keeping Charles VII securely in his proper place as ruler. This reading certainly makes sense within the context of the manuscript: one illustration shows Charles VII as one of the magi adoring Christ, with the French routing the English from a castle in the background. Another, alluding to the liberation of Paris, shows the faithful kneeling in the foreground and gazing across the Seine at Paris, while the Holy Spirit's rays disperse demons in the sky.[56] Apollonia's gender would hardly seem to matter in this historically grounded interpretation of Fouquet's image within its manuscript context.

Yet Apollonia is female, and we can productively trace out additional meanings for this image without losing our historical grounding if we shift the frame of analysis from political history to women's history. To begin again from a familiar model for spectator response, a female spectator might identify as victim, in the center of the circle, powerless before the objectifying male gaze. But the virgin martyr is a special kind of victim: although she is subjected to violence, the violence degrades only those who inflict it. Both and Nerida Newbigin and Elizabeth Lalou point out that dramatizations contrast the comical frenzy of the pagan tormentors with the serenity and faith of the martyrs.[57] Perhaps this sort of identification with the virgin martyr made it easier for a late-medieval woman to endure the suffering in her own life by considering it a sign of her moral superiority. Indeed, Wogan-Browne says that the hagiography from which she extrapolates the virgin-martyr profile was aimed at women. But she discounts the possibility that the audience for what she calls a "diet of licensed 'body-ripping'" might be "colluding with its own worst interests"[58]—echoing, of course, more recent arguments about romance novels, or bod*ice* rippers.[59] She suggests instead that the torments withstood by virgin martyrs served to augment strength of will for their female audience; thus, identifying with the virgin martyr's resistance and bravery might well produce a sense of empowerment rather than acquiescence.

Wogan-Browne analyzes texts written to edify young ladies during the twelfth and thirteenth centuries, at the same time as the church was taking control of marriage away from the secular aristocracy by making it into a sacrament. This change made the woman's consent "at least theoretically essential," and hagiographic convention demonstrated the terms within which a woman could reject marriage. A young woman might see the life of a virgin martyr as a critique of courtly love conventions and find the message: "Defy authority if it elides you...you do not have to marry, and there is a legitimate career of consecrated virginity available to you with its own emotional and ethical satisfactions."[60] The virgin-martyr narrative makes the possibility of choice for women explicit, even if it falls short of imagining any choice lying outside of patriarchal structures. Although narratives initially present the female saint as a marriageable property, those who would view her as such are pagans, and the story always shows them to be wrong. The typical virgin-martyr narrative thus denies that women are chattel even while reiterating the equation, which would seem to encourage a higher appreciation of the religious alternative to marriage.

On a less positive note, though, women's inheritance rights were being severely curtailed, with the rediscovered Salic law emblematic of a pervasive late-medieval denigration of women. Clovis, the first king of France, compiled this code between 507 and 511, incorporating elements of Roman law and Frankish custom. French scholars at the abbey Saint-Denis rediscovered it in the middle of the fourteenth century, and those supporting the Valois succession during the Hundred Years' War used it to establish that the kingship could not pass through the female line. The issue at stake was who should rule France after the demise of the Capetian dynasty. The sons of Philip IV (the Fair) died without children, and his daughter Isabella was married to Edward II of England. Salic law handily prevented the accession of Edward III to the throne in France.[61] The argument had theological as well as legal support; for example, François de Meyronnes argued in 1322 that royalty is a *dignitas* and that the biblical treatment of priesthood was proof that *dignitas* was reserved for men; therefore, women must be excluded from royal succession.[62]

The negative inscription of marriage in virgin-martyr narratives helped to reinforce this devaluation of women as property, to the disadvantage of real women who did marry: they were quite literally worth less than they had earlier been. The Parisian tax records show a corresponding constriction of economic freedom. In 1297, women were in charge of more than 14 percent of the city's households. Then in 1421, their percentage dropped to 9.6; in 1423, they dropped further to 4.5 percent; and in 1438, they rose slightly to 5.8 percent after the end of English rule in the city. Simone Roux argues:

> The drop cannot be underestimated, and it undoubtedly meant a degradation in the recognized role of women in the capital's society. Once peace had returned and business picked up again, it appears women did not regain the accompanying autonomy that had previously been recognized. Quite the contrary, in the great restoration of order during the second half of the fifteenth century, women's work was degraded and confounded with prostitution, for which it often served as a mask.[63]

Like the economic and political, the moral valuation of women grew increasingly negative during the later Middle Ages, finding justification in physiology.

Galen had derived from the Hippocratic corpus a system of humors based on the circulation of pneuma: the left chamber of the heart turns inspired air into *vital pneuma,* which then moves through the arteries. In the brain, this vital pneuma is transformed into *psychic pneuma* or *spiritus animalis.*[64] This animal spirit moves through the veins to the nerves, which medieval science thought of as hollow ducts, providing nourishment to the entire body. Drawing upon Arabic texts, medieval science adds to Galen's two kinds of pneuma a third, *spiritus naturalis*: the liver transforms vital pneuma into this natural spirit that supports vegetative functions. The process of elaboration that turns air into vital pneuma is analogous to the elaboration of blood out of food, and its subsequent transformation into animal or natural spirit is similar to the coction of blood into various other bodily substances such as bone and semen, which medieval medical texts never precisely explain but liken to boiling. The retiform plexus that Galen thought was present at the base of the brain and the choroid plexuses in its ventricles provided a network of vessels within which this transformation could occur, similar to the vessels in the testicles where blood was concocted to form semen.[65]

Female anatomy was understood to function in a similar manner, since the ovaries were understood to be small internal testicles.[66] But as a result of women's cold and wet complexion, the ovaries do a less thorough job than the testes of hot and dry men; therefore, women must expel their superfluous matter as menstrual blood. This matter is understood to be dangerous: a menstruating woman can cloud a mirror or dull bronze because her eye emits a poisonous vapor, and the gaze of old women who have stopped menstruating due to insufficient heat is poisonous and particularly dangerous to infants. Poor women are especially poisonous because of their diet.[67] Women were also understood to be inherently porous, a quality that combined with wetness to render their imaginations more susceptible to arousal.[68]

Late-medieval theology accepted and extended these physiological concepts, and affective spirituality differentiated between male and female imitation of Christ. Medical and theological writing equated male with the spirit and female with the flesh; however, this is not quite the same thing as a gendered opposition between mind and body. Augustine stresses the difference between body (*corpus*) and flesh (*caro*): one is necessarily corporeal during this life, but one need not behave carnally.[69] Sexual lust is the prototype for all desire (*concupiscentia carnis*), and orgasm is clear evidence of its sinfulness because "the original 'integrity' of the body dissolves into an undifferentiated ocean of flesh. Sensation—in a perfect inversion of the well-ordered body—overwhelms and subjugates the mind."[70] As Suzannah Biernoff summarizes Saint Paul's conception of the flesh, one can live "*kata sarka*, 'according to the flesh' or 'after the flesh' (2 Cor. 10.2–3; Rom. 8.1f.), where *sarx* refers to human (i.e. worldly, secular) concerns, values, and attitudes.... The alternative is to live *kata pneuma*, 'according to the spirit' (Rom. 8.4)."[71] Both Augustine and Bernard of Clairvaux take from Paul the concept of "flesh" as the entire, self-willed human being, separated by the Fall from the will of God. As Karma Lochrie argues, flesh is a matter of the will's orientation, or a mental disposition, and in the Pauline and Augustinian tradition both body and mind follow the rules of either flesh or spirit. The role of reason is to bring body and mind back into conformity with God. Thus when a man imitates Christ's suffering, he humbles himself with an awareness of his inability to transcend the flesh. Purified by reason and regulated by grace, a carnal love for Christ can provide the means for restoring *man* to God—but what about woman? Is a woman's only option to valorize her alignment with the flesh, reinforcing her exclusion from transcendence?[72] Lochrie says that "Christ's wounds, far from signifying the perviousness of the female body, serve to remind women of the need to dam up their own vulnerable bodies."[73] The religious woman is advised to close off her body through chastity, silence, and actual enclosure.

The silent martyr thus models the silent woman, epitomized by the anchoress but also desirable within late-medieval society at large. Restrictions on the freedom of religious women during this period paralleled those in the secular world. The church not only ended the tenth- and eleventh-century practice of women founding and administering their own religious foundations but even stopped them from dispensing charity. Jo Ann McNamara suggests that they turned to *spiritual* almsgiving: cloistered, silent, and dependent, they could give only their prayers and their voluntary suffering.[74] Carolyn Walker Bynum suggests that these limitations accounted at least in part for the growth of lay religious movements beginning in the thirteenth century: in northern Europe, beguines; in Italy and other parts of southern Europe, *tertiaries*; and in Spain, *beatas*. These women "set themselves apart from the world by living austere, poor, chaste lives in which manual labor and charitable service were joined to worship."[75] The beguines provided direct service to the living, by means not only of miracles but also with their physical labor.[76] Inside the cloister or outside, though, women's spiritual power was focused on Purgatory, what Dyan Elliott calls a "gray area" between Heaven and Hell that emerged during the twelfth and thirteenth centuries as a space of negotiation befitting the "burgeoning world of commerce" and was financially vital to the church because it brought in funds both through masses for the dead and indulgences for those still to die.[77]

The increasing restrictions on women during the high Middle Ages went hand in hand with a significant increase in ascetic mysticism, particularly among lay women. Throughout the Middle Ages, the majority of those categorized as saints were male, and among them heroic ascetic practices—fasting, self-laceration, and sleep deprivation—increased slowly but steadily from the fifth to the fifteenth centuries.[78] But the thirteenth to fifteenth centuries saw a huge increase in ascetic practices among women, with as many as a third of holy women engaging in them. During the same period, slightly more than 50 percent of female saints were mystics, again a huge increase from previous periods. More women than men always fit in this category; furthermore, the men who had mystical experiences were not the ascetics, whereas the categories were generally associated for women.[79]

The female mystic reaches toward purification and redemption through a process of abjection that reminds her of her great dissimilarity from Christ. She speaks, she cries, she starves and flagellates her body, she drinks the pus-filled water with which she has washed the feet of lepers. As Bynum argues, the purpose of such suffering was not to destroy or even to punish the body, but to comprehend the humanity of Christ at the moment of his dying. Both self-mortification and illness served as tools for fusing with Christ, and both merged with the ecstatic imagery of erotic union.[80] Affective spirituality encouraged ecstatic trance states, into which some individuals easily slipped at some times. At other times, or for other persons, transcendent experiences were difficult to attain. Kroll and Bachrach argue that self-injurious behavior served late-medieval religious women "both as a substitute for the emotional intensity that accompanies affective mystical states, and as a method of induction into such trances when ordinary prayer and meditation fail to work."[81]

The church supported the first flowering of lay women's mystical spirituality in the thirteenth century. Humble and thoroughly subordinate to their confessors, the beguines in the Low Countries not only modeled "the proper attitude to the clergy," as Elliott notes,[82] but their example also countered the dualism of the Cathars for whom women's reproductive capacity was an inherent link with evil. And their suffering reclaimed martyrdom for the Catholic church at a time when the inquisition was actively martyring heretics.[83] Beguine piety centered on penance and the Eucharist, which was understood not to enter the digestive tract when ingested, but instead to enter the heart directly to mingle with the vital spirit.[84] From the twelfth century onward, the spirit and the immaterial soul were increasingly conflated, and the term *cor* (heart) sometimes referred metonymically to the *anima* and sometimes to the *spiritus*. If the heart constricted, spirit overwhelmed the rest of the body with emotion or even came out in the form of tears, and it was finally exhaled at death. In contrast, demons were thought to enter the viscera and live in the body's empty spaces, moving around in them, disrupting the spirit's control over the senses by isolating the soul in the safety of the heart, which they could not enter. The soul would thus be rendered impotent for the time being, and demons could tempt the soul by sending it false information. Thus one could distinguish demonic possession from holy rapture by locating the spirit: divine if it were in the heart or demonic if it were elsewhere.[85] There was no easy way to see the difference, although when exorcism succeeded, an imp or toad might jump out of the demoniac's mouth. Iconographic and theatrical convention made holiness visible as well, showing a homunculus-soul leaving the mouth bound for Heaven at death, but this does not suggest that people actually expected to see the exhaled soul in such cases.

What we know about thirteenth-century mystics comes from the vitae written by male clerics, often their confessors, and none of the vitae was written until after the women's deaths. Elliott refers to women such as Mary of Oignies (d. 1213), Lutgard of Aywières (d. 1246), and Margaret of Ypres (d. 1237) as "relics before their time" who endured a "white" martyrdom through purity and voluntary suffering but were not violently martyred (the "red" martyrdom of an earlier age). Their bodies performed miracles during their lives, always associated with their pain, and their raptures were a state similar to death.[86] Rapture was understood as an "out-of-body experience that resulted from contact with the divine," and mystics were transported to other locations while appearing dead to the world or even to physically levitate above it.[87] The rapture might include extreme physical manifestations: Christina Mirabilis (1150–1224) "curled up like a hedgehog" when she prayed, and rapture caused her to "roll and whirl like a hoop."[88] In other cases, self-injury brought about rapture. When Mary of Oignies remembered having consumed meat and watered wine to counteract an illness in the past, for example, she cut a big chunk out of her side. The resulting pain induced a "mystical ecstasy in which Mary understood herself to be standing beside a seraph."[89] And the mystic's supporters might inflict further pain in the process of testing their raptures for authenticity, with an eye to helping the mystic stand up to the inquisition after death that they hoped would result in canonization. Franciscans threw Margaret of Cortona (d. 1297) around the room, and Charles of Anjou had Douceline (d. 1274) "jabbed with nails and chisels, and even had molten lead poured over her feet."[90] Mystics were quite likely to live as outcasts, performing their ecstasies, ascetic practices, and raptures under the close scrutiny of their skeptical neighbors in medieval cities. Nancy Caciola argues that the hagiographers were the only people venerating them during life.[91] And by the fourteenth century, they were losing the general support of the church hierarchy as well.

Both self-injurious behavior and mystical rapture continued to flourish through the fifteenth century although the church now discouraged them. All other evidence aside, the fact that devotional literature intended for female ascetics warned against active emulation of the martyr's suffering was a relatively sure sign of its popularity.[92] For example, Jean Gerson warned against overzealous confession, challenged Bridget of Sweden's canonization in 1415, and wrote against Marguerite Porete and the Free Spirit Movement. Elliott attributes the failure of his attempt to defend Joan of Arc at least in part to his own efforts against other female mystics.[93] As Chancellor of the University of Paris, Gerson's concern was scholastic reform and reinvigoration, but his effort to suppress female lay mystics "unites various strains that particularly contributed to the holy woman's downward spiral: the inquisitorial method, scholasticism, the manipulation of medical discourse"—that is, the theory of humors.[94] He diagnosed "a certain kind of spiritual duplicity or deception as a woman's problem."[95] Standards of behavior changed as lay women's mystical spirituality lost official support, and Gerson and others wrote manuals of discernment that discouraged the performance of pain: because the influence of the Holy Spirit leads the heart to open naturally and serenely, calmness became the behavioral benchmark of the saint.[96] As the late-medieval period slid into the early modern, women's ecstatic raptures were more likely to identify them as witches than as saints. Indeed, Callahan notes the fine line between the two groups and points out that Fouquet's image of Apollonia could as easily represent a public execution as a theatrical performance.[97]

The medieval spectator is supposed to accept the theological position that the saint does not suffer; nevertheless, while gazing at Apollonia's closed-off and inviolate body center stage, the spectator can compassionately experience the pain of torment. The miniature, the virgin-martyr play, and the memory image thus present both a warning against ecstasy and an opportunity to vicariously experience it. The dialogical spectacle of a tormented virgin martyr center stage offered a loophole through which compassionate meditation upon her closed-off, inviolate body could slide into imagined mystical rapture. Kristine Stiles finds similar loopholes in body art, arguing that its ambiguity makes it particularly suitable as a vehicle for "the languages of the oppressed who long to speak for themselves" in the face of those who seek to "impose a uniform language."[98] Double-speak and heteroglossia are as important for reception as for articulation. Bakhtin himself had to write carefully in order to avoid censure under Stalin, and he in turn seeks out the hidden polemic of writers oppressed by Renaissance or czarist structures of power. He uses the loopholes in texts by Rabelais and Dostoevsky to imagine differently. The same tactic is available to those who watch the virgin martyr's or conceptual artist's body in pain. Indeed, Stiles maintains that art actions draw the spectator into a "committed relation" because they require the viewer to engage in active interpretation rather than passive contemplation or consumption.[99] Similarly, Amelia Jones argues that body art "provides the *possibility* for radical engagements that can transform the way we think about meaning and subjectivity (both the artist's and our own.)"[100] The possibility comes about because the artist's body/self is implicated in the work in all its particularity, and as such solicits the spectator's engaged response, in all its particularity as well, including embodied desire (or repulsion). Jones argues that body art makes it difficult for the critic or historian to maintain a "disinterested" position and from that position pronounce upon the meaning and value of the work. As a result, body art has the capacity to "destabilize the structures of conventional art history and criticism."[101]

Mysticism blossomed during the transition into modernity, and we should hardly be surprised to see it again at modernity's end. The late-medieval church's authority was weakened by the existence of two or at times even three popes, each claiming sole leadership of Christendom; moreover, social controls were generally disrupted by plague, famine, and seemingly interminable war. In a similar pattern, grotesque bodily performance infiltrated the visual art world and experimental physical theatre as social controls loosened after World War II, then burgeoned during the social protest movements in the late 1960s and early 1970s. For the body artist as for the mystic, pain has been a source of empowerment and guarantor of authenticity. But at the same time, it generates material for collecting by hagiographers and connoisseurs, and they can rework these dialogical and heteroglossic performances of suffering in ways that might appall the women who created them. Ambiguity has a negative side as well: many of the women using their bodies in art actions during the 1960s and early 1970s were beautiful and were criticized for being easily co-opted. Hannah Wilke and Carolee Schneemann were dismissed and even vilified during the 1980s, until a terminal illness and age, respectively, rehabilitated them as serious feminist artists.[102] Karen Finley ran into the same difficulty in the 1990s when right-wing politicians' characterization of her as the nude, chocolate-smeared woman helped them to eviscerate the National Endowment for the Arts even though it totally missed the point of her hilarious and rage-filled performance, which they had not bothered to see. To rephrase Schneemann's complaint, she could be an image maker, but couldn't control the use of her images or determine their meaning with any fixity.

Abramović's *Seven Easy Pieces* largely effaced the oppositional intent of historical body art, now reperformed as a fleshly retrospective and an intersubjective merging—a mystical but secular compassion, in the medieval sense of the word. Feminist body art nourished a community of sentiment, whereas Abramović's energy exchange with her audience leaves each spectator to respond within a privatized realm. The heteroglossia of her pain threatens no one. Fortunately, the body artist has more power than the medieval mystic. Abramović can and does speak for herself, controlling her own documentation and obsessively rewriting her own work, and—we hope—she is less vulnerable to the witch hunt than the medieval ecstatic proved to be.

4. Whipping Up Community ∽

Plate 6 Photograph of Ron Athey atop wooden pyramid in performance *Judas Cradle*, Ljubljana, 2004. © Manuel Vason.

We face one another in metal folding chairs, about three feet separating the two lines of spectators seated in the mezzanine performance space on New York's Lower East Side. In breastplate and studded leather codpiece, Ron Athey prowls around the tiny space, singing at and with Juliana Snapper, her voice more musically developed but his impressive in its own way. She hangs upside down, he strides about, they face off and screech. He opens a can of Crisco and shoves handfuls into the wire breast-forms attached to his corset, ends the performance on his belly, dragging himself down the narrow corridor between us, smearing grease on the floor at our feet, leaving a shortening memento on my shoes.

—*Judas Cradle*[1]

Plate 7 Giovanni del Biondo (fl. 1356–1399), *Martyrdom of Saint Sebastian and Scenes from His Life*. Triptych. Museo dell'Opera del Duomo, Florence, Italy. Photo credit: Scala/Art Resource, NY.

Whipping Up Community 105

> The central panel of the altarpiece shows a plump and modest Saint Sebastian raised up on a pillory. His naked body draws less attention than its covering of arrows so numerous as to suggest a porcupine's quills. He gazes slightly downward, eye to eye with the small angel hovering over his left shoulder to guide him through this assault. The archers grouped below his feet fire off more arrows or survey their handiwork. Jesus gazes out from the panel's peak above the saint. Mary occupies the top of the smaller right-hand panel, above two depictions of the death that follows Sebastian's stint as archery target: the first shows him beaten with clubs and dumped into the sewer; in the second, an angel-sent dream enables Christians to retrieve the saint's body. An angel surmounts the posthumous scenes on the left-hand panel: in one, a woman is stricken down for desecrating a church consecrated to Sebastian; in the other, the saint and Mary intercede for the citizens of Pavia when an outbreak of plague leaves the streets littered with corpses.
>
> —*St. Sebastian Triptych*[2]

This chapter analyzes men's formation of group identity through voluntary suffering in negotiation with specific structures of power, especially in the register of plague. Ron Athey embraces pain as a way to form bonds in opposition to homophobia, his work first coalescing around the post-modern plague of AIDS. I'll read his eroticized performance of pain against the background of heterosexual, mainstream masochism in the twentieth and twenty-first centuries in order to understand his limited viability as a commodity. Athey's imagery has often featured Saint Sebastian, this chapter's medieval focal point. He identifies the saint's homoerotic appeal as his reason for using Sebastian and cites Yukio Mishima's *Confessions of a Mask*, a story in which an adolescent boy has his first ejaculation when he sees a picture of this saint in a book.[3] It was the early modern period that eroticized both Sebastian and the practice of self-flagellation. Yet we've tended to displace this eroticism backward onto the medieval, where we can indeed locate the roots of economic and religious changes that rewrote masculine pain and laid the groundwork for modernity's masochism. The evidence strongly suggests significant differences in late-medieval spectator response to the male body in pain offered up as an appeal for protection against plague—differences from the early modern as well as the post-modern.

There's no historical evidence for Sebastian's existence. His vita in the *Acta Sanctorum* dates from the fifth century, and medieval Christians would have been most familiar with the similar version in Jacobus de Voragine's *Golden Legend*.[4] Nigel Spivey considers Giovanni del Biondo's altarpiece, shown in plate 7, to be the best available representation of Sebastian as late-medieval Christians would have imagined him. In contrast to later images, the body is rounded, no throat visible, ankles bound together, knees turned to one side, bristling with the arrows that leave him still alive but his skin covered with wounds like a plague victim's sores.[5] Louise Marshall argues that Sebastian functioned as a sort of "lightning rod" who drew the arrows of pestilence toward himself and thus away from those who appealed to him for protection.[6] Some scholars have maintained that the arrows link Sebastian to Apollo and thus to plague, replacing a pagan protector with a Christian corollary. But Sheila Barker notes that seventh-century mosaics show him as an elderly man with a white beard, in no way Apollonian, and with no arrows in sight. The arrow became his attribute some time between the late tenth and mid-thirteenth centuries, Barker suggests, due to "his spiritual role as militant defender of the church and his worldly career as a professional archer."[7]

Sebastian supposedly held a high military position under Diocletian, who martyred him. His reputation as defender against plague derives from the 680 outbreak in Pavia, which ended when Rome sent his relics to a local church. But even when the Pavian cult, likely influenced by the *Golden Legend*, began to celebrate Sebastian's feast day by eating rolls called *avicule* and wearing miniature golden arrows, the rolls rather than the arrows gave protection from plague. Barker suggests an underlying political motivation for the translation of relics, as 680 saw plague in Rome as well. Pope Agatho used the occasion to cement an alliance with the region, and Sebastian's youth in Lombardy and martyrdom in Rome made him a particularly appropriate intermediary.[8] After a recovery from plague in 1348 that he attributed to the saint's intercession, Filippo di Neri dell'Antella brought Sebastian's cult to Florence, where he was bishop from 1357 to 1363. When plague returned to Florence in 1353, dell'Antella donated a relic to the cathedral, most likely an arrow. Then during another episode in 1362, he consecrated an altar to Sebastian and commissioned an altarpiece that included the saint on a side panel, now known as the Wildenstein Panel. Holding an arrow (his attribute) and a palm (signifying marytrdom), the saint is bearded and dressed as a soldier. After another plague in 1374, Giovanni del Biondo's triptych replaced this one. Barker observes the "meaningful juxtaposition between the scene of the saint's own salvation from a bad death" and the posthumous scenes "portraying plague as a sudden, unpredictable mortality that threatens a whole community with the danger of a bad death."[9]

For Marshall, later images of Sebastian alive and impassive shift the focus to his *double* martyrdom—what Spivey calls his "recovery against all odds."¹⁰ Left for dead by the archers, Sebastian revived for another confrontation that left him bludgeoned to a second death and dumped into the Cloaca Maxima. As Sebastian's cult became more popular and more closely associated with plague, a mixing of secular medicine with belief in religious causality gave him a further association with public health. People came to believe that he could save entire cities, since he interceded on behalf of Pavia's entire population and was known as a defender of the Roman Church. This relation to collective salvation also made him a particularly useful counterforce to the individual conception of penitence spread by the flagellant cults after 1348. Barker notes that the devotional imagery simultaneously

> discouraged the individual from viewing his body as an autonomous instrument of conversion and salvation by demonstrating to the flagellant that he or she was not in a closed, reciprocal relationship with Christ, but part of a larger Christian hierarchy, in which the suffering saint occupied an intermediary position between the flagellant community and the perfection of Christ.¹¹

Even though penitents might take inspiration from images of Sebastian's suffering body, the saint's cult helped to contain such devotional energies within orthodox channels.

The Middle Ages saw a variety of penitential processions intended to be efficacious—to affect divine will, not public opinion as a modern protest march would do. Throughout the *Parisian Journal*, for example, the masses endure physical hardship in the hope of producing a more stable kingdom. On notable occasions, they voluntarily undertake an endurance ritual. While Charles VI besieged Bourges in 1412, for example, the citizens of Paris supported him with a series of processions "arranged by common consent." The *Journal* describes more than twenty of "the most touching processions that anyone had ever seen in living memory," reiterating many times that the people were barefoot and that each carried a candle. Relics were carried in some of the processions, the Eucharist in some, various masses were sung, and the text mentions the participation of various clergy, emphasizing the tears and devotion of everyone involved (62). The mass flagellant movements of the late Middle Ages differed in scope and organization but were hardly sui generis.

The phenomenon of lay movements traveling from town to town and flagellating themselves in public without official church sanction appears to have begun in Perugia around 1260, a time of civil and religious strife within Italy. These flagellants were pacifist and millenarian, and their behavior suited the growing emphasis upon confession and Eucharistic devotion.

The church condoned the processions and attempted to contain the practice within the newly formed confraternities. Then a much larger and more autonomous movement arose in 1349 in northern and eastern Europe. In Austria and Hungary, the flagellants appear to have arrived a few months prior to the plague; in the Low Countries, a few months after. There were large movements in 1349 at Avignon and 1350 at Tournai that alarmed both civic and ecclesiastical authorities. Because the King of France intervened with harsh and effective measures to suppress them, the flagellant movements essentially disappeared from France, although they flourished in Germany. A resurgence in the Low Countries in 1400 was effectively suppressed.[12] Like praying before a devotional image of Saint Sebastian, the flagellant procession was in many cases intended to stop the plague; in others, to atone for sins in preparation for the end of the world, plague being one of the signs within a millenarian framework.

Individual penitents entered a group of flagellants for a period of thirty-three and a half days—corresponding to the number of years that Jesus lived on earth—during which they flagellated themselves twice daily. They abstained from sexual intercourse; ate only what they were given; dressed in a white tunic with a red cross on the front and another on the back, a cowl covering the head, and a hat with the same crosses as the tunic; and around the waist wore a scourge ending in three knots with iron points. Chanting, led by a cross, candles, and banners, the procession entered a town. Once they reached a large enough open space, they removed all clothing except for a sort of skirt, chanted songs to the Virgin, and flagellated themselves, interrupted by several prostrations with arms outstretched as if on a cross. They finished by kneeling to say several prayers, most often addressed to the Virgin. When they arose, companions covered them and the ritual ended. Most of the prayers and the songs were in the vernacular, but they recited others from the Latin liturgy as well. Although some groups included or were aided by clergy, others were violently anticlerical, and some compared themselves favorably to the early Christian martyrs due to their free choice to suffer. After thirty-three and a half days, the flagellant group disbanded, and its members were to flagellate themselves on Good Friday for the rest of their lives.[13]

Flagellation by these lay penitents was quite different from monastic discipline. Religious self-flagellation had been unknown during the early Middle Ages. The abbot meted out discipline to correct faults; the bishop and the pope, as penitence prior to forgiveness of sins. In spite of Peter Damien's eleventh-century efforts to popularize discipline as part of his reform project, a fourteenth-century monk who wished to engage in this type of penance asked another monk to ply the whip. The practice was quite similar in form to punishment in the chapter house: for less serious faults, the penitent was prostrate and removed outer garments but retained a woolen chemise. For more serious faults, he remained seated but pulled up all of his garments over his head and took the lashes on a bare back, wearing only underpants.[14] Medieval medical texts prescribed flagellation as a means for disciplining the sort of wandering imagination that leads to involuntary ejaculation. According to Albert the Great, where such emission occurs without erotic imagination, it can be controlled by diet and bleeding. But if the imagination is involved, fasting and flagellation are required.[15] Jacques Despars recommends this in his commentary on Avicenna as part of a regimen to destroy the desire for passive sodomy—a desire that Despars condemns although Avicenna does not:

> The first means is the depression that one must harshly rouse in them through invective, criticism, and hatred of their thoughts and their vile acts. The second means is torturing them with a strong and constant hunger. The third is tiring them greatly by means of depriving them of sleep. The fourth is throwing them into a horrible prison. The fifth is beating them frequently, until the blood flows, with whip or rod.[16]

Whereas early medieval flagellation within the monastery had as one of its goals the suppression of sexual desire, later medieval lay penitents renounced all sexuality during their period of participation as part of a larger renunciation of the flesh.

Merback argues against any interpretation of the rituals as frenzied flagellation, with severity of action, intensity of pain, or profusion of blood as the goal. The processions were disciplined and orderly, and the participants beat themselves just to the point that blood began to flow. The point was "the visible, *stylized* combination of these bodily techniques with other gestures, sights, and sounds in the overall staging of the spectacle."[17] Communities generally welcomed the flagellants, and conversions were common as the rituals quite literally dissolved boundaries and spectators were moved to join the group.[18] As a mass mobilization of lay piety, however, the processions presented a challenge to ecclesiastical control and a source of disorder—this was why King Philip VI de Valois suppressed them in fourteenth-century France. Flagellants proved as difficult to suppress as mystics, though, leaving Jean Gerson to argue against this disruptive practice in his 1417 tract *Contra sectum flagellantium*, urging adherence to doctrinaire Christian practices under the close supervision of the ecclesiastical hierarchy.[19]

Displacement often proves more effective than suppression, and Barker notes that orthodox confraternities of disciplinati soon replaced the lay flagellant movements in Italy. As foci for compassionate suffering, fifteenth- and early sixteenth-century processions replaced living penitents with wooden statues of Saint Sebastian. These were nude, pierced with arrows, and nearly lifelike, their prototype possibly a nude statue of Sebastian that cured a leper after it washed up on shore in Melilli, Siciliy, in 1411.[20] Marshall notes, as does Barker, that fifteenth-century devotional images of Sebastian with a sparse scattering of arrows and no archers in sight closely resemble images of Christ as the Man of Sorrows. Like the latter, they elicit an intimate and direct engagement with the viewer. Reading them in the register of recurrent plague, Marshall notes that "historical time is suspended and inverted, transforming the narrative into a devotional image that exists outside of time and place."[21]

Barker makes the interesting suggestion that the saint's beauty may have had a prophylactic function, according to the Renaissance medical theory that looking at beauty helped to preserve health and even to protect against plague.[22] The beautiful and homoerotic Sebastian first appears in late fifteenth-century Italian images that focus on the modeling of the nearly nude body, "stripped to loin-cloth or diaphanous briefs" and always in much the same position, "one leg relaxed, and the hip consequently pronounced." As Nigel Spivey describes him, "whether dandy, ephebe or trooper, St. Sebastian...is rarely bereft of erotic allure."[23] Robert Mills notes that the stillness of the saint's body, along with its lack of appropriate affect (that is, no expression of pain), creates narrative tension and suspense. He argues that suspension between life and death—not only in these images but also in the hanging of a criminal—creates for the viewer the potentially masochistic pleasure of indefinitely postponed release and, therefore, prolonged excitation.[24] To my eye, the head typically thrown back in passive surrender presents the strongest erotic suggestion. The sight of suffering can arouse us—pleasantly or not—because our reactive squirm puts us back in our own bodies but also because it evokes the murky interplay of power and desire. Overlapping neuroanatomical pathways and mechanisms may be responsible, as Richard Bodnar and others suggest. They argue that both painful and sexually related stimuli heighten certain central nervous system states, which in turn dampen responses to pain and facilitate sexual behavior.[25] Regardless of the neurological mechanics, a person with the power to cause one pain has the power to cause and control pleasure as well. I would venture that modernity heightens the erotic investment in pain as social and economic changes lead to more complex and abstract power relations: pain returns power to the tangible ground of embodied experience.

Northern Europe underwent a far-reaching commercial transformation during the long thirteenth century (1180–1320) that included, together with the urbanization and growth of trade already touched on in chapter 1, the development of a money economy. Money created new habits: concern with profit and loss, keeping accurate written records, and quantification of values that had previously been qualitative. As money and bureaucracy grew together, merchants gained not only wealth but also social and political power. Others gradually adopted their outlook; for example, lords began to think of their forests as income-producing resources rather than simply as sources of pleasure and status.[26] Money, lending, and profit came at a psychological and spiritual price, though, as shown by increased writing against usury. Within the contractual economy that prevailed until the twelfth century, credit came from monasteries: most often, the borrower used a building as loan collateral and the lender received income from the building. Lending money itself was a problematic innovation because the usurer sells time, which belongs to God, and furthermore makes money without working, contrary to the Creator's plan for us to labor.[27] Usury was one of the three "accursed professions," the others being prostitution and acrobatics.[28]

Penitential handbooks reveal great anxiety about fraud, about fair pricing, and whether it was acceptable to make money by selling goods that one had not produced or even augmented in any way—in other words, to be a merchant. The Franciscans and Dominicans produced most of these handbooks, because as urban friars they were the confessors for merchants.[29] Barbara Rosenwein and Lester Little argue that the money economy produced its opposite figure, the mendicant preacher, because the Benedictine and Cistercian clergy were too wealthy to assuage the medieval merchant's guilt about money. The mendicants depended upon the support of the urban middle and upper classes, and their lay followers remained engaged in the market economy but gained some measure of spiritual benefit by vicariously participating in the friars' renunciation. Yet even as the mendicant orders rejected the mercantile livelihood—what Francis of Assisi rejected with his conversion was the life of a cloth merchant—they participated in related discursive formations by persuading and negotiating. Rosenwein and Little point out that opponents criticized the mendicant orders in just these terms, and they judge the system of indulgences to be entirely in keeping with a market economy.[30]

Although Saint Francis was a popular model for ascetic practice—initiating a turn to poverty and service, living by begging, sleeping on the floor—and is also the first Christian to manifest stigmata, the mendicant friars typically documented the popular mass religious revivals such as the flagellant movements rather than actively participating in them.[31] The paradoxical eroticization of men's suffering and simultaneous suppression of any potential incitements to arousal began in earnest only after the Tridentine reforms (1545–63) put priests in direct control not only of the individual Catholic's confession and absolution but also of conscience and of the religious confraternities as well. Vandermeersch notes the influence of the Jesuits and the notion of accountability: one kept accounts and atoned for specific sins, expecting God to balance the accounts in Purgatory.[32] Barker says that "by the close of the Council of Trent, artworks with a potential to inspire *eros* were often systematically removed from churches."[33] Open speculation that flagellation might have an unseemly sexual purpose arose initially in connection with Henri III, whose private Confraternity of Death from 1585 onward practiced a kind of flagellation quite different from either monastic practices or the fourteenth-century lay processions. Henri's flagellation took place in a semidarkened room, and although others were present, they were witnesses rather than participants in a group ritual. As a private matter, flagellation was sexualized and secularized, transformed through its new relation to personal desires that must be confessed, no longer a penance imposed or a public ritual that was at least partially joyful. This sixteenth-century transformation placed the practice within a heterosexual context and entailed a double displacement: not only did the site of flagellation move downward from the back of the medieval penitent to the buttocks, but the related discourse elided the desire of the man who bared this clearly erogenous zone and instead conjured up a lusty woman wielding a whip.[34]

This picture of erotic flagellation by a dominatrix aligns so well with modern fantasy and practice that we may find it difficult to imagine the alterity of a late-medieval masculine investment in suffering. But if we accept the premise discussed at length in the previous chapter that the female mystic's ecstasy was an erotic spirituality, clearly separate from carnal eroticism, then can we not accept a similar characterization for the male penitent's self-flagellation? Although the chronicles note the diversity of fourteenth-century participants in some cases—male and female, young and old, healthy and sick, lay and religious—other groups appear to have been restricted to men. Some were so thoroughly exclusionary that if a woman or a priest were to enter the flagellant circle, the entire ritual sequence had to begin again.[35] Merback says that only very rarely did men and women participate in the same procession, that men predominated overall, and that when women did self-flagellate, they appear to have done so indoors.[36] Lisa Silverman suggests that according to the high-medieval intellectual framework within which flagellation grew popular, penitential suffering was a male prerogative precisely because women suffered in childbirth as punishment for Eve's sin; in other words, it meant little for a woman to choose that which was her fate anyway.[37] One major distinction between the mystic and the flagellant would seem to be that the flagellants engaged in a public group practice rather than in the private individual ecstasy of the mystics. Another is that the mystic, as Ruth Karras puts it, is the "passive partner to whom God does something,"[38] whereas the flagellant is active, doing something to affect the world at large through his action upon himself—and the most visible practitioners were men, thoroughly in keeping with the standard conception at the time of masculine activity and feminine passivity. Religious women suffer for those in Purgatory, whereas male penitents make themselves suffer to prevent plague here and now.

* * *

When PS122 presented Ron Athey's *Four Scenes from a Harsh Life* in 1994, I heard the extreme reactions of my fellow graduate students: the straight man who felt dizzy and trapped and would have left if he hadn't been sitting where he was; the gay woman who was so moved that she wanted to drop what she was working on and just write about Athey. Public response focused not on the pain but on the blood: paper towels pressed into a design cut into the back of an HIV-negative performer were clipped to a clothesline and reeled out over the audience. In Minneapolis someone who walked out before this portion of the performance reported towels dripping with Athey's HIV-positive blood, the NEA was attacked for its $150 contribution in support of performances at the Walker Art Center, and conservative hysteria over purportedly dangerous bloody towels generated increased attention in the mainstream liberal press for a short time.[39] Yet there was pain aplenty: multiple varieties of piercing and cutting, the entire cast dancing until the bells and limes stitched to their skin with fishing line tore free. The piece begins with a naked, arrow-pierced Saint Sebastian figure (an androgynous but genitally female performer identified as Pigpen) trembling next to Athey, who is dressed as a holy woman from his childhood. He tells the story of this faith healer who supposedly bore stigmata and his disappointment that she did not actually bleed when he met her.

Much of what I know about Athey's early work comes from Catherine Gund Saalfield's documentary, *Hallelujah! Ron Athey: A Story of Deliverance*

(1998).[40] *Four Scenes* is the middle section of a trilogy, preceded by *Martyrs and Saints* (1992), which Athey describes as an attempt to understand why his HIV-positive status makes him feel like a martyr and how that relates to his religious upbringing. *Deliverance* (1995) follows, dealing with death, healing, and mysticism, zipping its martyrs into body bags and burying them under a pile of earth. Although the narrative content of these pieces comes from Athey's life experience, he draws inspiration from diverse literary and historical sources. I've already mentioned Saint Sebastian: *Martyrs and Saints* ends with "nurses" slowly pushing darts into Athey, who also bears a crown of surgical-needle thorns. *Solar Anus* (1998) was inspired by Pierre Molinier's photographic self-portraits and an essay by George Bataille. The imagery of *Incorruptible Flesh* (2007) layers Sophocles' *Philoctetes* together with John Jesurun's 1994 reworking of that play for Ron Vawter, James Bidgood's 1971 film *Pink Narcissus,* and Wagner's 1882 opera *Parsifal*.[41] The unifying themes are pain and queer relatedness.

Judas Cradle owes a great deal to Athey's interest in historical torture devices—apparently early modern in this case, like the homoerotic Saint Sebastian, although I haven't found any scholarship to support Wikipedia's claim of invention by the Spanish Inquisition. The eponymous device is a large wooden pyramid upon which Athey anally impales himself during the full version of the piece, as shown in plate 6. Snapper suffers as well, stretched upside down on the rack and singing until her voice collapses. Amelia Jones describes performances of *Judas Cradle* in Ljubljana (2004) and Manchester (2005): "The woman flutters through a weird hysterical version of some bad, miscast 1970s BBC drama (with wispy ahs and huffs), the man impales himself slowly on the pyramid." Later, "they both rejoin at the central altar in a climax of cacophonous, operatic union.... They *come* through their screeching, rasping, chortling voices: Sound as sex."[42] Taking off from Wayne Koestenbaum's throat-as-cunt analogy, Jones talks about the eroticism of the glottis vibrating to make sound and equates Snapper's throat with Athey's anus. She says that watching this performance opened her up, repeatedly, making her a "body of holes."[43] Clearly, the painful eroticism of the piece overwhelms its topical referents for Jones, because she never mentions the Abu Ghraib video projections that serve as background for the live performance. Yet Kateri Butler describes *Judas Cradle* as "a response to Homeland Security, Iraq, Afghanistan, Guantanamo Bay, Abu Ghraib, American guilt and Ron's long obsession with instruments of torture."[44]

The excerpt that Athey and Snapper performed as part of the PERFORMA05 festival curated by RoseLee Goldberg included neither the judas cradle nor the section that Dominic Johnson describes as "Juliana abusing [Ron] in orange boiler suits in the high desert."[45] The evening's relatively mild discomfort called to mind Athey's more extreme work and pointed at the pain of the full opera, seen in Europe and Los Angeles but not New York. Athey's one-night stand at Participant Inc was a low-rent counterpart to Abramović's appearance uptown at the Guggenheim during the same week, documented not only with an expensive catalogue but also on film in Babette Mangolte's *Seven Easy Pieces* (2007). Abramović also features in Chiara Clemente's *Our City Dreams* (2008). The gender balance has shifted now from what it was when Athey performed in New York during the late 1990s. The last fifteen years of the twentieth century saw a fascination with male masochists: during this period, male pain artists Fakir Musafar, Bob Flanagan, and Ron Athey all "came out" into a performance genre that had been prepared by conceptual and performance artists. All three then became the subject of documentary films with enough commercial potential to warrant a home video release.[46] Although they are obscure by industry standards, even an obscure film gets more exposure than an art performance. No one was making documentaries about the comparable body artists Gina Pane, Marina Abramović, or Orlan at the time. Video documentation of their work was handled by nonprofit media arts organizations.

I think that Abramović sells now whereas Athey doesn't for the same reason that he got more attention in the 1990s; that is, the sexuality of his performances. Fakir, Flanagan, and Athey were presenting themselves as *sexual* masochists, whereas Pane, Orlan, and Abramović were keeping their sexual practices private. Flanagan, Fakir, and Athey were perceived as speaking for a sexual-preference minority at a time when a great variety of queer voices were being allowed into mainstream discourse—at least on its fringes. But then conservative backlash during the two Bush administrations combined with efforts to work within the system typified by the struggle over same-sex marriage laws, and funding to present this sort of work dried up. As Athey so eloquently puts it, "Action-wise, what started as piercing can be categorized as SM play, but live anal penetration in a non-sexual setting is blatantly not fakery, putting the very 'real' roots of homophobia on the table."[47]

In order to understand what has happened here, it will be well worth our time to trace out the central trajectories that brought punk and S/M culture, both transformed by processes of commodification, together with the performance art genres and venues that prepared a broadly based audience in the 1990s to watch men hurt themselves and to appreciate this as art. I discuss briefly four overlapping cycles of rebellion against normative masculinity, each of which can be characterized in masochistic terms and each of which was more or less neutralized and reabsorbed into mainstream culture: first, in a mid-twentieth-century reaction to art as commodity, the artist Jackson Pollock himself becomes the commodity in circulation; second, Chris Burden tries to move outside of this system of distribution by performing actions that cannot be merchandized; third, S/M becomes a fashion fetish; and fourth, punk culture reacts to the conservative excesses of the Thatcher and Reagan administrations.

The narrative of the action artist's descent from Jackson Pollock, centering on America and promulgated by Allan Kaprow during the generative phase, remains influential because of its coherence and explanatory value.[48] Its truth is almost irrelevant, because so many artists have understood the movement in these terms. As Paul Schimmel describes the causal chain, Pollock's paint flinging was an action intended to produce an object (a painting), but Hans Namuth's photos and films of Pollock emphasized the action itself (and with it, the artist's body). Other artists took this shift of focus farther, emphasizing the process of creation instead of the object and eventually eliminating the object entirely.[49] The historical narrative also highlights the role of the artist as hero, as maverick, as suffering genius. According to what Amelia Jones calls a "melodramatic myth," the completion of Namuth's film precipitated Pollock's descent into alcoholism and eventual death by car crash.[50] The European progenitors of action art also died prematurely, contributing to the appearance of a pattern: Yves Klein, the French artist who used models' bodies to transfer paint to canvas in the early 1960s, died of a heart attack at age thirty-four in 1963, the same year that Piero Manzoni, the Italian who sold balloons filled with *Artist's Breath* and cans of *Artist's Shit,* died at thirty of cirrhosis.[51]

None of this is exceptional: Romanticism and Modernism typically deployed the image of the tortured artist or poet as hero. If Pollock is the father of the post-modern pain artist, then Vincent Van Gogh must be the grandfather. Yet something had changed. A critical component of Pollock's creative crisis was that the film caused him to see himself "as a performer" and his actions as "histrionics" instead of as authentic acts of painting. Furthermore, his body was displayed not only in *Art Journal* but also in mass-market magazines such as *Life* and *Look,* alongside performers proper. The media fit Pollock into the mold shaped by (or for) Marlon Brando and James Dean; that is, "nonconformist hypermasculinity." But the display of virility for mass-market delectation in the 1950s paradoxically feminized these rebels and cowboys.[52] David Savran argues persuasively that the phantasm of the white male as victim plays a central role in twentieth-century American culture, beginning with the Beats imagining themselves in the 1950s as "white niggers"; developing into the hippie and the political radical of the 1960s; and culminating in "the angry white male, the sensitive male, the male searching for the Wild Man within, the white supremacist, the spiritual male." Savran says that the formerly dissident and marginal position of the masochist became central and hegemonic in the 1970s

> because it represents an attempt by white men to respond to and regroup in the face of particular social and economic challenges: the reemergence of the feminist movement; the limited success of the civil rights movement in redressing gross historical inequities through affirmative action legislation; the rise of the lesbian and gay rights movements; the failure of America's most disastrous imperialistic adventure, the Vietnam War; and, perhaps most important, the end of the post-World War II economic boom and the resultant and steady decline in the income of white working- and lower-middle-class men.[53]

To put it another way, the media began queering its rebels in the 1950s by positioning them as masochists, a queerness that remained veiled and contested until the late 1980s.

The early career of conceptual artist Chris Burden represents an intermediate step in the transformation of masculine masochism between 1949 and 1994. By the time Burden started college in the late 1960s, mid-century bursts of radical art experiment such as Happenings and Fluxus had significantly changed the academic art curriculum: as his thesis project at the University of California at Irvine in 1971, Burden spent five days in a locker.[54] *Shoot* (1971) remains his most widely known work, and he describes it in typically clinical fashion: "At 7:45 p.m. I was shot in the left arm by a friend. The bullet was a copper jacket 22 long rifle. My friend was standing about fifteen feet from me."[55] For *Bed Piece* (1971), Burden got into a bed in the Market Street Gallery and stayed there for twenty-two days. He gave no instructions, leaving it up to gallery personnel to figure out that they should provide essentials such as water and toilet facilities (which they did). He said that the first two days were very difficult and painful but that he began to enjoy the peacefulness by the second week and to consider staying; however, he knew that he would not be able to do so, even if he tried, and that people would think he was crazy. During *Bed Piece*, Burden noticed that he seemed to have a kind of power, like a repulsive magnet: there was a sort of invisible bubble around him, and people seemed afraid to come close.[56]

Burden's early actions bring the social contract into question, as Kathy O'Dell argues, not only by requiring the participation of others who are not always "performers" or "artists" but also by pushing the relation between performer and spectator into the foreground. In most cases, spectators did not participate physically in Burden's self-endangerment, but their presence and failure to interfere implied consent to his actions. O'Dell uses *Shoot* to introduce and explain her use of the label "masochistic" for 1970s body art because of its implied contractual relationship, not Burden's subjective relation to pain.[57] The masochist sets the terms of the S/M contract; therefore, in a peculiar and paradoxical way, the masochist suffers only physically but produces emotional suffering for any participant or spectator who doesn't enjoy filling the dominant role. Unwitting or naive spouses of masochists often enough end up miserable, drafted into dominance against their own inclinations.[58] If the Chris Burden of the 1970s qualifies as a masochist on any level, it is as the controlling drafter of contracts. According to O'Dell, the masochistic contract served artists as a metaphor for other contractual arrangements, those that structure political and domestic relationships. By causing spectators to question their participation in his self-damage, Burden stimulated a questioning of "the everyday agreements—or contracts—that we all make with others but that may not be in our own best interests."[59]

Like the story of Jackson Pollock's alcoholic postperformance regret, Burden's unemotional descriptions reinforce his gender conformity. Amelia Jones refers to the "tragic existentialist artist-hero" persona and says that "Chris Burden's body woundings act as tests to ensure and reinforce the ultimate impermeability of his masculine subjectivity."[60] His deadpan voiceover makes his actions sound like science projects: he posits that his "experiments" gave him "knowledge that other people don't have," asking, "How do you know what it feels like to be shot if you don't get shot?"[61] He has gone on to create art from the toys of a typical mid-century American boyhood, Erector sets and electric trains. Popular culture has even provided a new conceptual framework for his dangerous acts, positioning *Shoot* as a "proto-'Jackass' gesture."[62] The clean and controlled, intellectual nature of Burden's actions is far different from what Athey and other performers started doing in the 1990s. Burden's art may have been masochistic, but it held queerness at a distance.

The gay leather community was itself changing significantly at the time Burden was performing his early actions. Until the 1970s, "leather" was not about pleasure and pain or even dominance and submission but instead about masculinizing homosexuality and unifying a community.[63] Inspired by Marlon Brando in *The Wild One* and reflected in Kenneth Anger's *Scorpio Rising*, the leather world centered on motorcycles from the late 1950s until the 1970s, when the focus switched to clothing.[64] The gay movement to rehabilitate leather coincided with the human potential movement, and pain science provided useful tools starting in the late 1970s, when the discovery of opiate receptors on nerve cells, endorphins, and enkephalins led to research on endogenous pain-control systems.[65] The term "endorphin" quickly found its way into popular discourse, from the "runner's high" to S/M.[66] Leo Bersani observes that biochemical descriptions of leathersex in effect depain masochistic pain. In other words, an emphasis on the release of opioids as a result of painful practices leads to the conclusion that "the masochist, just like everyone else, pursues only pleasure"; in fact, the masochist wants *more* pleasure and is willing to tolerate the extreme pain needed to reach "that biochemical threshold."[67] Gilles Deleuze played a significant role recharacterizing S/M as a safe and loving role-playing game and banishing the "sadist." He first published his translation of Sacher-Masoch's *Venus in Furs* and accompanying essay in French in 1967, with an English translation in 1971 and a second edition in 1989.[68] Deleuze separates masochism from sadism and negates the combined term, sadomasochism. He argues that masochism is contractual, reciprocal, and exists in dialogue, whereas sadism is indifferent to the other except for the desire to annihilate.[69] After being transformed into a positive force for social and psychological health, S/M was further recuperated as politically subversive, fueled in part by Michel Foucault's explication of power relations and Judith Butler's work on gender performativity.[70] As Bersani notes, the "political rescue" of S/M depends upon the claim that it is a game, within which the master-slave relation is aesthetisized.[71]

S/M is a frontier (if surely not a last frontier): the battles for women's rights and gay rights made queer practices increasingly acceptable to many and increasingly visible to everyone. Yet visibility is not fashion, and S/M became fashionable in the 1990s. The gay "leatherman" of the 1980s morphed into neoprimitive "leatherfolk" and kinky (but not gay!) executives in need of release. Leather liberation and community formation led to criticism from mainstream culture and the psychiatric establishment, followed by feminist condemnation as the "sex wars" within feminism during the 1980s linked anti-S/M and antipornography efforts. Paradoxically, the Meese Commission's collaboration between antiporn feminists and political conservatives, followed by the attack on Robert Mapplethorpe (and other transgressive artists) by Jesse Helms, promoted acceptance and visibility for S/M as a form of liberal backlash.[72]

Mapplethorpe's photographs came to much wider attention than their fine-art context would otherwise have occasioned when the Contemporary Arts Center in Cincinnati was tried for pandering obscenity in 1990. The right-wing attempt to crack down on NEA funding for "obscenity" paradoxically brought bondage and discipline into many American living rooms, where Madonna's 1992 combination book (*Sex*) and CD (*Erotica*) followed them—or, if not the book itself, at least awareness of its contents. S/M was central to the film *Basic Instinct*, released the same year, and to one storyline on ABC-TV's *One Life to Live*. Fashion shows featured leather harnesses (Jean-Paul Gaultier), chain-mail bracelets (Perry Ellis), and studded collars (Claude Montana). Celebrities wore leathers by Gianni Versace to benefits. *Vogue* published a "Women in Chains" layout and *Cosmopolitan* paired a bondage-wear cover with an article on S/M.[73] Before long, *Redbook* found practitioners in its pages,[74] and reporters could make fun of the banality, noting that an annual European gathering was "more like a convention of Dracula extras than a scene from Caligula."[75] Mental health professionals identified AIDS and the recession as primary reasons: "You have a lot of men under a tremendous amount of pressure, trying to hold onto jobs, trying to run companies in trouble. They're exhausted. They go to these women and give up control for an hour."[76]

Bersani suggests that the inversion of power relationships in such representations of S/M simply solidifies the existing order of things:

> The transformation of the brutal, all-powerful corporate executive (by day) into the whimpering, panty-clad servant of a pitiless dominatrix (by night) is nothing more than a comparatively invigorating release of tension. The concession to a secret and potentially enervating need to shed the master's exhausting responsibilities and to enjoy briefly the irresponsibility of total powerlessness allows for a comfortable return to a position of mastery and oppression the morning after, when all the "other side" has been, at least for a time, whipped out of the executive's system.[77]

In a similar line of argument, Savran notes that masochistic fantasy "allows the white male subject to take up the position of victim, to feminize and/or blacken himself fantasmatically, and to disavow the homosexual cathexes that are crucial to the process of (patriarchal) cultural reproduction, all the while asserting his unimpeachable virility."[78] Far from seeing masochism as a route to radical subversion, Savran calls it "a kind of decoy" and points out that "the cultural texts constructing masochistic masculinities characteristically conclude with an almost magical restitution of phallic power."[79] In short, placing oneself temporarily in the victim role makes it easier to cope with one's actual role as victimizer. Note also that mainstream S/M is largely heterosexualized. Bersani's and Savran's analyses go far toward explaining the fascination with masochists that opened a tiny niche at the end of the twentieth century for documentary films about male pain artists.

The S/M club scene in Los Angeles nurtured Fakir Musafar and Bob Flanagan as well as Athey, and *Hallelujah!* helps to place that scene in the context of post-punk alternative culture. Piercing, branding, and tattooing were logical extensions of the punk body-marking of the late 1970s and early 1980s that affirmed unhappiness, disenfranchisement, and lack of a viable future and displayed them as quasivirtues. Turning to "primitive" sources made sense, particularly given the birth of punk in Britain: what better affront to neoconservatism than to honor the civilizations that the British empire tried to eradicate? Philippe Liotard points out that the neoprimitives take their inspiration from bodies "that were stigmatized and displayed during colonial exhibitions in Europe and the United States right up to the early 20th century.... Seen through European eyes, piercing, body scars and elongated lips, necks and ears were evidence of 'barbarism,' justifying the West's self-appointed duty to civilize."[80] As Talal Asad points out, the colonial project could not tolerate a practice such as hook swinging regardless of the fact that it was a religious ritual whose participants claimed to feel no pain, because the spectacle was demoralizing to European spectators.[81] Such spectacle also flies in the face of empathy as tool of conformity, at least with respect to "civilized" and heteronormative Western culture.

Hook swinging in India and the Native American Sundance ritual inspired Fakir Musafar, who is commonly called the father of the modern primitive movement and has avidly documented his own pain performances since his early teens. He has piercings all over his body and various genital modifications. Sometimes he severely constricts his waist or inserts close to a hundred spears into his torso.[82] Growing up with the name Roland Loomis on an Indian reservation in South Dakota, Fakir began to experiment secretly with body modifications gleaned from encyclopedias. He discovered that painful body play produced a tremendous relief from intense experiences of dissociation, hallucinations, and loneliness. His first out-of-body experience, alone and lashed to the wall of his family's coal bin at age seventeen, produced the insight: "Your body belongs to you. Play with it." Repeated dreams convinced him that he was the reincarnation of an Indian mystic who died in a gruesome accident, and he took the name Fakir Musafar. By coming out as both masochist and spiritual seeker in 1977 at a tattoo convention and continuing to proselytize for body play,

Fakir changed the context for his own subsequent actions *and* for anyone self-consciously performing within the context that he helped to establish. Rebecca Novick describes him as "a misfit who, unable to find a mold to fit into, simply fashioned one for himself."[83]

The "mold" took some time to fashion, however. Notably, Fakir did not find his way into the conceptual art world; rather, he met like-minded spiritual seekers when he moved to San Francisco to do graduate work in technical theatre. (As he tells the story, the connection to theatre is purely incidental.) In the mid-1960s, he became involved with the Janus Society; in the 1970s, with tattoo and piercing show-and-tell parties in Los Angeles. Charles Gatewood, a photographer documenting the tattoo and body-modification subculture, brought him wider attention. Interest in Fakir is to some extent a product of cultural trends, but he has been instrumental in promoting these trends—his career as an advertising executive should not be overlooked. The release of Dan and Mark Jury's film *Dances Sacred and Profane* and publication of *Modern Primitives* in the mid-1980s fed into a growing interest in body modification within youth culture.[84] At the time that the film was made, Fakir felt it necessary to tone down his conversation and to couch his pursuits in primarily spiritual terms reminiscent of Joseph Campbell. Even "neopagans" perceived the pursuit of pain in negative terms, as mortification of the body. Only within S/M circles did Fakir find understanding and acceptance. By the mid-1990s, though, he could talk openly and enthusiastically to audiences of young people searching for "new ways to reclaim their bodies, to do their own rites of passages, to do group rites of passage."[85] Fakir began to publish *Body Play and Modern Primitives Quarterly* in 1991 and instituted the *Fakir Body Piercing and Branding Intensives* in 1993. By 1996, *Modern Primitives* had been reprinted 6 times and 60,000 copies were in circulation.[86] Fakir retired from advertising to devote himself to publishing and teaching, with workshops that fill up far in advance.[87] He calls *pain* a "prejudicial word" for intense sensations which, *if* actively sought and expected, are not aversive.[88] Pain alone is not sufficient for the type of experience that Fakir describes, nor is it reliable. He stresses the need for an experienced guide and proposes that a modern primitive shaman (such as himself) can provide much-needed new rituals for modern tribes.[89]

Modern Primitives also includes a profile of Sheree Rose, who discusses her transformation from discontented Southern California housewife to happy dominatrix. In 1993, Re/Search published a volume dedicated to Rose's slave, Bob Flanagan.[90] Flanagan described his sexual masochism as a way to take control of his bodily experience—that is, to feel pain that he controlled, in contrast with the painful and depersonalizing medical treatments for cystic fibrosis (CF) that he endured from his earliest childhood. CF is an inherited disease characterized by chronic respiratory infections, pancreatic insufficiency, and malfunctioning sweat glands. Two of Flanagan's sisters died of CF, one as an infant and the other in her twenties. People with CF rarely live much beyond thirty, although the development of better antibiotics has extended the lifespan of many. During his last years, Flanagan hoped for a heart and lung transplant, but his lungs had deteriorated past the point at which that was possible, and he died in 1996.[91]

Like Fakir, Flanagan began as an adolescent to experiment with pain in his family home. He was a poet, exhibitionist, and aspiring stand-up comic; Rose, a photographer and video artist. They began to perform in Los Angeles in the late 1980s first as an outgrowth of poetry readings and then in S/M clubs. Flanagan apparently made the transition into a sort of show business at some cost to his pleasures—his *Pain Journal* recounts masturbating for spectators, although he feels too sick to enjoy anything, because the show must go on.[92] Performance had its compensatory pleasures, however. Linda Kauffman says that although Flanagan was a Bottom, "when he performs, he relishes the opportunity to go over the top" by confronting the audience with their investments in (male) flesh.[93] Dennis Cooper describes him as "a complex man who wanted simultaneously to be Andy Kaufman, Houdini, David Letterman, John Keats, and a character out of a de Sade novel."[94]

For Flanagan and Rose's installation *Visiting Hours* he was present in the museum, sometimes talking with visitors as he lay in a hospital bed, at other times hoisted up to the ceiling by his ankles, naked. Aside from this suspension, performative pain was limited to video and photo installations.[95] To Flanagan's surprise, strangers sat by his bedside in the museum and talked about their own experiences with grave illness,[96] inspired to such intimate exchanges by the charm and humor that were even more notable than his masochism. During the footage of *Visiting Hours* in Kirby Dick's film *Sick: The Life and Death of Bob Flanagan, Super-Masochist*, for example, Flanagan explains that although the bed and the suspension resemble events performed by Chris Burden, and the video scaffold is similar to work by Nam June Paik, he invented these things in his "Der Ivative" artist persona. For *You Always Hurt the One You Love* (1991) at QSM in San Francisco, he chatted about illness and pain while nailing his penis to a stool.[97] *Sick* includes a hilarious excerpt from another performance in which he talks about doing this for the first time and accidentally hitting his penis with the hammer. The film also includes Rose's narration, footage of Flanagan at a CF summer camp singing "Forever Lung" in the style of Bob Dylan, interviews with his parents and brother, and his deterioration and death. Kauffman points out that Flanagan focused attention on two aspects of sexuality that are usually denied: the sexuality of children and of those who are sick and dying.[98] *Sick* turns S/M into the everyday backdrop that makes it possible to communicate about the normally hidden, even taboo, experience of terminal illness and grief. The documentary presents Flanagan's illness as, finally, wrenching and unmitigated by his attempt to control bodily experience through volitional pain.

Flanagan's performative affirmation of masochism is less radical than Fakir's because of the explanatory apparatus available to create a comfortable distance for the spectator. Fakir describes dissociation in early childhood, and one can speculate about neurological imbalances or traumatic experiences, but Flanagan identified an originating trauma of sufficient magnitude to explain his behavior. Furthermore, because the trauma was an illness and its painful medical treatment, no blame needed to be assigned. Athey likewise identifies the traumatic origins of his painful art, but unlike Flanagan he assigns blame to both his family and the culture at large. In his performances and in his writing, Athey links childhood damage and the AIDS tragedy. His family were Pentecostal Christians for generations back, and the grandmother and aunt who raised him in Southern California believed that he was born to fill the role of John the Baptist for the second coming of Christ. His aunt was to serve as the new Virgin Mary. As a child, Athey cooperated by speaking in tongues, having visions, and preaching. When he was fifteen, he revealed his "Calling" to his girlfriend. "Under the weight of her incomprehension, the house of cards suddenly collapsed" and his faith was shattered.[99] He began to self-mutilate in order to dissociate while praying because the kind of psychic transport to which he was accustomed was no longer available to him and also to connect with reality.

Athey spent ten years addicted to heroin, tried to kill himself a number of times, and was finally redeemed by a vision of himself covered with black tribal designs. He began getting tattoos and also began to perform again in 1990, but in a venue much different from the revival tent—that is, he began go-go dancing at Club Fuck in Los Angeles among "a lot of extreme people who were extreme for private reasons, and the private went public." Before long, he began to include live piercings and his new performance career was underway. Invited by Dennis Cooper to present work at LACE in 1992, Athey compiled scenes he developed at Club Fuck into *Martyrs and Saints*. Athey's performance trilogy reworked the relation between voluntary suffering, homophobia, and the plague of AIDS in order to present a new martyr who rejects Christianity but finds a sacred subject in himself. In the absence of religion, a functional belief system, or an effective support system, borrowed ritual practices provide Athey and his fellow performers with the means to perform *communitas* on stage in defiance of a homophobic culture. During the 1990s, Athey brought onstage just the sort of modern tribe that other so-called neoprimitives were talking about, and both the tribe as a whole and the individual performers were remarkable for confounding any binary gender analysis.

Athey, Flanagan, and Fakir all use their performative suffering to take control of their own experience and also to form connections with other people. Their adolescent experimentation with pain is not uncommon; in fact, self-mutilation as a "feminine" practice closely followed "masculine" masochism into the news.[100] The psychiatric literature posits a traumatic origin for most deliberate self-harm. Many trauma survivors habitually dissociate from their immediate bodily experience as a way to cope with what they have been through. Some of them then cut their skin in order to produce a sense of reintegration:

> The cutting causes blood to appear and stimulates nerve endings in the skin. When this occurs cutters first are able to verify that they are alive, and then are able to focus attention on their skin border and to perceive the limits of their bodies. The efficacy of this process is startling; skin cutting almost always terminates episodes of depersonalization.[101]

The act of wounding initiates a healing process, with the pain often less important than the production of blood or some other visible sign. Self-injury can also give a sense of control that is otherwise missing, and produce sensation for those who feel benumbed. Finally, cutting serves to define the body's boundaries. Didier Anzieu suggests that self-inflicted pain is a strategy for reclaiming a body experienced as existing only "on sufferance." When one's body is "emptied of affect, reduced to a mechanical functioning, adequate but bringing no satisfaction...merely a body of need, of mishandled need at that," then the voluntary embodiment of pain is an experience lived "in one's own name."[102]

Regardless of its psychological etiology or function for the cutter, self-cutting also communicates. Clinicians describe the ways in which cutters manipulate family, friends, and therapists. At the very least, cutting communicates distress and does so very effectively, *if* it can be received. Often those surrounding the cutter cannot tolerate the message being sent; in fact, dysfunctional communication is often what makes such an extreme method necessary—the cutter has no other way to speak. Athey talks about his own adolescent cutting as a desperate, self-destructive prelude to his heroin addiction, in sharp contrast to the redemptive force of his later tattooing and piercing. Yet he acknowledges that they are linked. The difference is the context within which they are performed. Although Armando Favazza cautions against reading body modification as a psychiatric symptom, he argues that culturally sanctioned and pathological self-mutilation in fact serve much the same purpose; that is, "to correct or prevent a pathologically destabilizing condition that threatens the community, the individual, or both."[103] When Fakir worked as a commercial piercer in the early 1990s, he found that a surprising number of clients sought to reclaim their bodies from abuse. He suggests that many cutters would benefit from an accepting and supportive setting in which to carry out their rituals.[104] We can easily see this as a positive channeling of the cutter's impulse and similarly view as a correction of socially destabilizing conditions the more common choice to get pierced as a sign of group affiliation, as a rite of passage, or as a memorial to someone.

Body modification is a way to claim the body for oneself, and showing the marks of pain asserts in a positive fashion that one doesn't belong to the mainstream—Victoria Pitts calls it "queer anti-assimilation" and says that "queer body marks rely on provocation as a symbolic resource for *un*fixing *heteronormative* inscriptions."[105] As Kaja Silverman argues, masochism provides men with a mechanism of disavowal, but it requires display.[106] One gay male masochist told Pitts that he valued his stretched earlobes as marking a point of no return: because they can't be concealed, he can no longer pass for normal.[107] More crucially, Pitts notes that these performative practices embrace and explore pain rather than relying on the anesthesia typical of mainstream body modification.[108] Yet there are limits to willful recontextualization. For example, Athey finally covered the Tibetan swastika tattoo on the back of his neck because he couldn't bear having it misinterpreted as a hate symbol, an interpretation all too easily reinforced by his shaved head and leather jacket. I suggest that Athey has run into larger limits on recontextualization, which helps to explain why mainstream S/M fashion could not assimilate Athey—in fact, PERFORMA05 was his first appearance in New York since 1998, and he's presented his work mostly outside the United States since 1995.[109]

Athey's performances typically put the tattoos that cover most of his body on glorious display—including the sun image featured in the eponymous *Solar Anus*. The designs mark the corporeal boundary, serve as a reminder that the skin contains the "person." But even as Athey's performances display this outer border, they typically trouble it with multiple penetrations. Even the tattoo is a reminder of the skin's permeability, after all, accomplished by piercing the outer layer with a needle and infusing the body's covering with the foreign substance, ink. And Athey stages deeper penetrations, so often locating his actions at the anal sphincter: pulling out pink fabric to festoon the set, expelling an enema into containers of glitter, riding a double dildo (*Deliverance*); pulling out a string of pearls and then lowering himself onto dildo-bearing high heels (*Solar Anus*); impaling himself on an inquisitorial pyramid (*Judas Cradle*).[110] Athey embodies boundary confusion: violated but confirmed, over and over. As Dominic Johnson says with respect to the relative neglect of Athey in performance scholarship, "the faithful reproduction of the canon takes place at the expense of those artists who consistently evade official culture, in its delimited estimations of the appropriate—and culturally urgent—horizons of cultural reception."[111]

Athey and Fakir work with but are not entirely encompassed by the body-mod commodity culture: they remain too radical for complete assimilation, not a game or a pose, quite distinct from the 1990s S/M vogue. And even as S/M was losing its gloss, the suffering male body was being reclaimed for conservative religious and political agendas. Consider Mel Gibson, an actor who fit the macho-but-suffering male stereotype as outlined by Savran. The fetishizing camerawork of *Mad Max* (1979) introduces him in bite-sized portions for visual delectation: tall black leather boots, leather-encased midriff, hands pulling on leather gloves. The film progresses to a climactic confrontation, with "Max" shot in the knee, his arm run over, and a long straight-on shot of his leather-clad buttocks as he pulls himself up from the ground, legs spread wide, and drags himself toward his car. The motorcycle gang overtly echoes *The Wild One*, and both the bikers and the police force to which Max belongs look like the denizens of a late-1970s San Francisco leather bar. In one particularly curious scene, Max delivers his resignation from the police force to a boss who is wearing leather pants but no shirt, with a black silk scarf around his neck. The 1981 sequel *Road Warrior* manages to seamlessly combine homoeroticism and homophobia. Here Max's antagonists are done up in full dungeon drag, sporting various masks, chains, and bottom-baring leather chaps. The most agile and angry of them carries a blond boyfriend on his bike.

After this auspicious beginning as a cinematic body in pain, Gibson worked through numerous iterations on and behind the camera. Peter Boyer notes that *The Passion of the Christ* (2004) is not a religious movie but a war movie,[112] and I propose that Gibson waged this war at least in part to take back the suffering male body from the queering to which performers like

Fakir, Flanagan, and Athey had subjected it. Quite apart from Gibson's personal spiritual relationship to the Passion, his film's unrelenting laceration provides a community-building focus for Christians. Groups and churches bought up tickets and distributed them free to anyone who would attend a prayer meeting. After watching Gibson's *Passion*, devout viewers said that it was hard to get the film's images out of their minds. Invoking another star who has flickered through this chapter, one young woman compared it "to visualizing Marlon Brando when reading 'A Streetcar Named Desire.'"[113] Some priests commended its persistent memory images; others resented them. Attacks on Gibson (motivated by fears that the film would incite anti-Semitism) enabled Christian spectators to feel like they were supporting a brave warrior for the faith: he became the "Mad Max" of evangelical film. His production company went on to produce *Paparazzi* (2004), replaying the masochistic revenge scenario in a frenzy of paranoid amorality, with the bikers transmuted into unscrupulous photographers of celebrities; the policeman hero, into an action-movie star. *South Park:* "The Passion of the Jew," which manages to combine *Road Warrior*, *The Passion*, and *Paparazzi*, offers up a surprisingly insightful comment on Gibson's spectacular masochism. This cartoon also presents a broad panoply of spectator response, from devotional tears to antisemitic frenzy to vomiting and demanding a refund.[114]

The brand of Catholicism to which Gibson returned from despair has not been exactly doctrinaire. He is a traditionalist who rejects the reforms of Vatican II (1962–65). But Pope John Paul II rolled back those reforms and returned suffering to the center of the Catholic faith, demolishing liberation theology and discouraging debate but failing to address the scandal of sex abuse by priests. His early experience as actor and playwright Karol Wojtyla in Soviet-bloc Poland helped this pope to understand the "iconic nature of power" very well indeed, as Terry Eagleton points out. Long before becoming pope, he presented an "odd mixture of the theatrical and the ascetic."[115] After surviving a 1981 assassination attempt, he wrote in 1984 that "human suffering evokes compassion," but "in its own way it intimidates."[116] Although the Vatican denied reports of illness until very close to the end of his life, the pope announced a change in leadership style as early as 1994, saying that he would lead the church with suffering: "The pope must suffer so that every family and the world should see that there is, I would say, a higher gospel: the gospel of suffering, with which one must prepare the future."[117] As he "'serenely abandon[ed]' himself to God's will" during the weeks before his death, the Vatican issued no statements but broadcast images of the physically frail pope in pain, explicitly glossed as reminders of Christ's passion.[118]

Both John Paul II and Mel Gibson understood the performative power of pain and worked to wrest its mainstream incarnation away from the overtly sexual, openly pleasurable masochism so visible during the 1990s, providing renewed opportunities for bonding among fundamentalist spectators of every stripe. But they did not simply revive the medieval Passion play. Their pain exists in dialogue with queered Passions as well as with Christian tradition and also the ever more revitalized tradition of martyrdom within Islam. There is no single meaning for the voluntarily suffering male body. The difference between Ron Athey and John Paul II is huge, but so is the difference between Athey and Chris Burden. We can quite easily see these performances of pain as contentious, even struggling to invalidate one another; for these men, celibate, heteromasculine, and queer do not peacefully coexist. As private practices, the suffering of Athey and Fakir may be both spiritual and sexual. As performances, though, Athey's work is resolutely political: he performs new rituals to form new communities. Unlike the antitorture plays discussed in chapter 1, Athey's uncompromising work is increasingly unlikely to be seen by mainstream audiences and contributes to a politics of outrage rather than pity. Athey still frames his work in terms of community and in opposition to homophobia. His early work sought attention for the AIDS plague, *Judas Cradle* responded to Abu Ghraib, and *Incorruptible Flesh (Perpetual Wound)* interrogates queer relations across generations. The work has changed as the world and his life have, as HIV infection has become, for many of those with the necessary resources, not a death sentence but a medical condition to be managed over the long term. Although many would like to believe that HIV no longer presents grave problems at either the personal or the social level, Athey's work provides affirmation for those who know otherwise.

Like these post-modern performances of suffering, the mass penitential movements of the later Middle Ages arose in response to plague. Extreme circumstances during a time of loosened social controls—as discussed with respect to mystics in chapter 3—led laymen to take matters into their own hands or, quite literally, onto their own backs. This mass mobilization threatened the authority of the church-state apparatus, not exactly a single administrative entity in practice yet theoretically unified and certainly dependent upon the image of unity. As populations increased and nations stabilized under the leadership of divinely anointed kings during the late-fifteenth and the sixteenth centuries, this devotional energy was channeled away from the bodies of assembled lay penitents and toward the body of Saint Sebastian.

The flagellant and the body artist display similar marks of suffering: whips, tattoos, stigmata, piercing, and plague sores all mark the body's boundaries and its pain as these men performatively bind together a community and ward off danger. The most important difference is in their intended audience. The flagellant procession gets God's attention and makes converts—if others join the procession, then his attention will even more surely be drawn. The dramatization of Saint Sebastian's martyrdom serves the same ends, bringing the saint and perhaps also the Virgin Mary to intercede on behalf of those presenting the play. In contrast, a post-modern pain artist performs for other people. Rather than supporting a coherent theological doctrine, as the medieval saint play and flagellant procession do, Athey's performances of physical suffering counterpose bodily practices borrowed from non-Western traditions against a backdrop of rejected and reworked Christianity. Because both the late-medieval flagellant and the post-modern body artist present a threat to the existing social order, their respective cultures overwrite their pain with less dangerous figures of masochistic masculinity.

5. Containing Chaos ❦

Plate 8 Photograph of Reed Birney (Ian) and Marin Ireland (Cate) in Sarah Kane's *Blasted*, Soho Rep., New York, 2008. © Simon Kane 2008.

> Reed Birney gropes his way out from under the wreckage that was a hotel room. Louis Cancelmi lies crumpled on the platform, in the previous scene a rapist, now a corpse. Marin Ireland returns to the scene holding a baby that she doesn't know how to care for. When it dies, she pries up floorboards to make a grave. She hands Birney the pistol that he's been begging for, and he tries to shoot himself in the mouth, but she has removed the bullets. She leaves again. In a series of short blackout scenes, Birney tries to comfort himself: masturbating, defecating, laughing, crying, finally crawling down into the hole to eat the baby's corpse. Then he's quiet, his head sticking up through the floorboards. Rain starts to fall on him through a hole in the ceiling. With the word "shit," he reluctantly revives.
>
> —*Blasted*[1]

> Two women watch the actor playing Saint Sebastian stripped to a suit of "nude" skins and bound to a pillar, enjoying their wine and keeping up a ribald conversation. Henchmen fire twice, arguing about who's best, make sure that he's dead, and then make an obligatory report to Diocletian before they return to their drinking. A vulgar peasant gives incredulous witness as a Christian widow pulls out the arrows and a revived Sebastian comes down off the pillory for a final confrontation with Diocletian. This miraculous resurrection only infuriates the emperors, who command a second death. While the henchmen stretch him out facing the earth, Sebastian asks Jesus to protect the inhabitants of the city from epidemics, war, and pestilence. Then they pierce him from both sides with their lances, dump the body in the sewer so that no one will remember him, and return to drinking yet again.
>
> —*Le Mystère de Saint Sébastien*[2]

This chapter returns from performance art to dramatic theatre to analyze the relation of pain to laughter in the midst of violence that seems to turn the world upside down or inside out. Playwright Sarah Kane typically elicits an empathetic squirm but blocks sympathetic imagination, so that we react to horror but must find our own place to stand with respect to violence. She purposely gives us no viable position, drawing us into an experience of abjection. Her dark humor draws some lines around this unmanageable experience, but the shape remains provisional, subject to fresh rupture. Like Kane's plays, medieval theatre juxtaposes humor of a sort with violence that has been compared to the horror film. Unlike Kane's plays, though, the saint plays with which this book is concerned present a clear-cut hierarchy and unambiguous moral valuation. The spatial schema within which they operate encompasses vertical hierarchy and circles of containment, both susceptible to inversion. The humor (if that's what we want to call it) and chaotic violence in medieval performance operate according to a logic similar to the post-modern abject but to different ends. As *Le Mystère de Saint Sébastien* illustrates, the medieval grotesque serves to affirm order and to position the spectator more firmly within a coherent hierarchy.

Just as inversions reinforce hierarchy, expulsions and marginal figures reinforce the coherent social body by defining its boundaries—a particularly urgent need during and after a time of upheaval. Without pushing the metaphorical relation of human body to social body too far, Mark Johnson's model of embodied experience provides a particularly appropriate basis for the conceptual structures at issue. He argues that containment is one of the fundamental image schemata that humans use to understand experience. Based in bodily orientation and processes, these embodied gestalts are easily abstracted to structure thought—even reasoning and logic.[3] The experience of one's own body as a container with an inside and outside thus provides a metaphorical structure for the psychological and social process of abjection. Julia Kristeva defines the abject as "what disturbs identity, system, order. What does not respect borders, positions, rules. The in-between, the ambiguous, the composite."[4] In terms of individual development, that which is cast out or rejected during the process of shaping the self forms the abject. What is jettisoned does not coalesce to form an object—thus, it does not serve to form the ego, because the ego forms in relation to objects (desired and in some cases prohibited). As Kristeva puts it, "To each ego its object. To each superego its abject."[5] The amorphous abject serves as a border between the self and the world, a boundary outside of the self. Sometimes the abject expands and takes on the quality of an object, but this remains a phantasm. Sometimes an object stands in for the abject—for example, feces, a corpse, a wound. But the abject always overflows the borders of its representation. Kristeva thinks of this in theatrical terms: "As in true theatre, without makeup or masks, refuse and corpses *show me* what I permanently thrust aside in order to live."[6]

The most extreme abjection, that of the self, occurs when the "subject, weary of fruitless attempts to identify with something on the outside, finds the impossible within; when it finds that the impossible constitutes its very *being*, that it *is* none other than the abject."[7] Existing thus both without effective borders and in a perpetual borderland, this subject who Kristeva now terms the "deject" has no location, cannot find her bearings, is a peripatetic psychic traveler: "The *deject* never stops demarcating his universe whose fluid confines—for they are constituted of a non-object, the abject—constantly question his solidity and impel him to start afresh."[8] In this nowhere land, only the self-shattering pleasure that Lacanian psychoanalysis calls jouissance can conjure up the abject: "One does not know it, one does not desire it, one joys in it [*on en jouit*]. Violently and painfully. A passion."[9]

The system of inversions that Kane uses to stage abjection are most easily seen in *Blasted* (1995), at the end of which the character who initially seemed a victim perseveres as the one effectual agent in a world where all boundaries have been destroyed. This is a world defined by pain, in which all relations involve violence. Thematically, it works out an ethics of abjection on and through the body of Ian, a forty-five-year-old white journalist. *Blasted* includes a dazzling array of suffering over the course of two days in the hotel room to which he has brought twenty-one-year-old Cate, with whom he shared an intimate relationship in the past. Although Ian inflicts some pain on others, he himself embodies most of the suffering that the play actually stages (as opposed to describing). The first half of the play keeps him busy with self-inflicted pain. Although he has lost one lung and knows that the other is diseased, he drinks gin and smokes between coughing fits. His morning drink brings on an attack of pain that "*looks very much as if he is dying. His heart, lung, liver, and kidneys are all under attack and he is making involuntary crying sounds.*"[10] He lights a cigarette as soon as the pain subsides.

I had been thinking and writing about this play for a decade before I finally had a chance to see it at Soho Rep. in 2008, in between drafts of this chapter, and this first major pain episode was more extensive than I had imagined it. The lights came up for this scene on Reed Birney as Ian sitting downstage at the start of the second day. Shirtless, his lung-surgery scars visible, his stiff-legged walk of a prematurely old man in pain pulled me close more effectively than his more spectacular moments of suffering did. He had to search for his gin bottle, found it under the bed and drained the dregs standing and facing us directly so that we saw his left abdomen spasm as gin hit his stomach. He doubled over clutching his side, collapsed on the pillows and blankets at the foot of the bed, and coughed until he retched. His dribbling mouth was close by and pushed me away from empathy to a more distanced recognition that really gross and disgusting people suffer too, which made me wonder just why Kane wrote this character to be as sick as he is in every sense of the word. At an allegorical level, he represents a dysfunctional, misogynistic, racist culture, violent and irresponsible, continuing to savage the world even while rotting away from within. Just as importantly, though, his pain and loathsomeness put conflicting emotions into play for the spectator right from the start. Even sex is thoroughly imbued with pain. Cate, no longer willing to have intercourse with Ian, resists his overtures. After an early kiss, Ian "*appears to be in considerable pain*" and complains, "Don't give me a hard-on if you're not going to finish me off. . . . If I don't come my cock aches." Because Cate apologizes but remains adamant, he grabs her hand and uses it to masturbate "*until he comes with some genuine pain*" (15). Thus both the desire and the relief are painful. Cate later fellates (and bites) Ian—apparently paying him back for cunnilingus that drew blood the previous night (between scenes).

Designer Louisa Thompson created a very posh hotel room at Soho Rep., and Marin Ireland's entrance as Cate created a powerful relationship with that environment. She stood in the doorway for quite a long time, still, neither speaking nor moving. While Birney was present it seemed that she was hesitant or perhaps even afraid. But when he disappeared into the bathroom for a shower, it began to seem that Ireland was just slowly taking in this expensive physical world. Her feet moved slowly, feeling the plush carpet, as she crossed to a dresser nearby and ran her fingertips over its polished surface. She crossed to a table on the opposite side of the stage and touched the lilies there: "Lovely," she whispered, then sat on the bed and bounced like a small child. This production appeared to take Ian's word for Cate's cognitive deficit and to interpret her as slow witted, at the very least. Ian angrily calls her "stupid" and "thick" after she laughs at his request to "put your mouth on me" as he stands before her (7–8). A counterexample to the observation that the naked and suffering body on stage is typically female, Ian's nudity within the first five minutes establishes his body as the play's ground—as Sean Carney puts it in analyzing a different production, "the pale, soft, slightly corpulent, anonymous flesh of a male human being, notable most of all for its banality."[11] Perhaps it's difficult to understand why Cate is in the hotel with him unless she really is stupid. But when his aggressive questions in this scene start her stuttering and precipitate her first fainting fit, she says that they've been happening "all the time [...] since Dad came back" (9–10). Cate is epileptic, not stupid, and the fact that her father's presence at home has either caused or intensified her seizures quite clearly implies a stressful relationship. Such a problematic father goes much farther than diminished mental capacity to explain why this young woman has come to a hotel with an abusive and significantly older man.

Cate claims to have come for the weekend because she feels sorry for Ian, but his suffering is not effectively seductive, and his behavior—especially toward Cate—consistently undercuts spectator sympathy. In addition to multiple attempts at coercing sex, he disparages her intelligence and appearance, and he uses a wide array of racial slurs to refer to the unseen room service waiter. Finally, he rapes Cate at gunpoint while she is unconscious. Cate seems fragile during the first half of the play, leading one to anticipate with a kind of nausea her victimization. But she escapes from Ian through the bathroom window just before the Soldier arrives to set in motion the play's second half, and she then returns twice, more effectual and assured each time. The Soldier, who is present (alive, that is) only when Cate is not, serves at the allegorical level as a mechanism for the revenge of the weak and oppressed (represented by Cate) upon those with power (Ian). More vital for the play's structure and what I see as its central theme, however, is the challenge that he poses to Ian as a journalist. He describes the rapes and other atrocities that he has committed in the course of war and the opposing soldiers' rape, murder, and mutilation of his girlfriend Col. He challenges Ian to write about these things:

> Soldier: Some journalist, that's your job.
> Ian: What?
> Soldier: Proving it happened. I'm here, got no choice. But you. You should be telling people.
> Ian: No one's interested. (47)
> [...]
> Soldier: Doing to them what they done to us, what good is that? At home I'm clean. Like it never happened.
> Tell them you saw me.
> Tell them...you saw me.
> Ian: It's not my job. (48, second ellipses in original)

When Ian refuses to accept this task, he is destroyed. Kane thus implies a choice for the spectator between morally responsible action and the violent destruction that she stages, challenging the spectator to find an appropriate response to intolerable actions. She considered it "crucial to chronicle and commit to memory events never experienced—in order to avoid them happening."[12]

Discussions of *Blasted* often suggest that the initial hostility of the press may have had something to do with the central character's age, race, gender, and profession.[13] Annabelle Singer points out that when *Blasted* premiered at the sixty-seat Royal Court Theatre Upstairs in 1995, all of the reviewers came to a single press night. The result was an audience of which "all but five members were critics, all but three of whom were white, middle-aged men."[14] Critics were horrified by what they saw, wanted to turn away, and as Singer notes, refused to analyze the play, instead just describing events and expressing outrage. The vituperation was comparable to that which greeted Edward Bond's *Saved* thirty years earlier—and in one case nearly identical, as a critic repeated his assessment that the play suffered from a lack of connection to any larger social context.[15] The run sold out, perhaps abetted by the resulting notoriety but undoubtedly owing precisely to its resonance with multiple social contexts. No alert spectator in 1995 could avoid making a connection to so-called ethnic cleansing and systematic rape in Bosnia. At the same time, setting the play in Leeds rather than Bosnia makes the connection to domestic violence impossible to ignore. Kane said explicitly, "one is the seed and the other is the tree. I do think that the seeds of full-scale war can always be found in peace-time civilisation [sic]."[16] The structure of *Blasted* corresponds to Kane's experience in writing it. While she was working on the first scene of a domestic drama, news reports about atrocities in Bosnia shattered her focus.[17] Solicited by the world's terror, Kane responded by writing Ian as a journalist who fails to respond.

The eponymous blast comes while the Soldier is pissing on the bed after eating both of the room service breakfasts that Ian has ordered. At Soho Rep., as Louis Cancelmi claimed the city as "our town now," he stepped up onto the bed facing upstage, unzipped, and let me wonder for a while whether liquid would appear. Because I was mesmerized by the rain of urine, supposed or actual and wondering which, the explosion took me entirely by surprise. It went on and on, covering the noise of the set change. Having been warned not to sit in the first row because then I'd see too much of the mechanics at this point, I wasn't really aware of any activity beyond the darkness and the sound that rumbled through me. During the opening scene I had thought that I knew how the room would come apart, but I was wrong. When the lights came back up, the set had been pushed back about six feet. The top and one side of the proscenium hung down at an angle in front of the room, and the main playing space shifted to the floor of the theatre, below and in front of this wheeled room-platform, at times even underneath it. Kane blasts open not only the hotel room in Leeds but also the familiar form of dramatic realism. In their fine analyses of the play, both Sean Carney and Alyson Campbell talk about civil war in Britain, assuming that the location in Leeds remains constant.[18] But I think the play blasts apart geography as well, that after the explosion there is no distinction between Britain and Bosnia (and New York). After the second scene of *Blasted*, the theatre becomes a global state of siege, and we are in its midst.

After the rape and blinding in the play's third scene, Birney crawled out from under the platform at the start of the fourth, calling for Cate. Cancelmi lay crumpled in the wrecked doorway, where he spent the rest of the play, a splat of red indicating that "*he has blown his own brain out*" (50) during the blackout—something that spectators unfamiliar with the text easily missed in this production. Cate soon returns, bringing the baby that a mother has handed her on the street. She helplessly holds it until it dies, then makes a grave in the floorboards. As she and Ian talk about God and the afterlife, he begs her for the pistol and tries to shoot himself in the mouth, but Cate has removed the bullets. Ian is left alone again for much of the play's progressively surreal fifth scene. He masturbates, tries to strangle himself, defecates, laughs, dreams, cries, hugs the soldier's corpse for comfort, starves, and finally crawls into the hole that Cate made in the floor and eats the dead baby. Only his head remains visible for the rest of the play, and rain begins to fall on him through a hole in the ceiling just before Cate returns, bloody from the sex that she has traded for food and drink—as shown in plate 8. The last words are Ian's simple thanks when she shares it with him.

After the blast, which we felt every bit as much as heard, sound designer Matt Tierney replaced the muted street sounds of the early scenes with an ominous rumbling under the dialogue, faint at first but growing in intensity through the blackout scenes until Ian *"dies with relief"* under the floorboards (60), upon which there was silence. The sound of running water created a throughline, starting with Ian's shower in the first scene and another in the second along with Cate's bath and the Soldier's piss. Kane's notoriously cryptic stage directions for scene breaks call for water: *"Blackout. The sound of spring rain"* (24); *"There is a blinding light, then a huge explosion. Blackout. The sound of summer rain"* (39); *"Blackout. The sound of autumn rain"* (50); *"Blackout. The sound of heavy winter rain"* (57). I can't say that Tierney made the seasons pass, but the sound of rain in the darkness was like the whole world or even the universe crying—or perhaps just the theatre that held us for the evening. We were all inside something that was crying its heart out. And when Ian crawled into the floor and died, the tears of rain came inside and touched him: *"It starts to rain on him, coming through the roof"* (60), continuing through to the ending: *"Silence. It rains.* Ian: Thank you. *Blackout"* (61).

Kane's written play texts pose impossible but irresistible challenges. *Phaedra's Love* (1996) ends with vultures descending to eat the body of a castrated and eviscerated Hippolytus. *Cleansed* (1998) requires a sunflower and daffodils to grow up through the floor and rats to carry off a character's severed feet (120, 133, 136). Taken chronologically, the plays become more and more difficult to stage as written, perhaps precisely because Kane doesn't intend for her gruesome images to be staged realistically; for example, she thinks that *Blasted's* baby-eating scene is harder to take on the page, because in the reader's imagined performance, the corpse of a baby is actually eaten. On stage, she says, "When you see it he's clearly not eating the baby. It's absolutely fucking obvious. This is a theatrical image. He's not doing it at all."[19] In a Hamburg production reminiscent of Tarantino in its graphic violence, and which Kane didn't like because the actor playing Ian was young and attractive, the baby was an edible prop (perhaps chicken) that the actor really did eat, prompting some walk-outs.[20]

Although the staging at Soho Rep. found visual and acoustical solutions to the problem of blasting open realism, the choice to maintain a realistic acting style rendered the sex scenes truly disturbing—more so than the edible chicken/baby used in this production. I had expected the impact of seeing violence onstage to be less powerful than some of Kane's descriptions such as "*he [the Soldier] puts his mouth over one of Ian's eyes, sucks it out, bites it off and eats it*" (50) or "*he [Ian] eats the baby*" (60). My anticipation of these moments certainly affected their impact. But the uniformly unpleasant sex was something that I had not taken the time to imagine:

> *The Solider turns Ian over with one hand.*
> *He holds the revolver to Ian's head with the other.*
> *He pulls down Ian's trousers, undoes his own and rapes him—eyes closed and smelling Ian's hair.*
> *The Soldier is crying his heart out.*
> *Ian's face registers pain but he is silent.*
> *When the Soldier has finished he pulls up his trousers and pushes the revolver up Ian's anus. (49)*

The stage directions are written like poetry, even to their placement on the page, but there's nothing poetic about the fucking on stage. What the description doesn't capture is the passage of time: for this and all other sexual activity, the actors took enough time to reasonably achieve orgasm. Watching for that long was a truly awful experience, with Birney's flabby, pale body shivering in all its vulnerability.

Identifying shock as Kane's "first technique in attempting to break down familiar perceptions," Campbell argues that witnessing certain moments makes one aware of their impact upon one's own body and thus brings one back to awareness of one's presence in the theatre at this particular moment—the reactive squirm discussed in chapter 1. Campbell describes her own reaction to a section of *Crave* (1998), somewhat tedious on the page but delivered in performance too rapidly for comprehension:

> The speed and intensity of this section produced a violent lurch in my stomach and sent a huge tingling down the length of my legs. This immediate visceral response was followed by a deepening sense of despair at the bleakness being played out. What becomes clear in "experiencing" this section in performance is that Kane is not making something meaningless. The phenomenal impact, the affect, of the whole produces an utterly devastating picture of abjectness, of bodies and lives routinely abused and completely without hope.[21]

Because Kane's dramatic technique developed over the course of her short writing career, we can more easily see with later works such as *Crave* her masterly use of images, sounds, and actions that are not entirely comprehensible but have a physiological effect.

Her final play, *4.48 Psychosis,* is a poem without stage directions or character designations, written shortly before Kane committed suicide in 1999. Claude Régy's 2005 production powerfully affected my companions even though they couldn't understand the French and had neither read the text of which the supertitles translated only a very small portion nor seen other productions: Isabelle Huppert stood in the middle of the stage for close to two hours, speaking rapidly, no bodily movement other than a slight turn, barely any gesture. Occasionally a hand clenched, then the fist released. Some tears rolled down her cheeks. When the time and text were done and the applause began, the effort and care with which Huppert slowly moved to take her bow and then limped offstage made apparent the physical pain that this tense stillness engendered. Her pain had been a subliminal accompaniment to the text's explicit psychological anguish.[22] This production gave certain lines to a male actor, implicitly in role as a therapist but concealed behind a scrim on which numbers were projected. Régy gave almost all of the text to Huppert, his production hearkening back to Beckett in its stripped-down rigor and the torment that the staging required the actor to endure. Although we saw Huppert's entire body during her performance of *4.48 Psychose,* we read her negative athleticism much as we might have read the invisible body of *Not I* or the potted bodies of *Play*. By connecting with Kane's images and image structures at a physical level, filtering their affective impact for the audience, Régy and Huppert drew us into Sarah Kane's psychic space, blurring the boundary between the physical and the psychological, between internal and external events.

Sean Carney argues that *Blasted* achieves its effect not only through shocking violence but because of the way that violence both defies comprehension and demands interpretation. Kane uses Ian's degradation to lead us farther and farther into what abjection feels like but at the same time pushes us to make meaning: "We have no choice but to interpret the image of Ian's head, because no 'literal' meaning is available."[23] Carney's discussion hinges upon the impossibility of Ian's living death although, as he acknowledges, no spectator without independent knowledge of the play would be able to perceive a death on stage—and indeed, those with whom I spoke about the Soho Rep. production did not. Kane says:

> He's dead, he's in hell—and it's exactly the same place he was in before, except that now it's raining. [...] Ian is deified in a way that I didn't really realise until I saw the play performed for the first time. When I watched the blood being

washed away by the rain I saw just how Christ-like the image is. Which isn't to say that Ian isn't punished. He is, of course, he dies, and he finds that the thing he has ridiculed—life after death—really does exist. And that life is worse than where he was before, it really is hell.[24]

Watching, one might think that Ian has taken a little nap or paused in despair. But if one knows that he is supposed to have died, then there's a moment of impossibly dark humor when he says "shit" in response to the rain. For me, Ian's head has become a grotesque echo of Saint Denis, separated from the body but still animate, the antirelic left by someone who is anything but a saint. If he's dead, he's in hell, then perhaps Cate is an angel. This suggests that the play is about responsibility: for how we touch and speak to and even refer to those whom we encounter. Ian is an exemplum of failure at every level and is punished at every level. He has to be utterly degraded, to the point of not simply cannibalism but of eating the body of utter innocence, a baby. Then his punishment can end. Cate is utter goodness, embodying not pity but the wish to alleviate suffering in the absence of sympathy. She won't share Ian's pain but will attempt to soothe it. This does suggest a reason to interpret her as simple minded, a holy fool in the Dostoyevskian epileptic tradition, wise as a result of knowing death in life. Carney most helpfully draws a parallel between Ian's live-dead existence in the play's final scene and Cate's epileptic fits in its first two. Cate likens fainting both to being dead—which Ian says he thought she was—and to orgasm. And unlike Ian, Cate has no unpleasant associations with any of these states. Her early fit initiates a discussion of life after death that resumes in the final scene.[25] Carney observes that "for Cate, her fits engender a loss of self, the annihilation of ego in *jouissance*" but "what for Cate is the mark of transcendence through the end of the self is for Ian the mark of death."[26] Cate lives easily in her jouissance. Ian must learn to endure his.

Kristeva's psychoanalytic and critical notion of the abject doesn't inquire too deeply into the nature of this self that jouissance shatters, because she's writing at a level of description that assumes the commonality and familiarity of this and other psychic structures. But neuroscience gives us some resources for conceptualizing the relation between the sense of self and pain. We've discussed the addition of painful punishments to public execution in order to make the events more memorable, and the notion that physical pain can help engrave knowledge upon a student's memory did not disappear with the end of the Middle Ages. Pain—whether experienced actually or empathically—makes events memorable, and memory contributes to one's sense of self. Yet pain also has the power to shatter the self, and research into hypnosis suggests some reasons for the connection of pain, memory, and self. Not only can hypnosis make painful stimuli less painful by breaking down communication between the neural structures involved in pain, as discussed in chapter 3, but it also produces the sensation that one's actions are not one's own.

Matthew Liebermann and Naomi Eisenberger argue that there are two forms of memory, episodic and reflexive, with distinct neural systems; furthermore, the two systems tend to inhibit each other. The *C-system* supporting *reflective consciousness* encodes the episodic memories of events about which we have to think because they involve conflicts, and we rely upon it when we need to make choices. The *X-system* supports the *reflexive consciousness* comprising habitual memory that builds up gradually with little conscious thought but a closer relation to affect—the memories that we commonly refer to as intuitions.[27] The concepts that we use to associate reflexive consciousness with the self seem to me highly dependent upon belief systems about consciousness: the authors mention intuition; one might substitute spirit, the unconscious, even the universal unconscious. The relation between the self and reflective consciousness is more direct. The more one has to think about an episode, the more lasting the memory. The C-system becomes increasingly important as the choices increase and both external guidance and useful habits decrease, which in turn leads to increased self-reflection and sense of an inner self.[28] Stimuli such as physical pain and social exclusion disrupt the sense of self, as do "discrepancies between perceptions and impulses, on the one hand, and current expectations and goals on the other hand," because conflicts cause the anterior cingulate cortex (ACC, part of the episodic C-system that monitors input) to signal another portion, the lateral prefrontal cortex (LPFC). But the LPFC is limited in the amount of data that it can process.[29] Kane's plays abound not only in pain to which the spectator responds empathically but also in discrepancies and other stimuli that activate the testing function of the ACC.

I would suggest that Kane's plays confront spectators with far more conflict than the LPFC can process along with a superabundance of suffering. She uses violence and confusion to push the spectator into empathic response and then pull her or him back out again into revulsion, over and over. *Blasted* demolishes known emotional landmarks along with its hotel room and its geographical localization. *4.48 Psychosis* gives us an abject consciousness, with no border between the inside and outside—as Ariel Watson puts it, "with the boundaries between self and other continually erased and reconstructed as they never could be in the convention of the 'mad scene,' which draws its power from a clear delineation between the sane observer and the insane observed."[30] Although Watson is analyzing the internalized relationship between therapist and patient in *4.48 Psychosis,* the description holds for Kane's formal structures generally. And Kane's humor is a tool for surviving in this world without order. I was not the only person who had a few surprising laughs watching *Blasted, 4.48 Psychosis,* or *Phaedra's Love.* The playwright referred to her sense of humor as "probably... life-saving":

> When I was first thinking about writing [*Phaedra's Love*] I read an article in a newspaper written by a man who'd been suffering from clinical depression for three years. And he said the only thing that he'd had to hang onto was this really morbid sense of humour. It was the only thing that made him bearable to be with. And that kept him rooted.... I think when you are depressed oddly your sense of humour is the last thing to go; when that goes then you completely lose it.[31]

Kane struggled with and eventually succumbed to depression, a psychiatric illness that is nonetheless familiar and able to touch something in those of us who are more resilient, who *do* go on with life. She also struggled with the horror that can appear to engulf the world, with the violence that people do to one another. All of Kane's plays project depression onto the external world, and all except the last also introject to a remarkable extent the chaotic violence around us. At those moments when one is sucked into depression, atrocity fascinates. Depression encourages an obsession with everything that's awful in the world and a response that veers between pity, laughter, self-righteous indignation, and despair. Responding to a world perceived as chaotic and violent also calls upon one's creative resources, and to stage the terror gives it shape by redrawing some borders around feeling. As Kristeva puts it, "laughing is a way of placing or displacing abjection."[32]

Kane's humor is, admittedly, not for everyone, and it certainly does not turn the plays into straightforward comedy: *Phaedra's Love* begins with an utterly repulsive Hippolytus watching television in his room amid junk food wrappers and dirty underwear, blowing his nose in a sock, masturbating into another, checking the socks to make sure that he doesn't reuse the same one. When Phaedra admits her love to her stepson, and he asks her why, she explains: "You're difficult. Moody, cynical, bitter, fat, decadent, spoilt. You stay in bed all day then watch TV all night, you crash around this house with sleep in your eyes and not a thought for anyone. You're in pain. I adore you" (79). When he sees vultures circling as he dies, Hippolytus says: "If there could have been more moments like this" (103).

It's the last line of the play. There is humor in the play's inversion of legend and dramatic tradition, turning Euripides' and Racine's righteous ascetic into a gross, selfish slob; in the citation of negative traits as a reason for love; in the understated and unlikely reaction to a dire situation. The production that I saw in 2005 played up the gross humor, employing a chorus that loudly sucked their thumbs onstage to create the sound effects as first Phaedra and then a priest fellated Hippolytus.[33] *4.48 Psychosis* expresses anger and exasperation at the

> Inscrutable doctors, sensible doctors, way-out doctors, doctors you'd think were fucking patients if you weren't shown proof otherwise, ask the same questions, put words in my mouth, offer chemical cures for congenital anguish and cover each other's arses until I want to scream for you, the only doctor who ever touched me voluntarily, who looked me in the eye, who laughed at my gallows humour spoken in the voice from the newly-dug grave. (209)

This voice from the grave soon thereafter articulates a plan to "take an overdose, slash my wrists then hang myself," employing "all those things together" because "it couldn't possibly be misconstrued as a cry for help" (210).

This humor certainly never outweighs the suffering in her plays, but Kane uses it to keep us (and herself) watching the unwatchable. She said: "I think to a certain degree you have to deaden your ability to feel and perceive. In order to function you have to cut out at least one part of your mind. Otherwise you'd be chronically sane in a society which is chronically insane. I mean, look at Artaud. That's your choice: Go mad and die, or function but be insane."[34] But instead of deadening, Kane's humor and the violence in her plays open us to witness real suffering, psychological, physical, and social. In the theatre of Sarah Kane, pain and violence constitute the real world; humor and grotesque beauty, creative means of resistance.

* * *

Like *Le Geu Saint Denis, Le Mystère de Saint Sébastien* stages a worldly hierarchy with pagan Romans at the top, martyrs at the bottom, and a range of ordinary folk in between. For both of these plays, some of the last group convert and thus cross the line from pagan to Christian, some of them making it all the way to martyrdom. Opposed to this order of the flesh is a spiritual hierarchy with saints at the pinnacle, answerable only to God, protected by him from suffering and rewarded with death. A vulgar quartet of henchmen torments the martyrs, adhering to stereotypes in order to set off the saints' purity and beauty by contrast: here they are called Machecothon (mace-accustomed), Tailliebodin (sausage-slicer), Rifflandoillie (filch-sausage or perhaps peel-dick or scab-penis), and Mal Feras (evil-doer).[35] The banter between soldiers in scenes of torment and their unrestrained gluttony have been considered grotesque because of the way they mix into a generally serious drama. I agree with Jelle Koopmans in considering these to be integral components rather than interpolations designed to keep the attention of audiences during the waning Middle Ages. He further argues that the understanding of such scenes as comic rests upon modern sensibilities, because we know next to nothing about the relation between fear and humor for the medieval public.[36] Also agreeing with Koopmans, Véronique Plesch argues that grotesque elements serve to alienate the spectator from the tormentors, to create an alienated revulsion.[37] The spectators must not merely know that these actions (and by extension their own) are wrong, but they must also *feel* the wrong.

Plesch suggests that the very characteristics that led modernist literary theory to disdain medieval drama were the means by which it engraved lasting memories for its spectators, because it was able to activate their emotional response on multiple levels. Medieval drama was chock full of mnemonic devices strikingly similar to the marginalia in illuminated books—as Mary Carruthers catalogues these, "grotesque creatures, the comic images..., images that are violent, ugly, salacious or titillating, noble, sorrowful, or fearful."[38] In other words, as Plesch argues, the plays mix emotional registers for the same reason that they become so extremely violent by the fifteenth century: to make them memorable. Medieval drama appears grotesque because it escapes the Aristotelian categories that have dominated Western dramatic theory since the Renaissance, when the term originated. Late-sixteenth-century Italy coined the term "grotesque" to designate a style of painting deemed appropriate for grottos, featuring the combination of animal and human forms. The plausible conjecture is that ancient chambers (grottos) excavated during the Renaissance were decorated in this manner. From this origin, the conception of the grotesque soon grew to include exaggeration and the combination of incongruent elements, with a generally ludicrous result.[39] Wolfgang Kayser points out that the combination can just as easily be sinister as ridiculous. He describes the grotesque as a structure that "presupposes that the categories which apply to our world view become inapplicable."[40] To employ a notion of the grotesque with respect to medieval drama, we must first have a clear picture of that drama's systems of categorization.

After reviewing the boundaries with which *Le Mystère de Saint Sébastien* delineates groups of characters and categories of experience, I will analyze its parallel hierarchies and then explore its use of devices that disrupt or exceed these structures. The play spreads its action over two days and frames its martyrdoms first with the ever-increasing frustration of the devils who ultimately lose the Christians' souls and second with the ribald marital squabbling between a fool (*Le Villain*) and his wife. A tavern keeper (*Dame Margot*) serves this pair as interlocutor and complicator. I will return to these grotesque elements and their function after first laying out the play's main thread. The manuscript, *Bibliothèque nationale de Paris Nouvelles Acquisitions françaises n. 1051*, appears to have been copied during the second half of the fifteenth century, perhaps from another manuscript existing at that time.[41] The long and rectangular shape of the pages suggests to Léonard Mills that it may have been used in staging, and its final pages are missing (li–lii). He notes spellings and rhyme schemes typical of Paris, Normandy, Picardy, and the north and east of France more generally (lv–lvii). Numerous spellings exhibit knowledge (albeit often erroneous) of Latin etymology, a common feature in fifteenth-century manuscripts (lix–lxi).

The play's first day features conversions, healings, diableries, foolery, and threats. Both Roman emperors, Diocletian and Maximian, take an active part, particularly infuriated by Sebastian's Christian activism because he is Diocletian's seneschal. Trouble begins when Sebastian comes to the aid of fellow Christians Marcus and Marcellianus, who are sentenced to death and waver in the face of their families' pleading. He shores up the martyrs' conviction, cures their father Tranquillinus of crippling gout, and converts not only the families but also the jailer Nicostratus and his mute wife Zoe, whom he enables to speak. The prefect Cromachius, also suffering from gout, then converts in order to be cured by Sebastian. He burns all of Diocletian's idols as part of the deal. On the play's second day, the martyrdom sequence gets underway with the flagellation of Sebastian alone.[42] Then Diocletian orders the execution of the play's Christians. Supervised by Maximian, the Romans first hang Zoe; then behead Nicostratus, Marcus, and Marcellianus; and stretch Cromachius out on the earth for death by stoning. The audience need not pay close attention—a character called Joli Corps announces each execution, calling all Romans to come and witness. Maximian and his henchmen report back to Diocletian between episodes. Sebastian prays, reassures each martyr, and expresses his satisfaction with the course of events. The play's penultimate martyr is Tiburcius, the son of Cromachius and a near double of Sebastian himself: during interrogation,

Diocletian asks Tiburcius to take pity on his own beauty, youth, and gentility (5224–26), repeating much the same request later to Sebastian (5705–6). Tiburcius replies that Diocletion is the one to be pitied and affirms that the Romans can do what they wish with his body but cannot harm his soul (5255–56). Stripped to his chemise—the henchmen fight over his clothing, much like Christ's cloak in Passion plays—he walks barefoot over burning coals, making the sign of the cross and feeling nothing, before his death by decapitation. The emperors are well pleased, the henchmen return to their wine, and a Christian widow named Luciane summons the bishop Policarpus to help her bury the martyrs (5447–5529).

The archery scene does not begin until three-quarters of the way through this second day. When Diocletian requests something more horrible than anything yet seen, Maximian suggests stripping Sebastian entirely nude, tying him to a pillar, and having the archers shoot him full of arrows. The soldiers all think this is a great idea (5775–5822). Although Joli Corps calls for all Rome's archers to assemble and for all citizens to witness, the same four henchmen arrive with their bows, and only the Villain's wife and the tavern hostess come to watch—along with the play's audience, of course. As they argue about which of them is best, the henchmen fire twice. Then, after repeated assurances that he's dead, everyone except the Villain returns to drinking (5850–6093). Luciane comes to the gibbet, mourns Sebastian's death, and prays for his restoration. Pulling out the arrows, she tells Sebastian that she'll cause him pain because they entered just to the heart and up to their plumes. As Sebastian comes down off the pillory saying that God has restored his health, the Villain voices his shock (6094–6177). This miracle and Sebastian's ensuing attempt to convert the emperors makes Diocletian so furious that he accuses his coemperor of being a Christian, and Maximian tells his henchmen to turn Sebastian over facing the earth, tie him up, and pierce him with lances on both sides. As he prepares for this second death, Sebastian's prayers include protection for the people of Rome from epidemics, war, and pestilence (6212–54). Although the henchmen dump his body into the sewer, Luciane and the other Christians have the angelic information that they need to recover the body and place it in the catacombs near the apostles Peter and Paul.

As one would suspect, Sebastian does not suffer. But in contrast to Saint Denis, Sebastian's torment is not prolonged; instead, other bodies are subjected to an increasingly inventive series of punishments while he remains busy reassuring, preaching, and praying. Spectators have most of two days to anticipate the naked saint bristling with arrows, but he appears in this emblematic guise only briefly. The play stresses his power and efficacy, not his martyrdom, giving the audience little time to view him pierced, restoring him quickly to wholeness. In fact, Sebastian is that rare martyr who escapes beheading, almost as if Tiburcius loses a head for him. As we saw in the previous chapter with respect to late-medieval devotional images, the play focuses on Sebastian's miraculous survival. Performances of *Le Mystère de Saint Sébastien* might have appealed to a heavenly audience to help the sponsoring city achieve similar survivals in the face of plague's devastation.

Like *Le Geu Saint Denis,* this play uses a temporary inversion of power to represent the upheaval of categories, giving us mirrored hierarchies of good and evil and restoring the good to preeminence over the course of the play. Active interventions from both Heaven and Hell are plentiful, and each of these supernatural realms has its own hierarchy. Jesus begins the play with the instruction to remember his death but never leaves Heaven, nor does Mary. She intercedes on behalf of the martyrs, persuading Jesus to send angels to Earth when necessary: Gabriel to help Sebastian and comfort the other martyrs as they resist the temptation to recant and live (1968–2077), then both Gabriel and Raphael when Sebastian returns to life after being shot full of arrows (6178–6211). Just as Jesus occupies a stationary position in Heaven, Lucifer does so in Hell and sends Satan out to act in the world. And Hell acts first, when Diocletian appoints Sebastian as his seneschal: Astarot calls all the devils together and warns them that the presence of a Christian in this position of power threatens their supply of damned souls. After a clamorous conference of devils, Satan appears to Diocletian and plants the idea to persecute Christians generally and Sebastian in particular (1373–1502). Sebastian's preaching, prayers, and miraculous cures lead to multiple baptisms and finally the burning of 200 idols, sending Lucifer and Satan into paroxysms of despair. They agree to send all of Hell's denizens to work against Sebastian (3260–89), and the first day ends shortly after this.

Having set the evil machinery in motion on Earth, the powers of Hell need be less active during the second day's martyr killing. Satan returns to the scene only when Sebastian remains alive, calling himself an enraged dog as he reports to Lucifer on the dismal state of affairs and swearing to burn the entire Earth (5566–5604). As the henchmen pierce Sebastian with their lances, the angels tell him to take heart because this second death will bring him face to face with Jesus (6354–57), and the play ends with simultaneous bursts of activity from Heaven and Hell: the angel Michel fetches Sebastian and sings the martyr's hymn, and Gabriel directs Luciane in the discovery and burial of Sebastian's body—presumably Michel interacts with the actor who now represents the martyr's soul, while Gabriel has a dummy body deposited in the catacombs. Satan wails that he's dying, the Christians are lost, and all the devils should come from Hell for their mopping-up operation. Diocletian rages, mad, calling upon his gods and upon the devils to end his torment, finally hanging himself. Maximian compels the henchman Machecothon to kill him. When the others challenge what he's done, Machecothon kills them and then dies as well. The devils take them all into Hell, where Satan must report to Lucifer that he's lost Sebastian's soul (6406–6642).

This play's implied scenography resembles that already described for *Le Geu Saint Denis*, starting in Heaven and ending in Hell, with Diocletian's palace in Rome as the only earthly location that clearly requires a mansion. Like Lucifer in Hell or Jesus in Heaven, Diocletian stays put and sends his coemperor Maximian out to supervise the interrogations and report back, to bring Christians before him at various points, and to direct the actions of the henchmen. The overall spatial arrangement has a stationary Diocletian orchestrating the play's overwrought physical action in the neutral playing space, with Jesus and Lucifer periodically sending in angels and devils, while Sebastian gathers more and more calm Christian converts to its spiritual center. The limited staging directions suggest a powerful visualization of the martyrs' quietly mounting power in numbers, mechanics interestingly enough facilitated by the play's fool.

This character, initially identified as "Rusticus" and thereafter as "Villain," binds the martyrdom drama together with its diableries and "accents the contrast between the action's material and spiritual registers," as Léonard Mills points out in his introduction to the play (xlii). The Villain floats, either at the bottom of all hierarchies or outside them, unconstrained. Does he embody the grotesque, in Bakhtin's terms a clown or fool "characteristic of the medieval culture of humor" and standing "on the borderline between life and art?"[43] Whatever the performer's real-life role may have been—and we know nothing about this—the *Mystère de St. Sébastien*'s Villain serves as a metatheatrical guide for the audience in addition to playing his scenes of lust, anger, and drunkenness. His is the first scene after the opening prayer in Heaven and the last before the closing scene in Hell. The Villain begins the play by wishing his wife to be tormented with a long list of illnesses. He voices anxiety about being cuckolded, describes the torment of recurrent erections that he must relieve on his own, and wishes to have all the women of Savoy right there—presumably to afford him more satisfactory relief. His wife returns his insults and tells him to shut up, cursing marriage (386–417).

Soon enough, the enraged Villain welcomes Sebastian and his companions to Rome. He claims that he could have killed both his wife and the hot young stud with whom he found her in bed, even though his wife threw him down and hit him with a big stick. Using multiple terms of measurement, he makes repeated and colorful references to the size of her lover's genitalia, so hairy that he could have shaved the fellow's ass and sold the hair as wool (1039–76). The knights put an end to this diatribe by inquiring politely for directions to Diocletian's palace. The Villain instead offers them his wife, so far enjoyed only by the curate. When this leads to a fight, the Villain raises an alarm claiming that they tried to abduct his wife, who then appears and takes the side of the knights (1077–1140). He returns to the scene shortly after the persecution of Christians begins, drinking with the henchmen (1860–1916) and then remaining in the tavern. He propositions the tavern hostess, and three-way abuse develops when his wife joins the scene (2705–76). These scenes make tangible the martyr Marcellianus's observation that the world is "nothing but sin and filth, short joy and long sadness" (1648–49).[44]

From this point forward, though, the Villain increasingly directs his attention to the play's main action as first the miracles and then the martyrdoms get underway. He brings the first day's performance to a close with direct address to the audience about the great mess and noise, promising that arrows and the like will reward a return the next day (3290–3356). The second day does indeed bring arrows, but also a shift in the Villain's relation to the play's main action. As the saint is stripped, bound, and beaten, the Villain begins to change his tune. He deplores the action:

> By our lady, that's badly done. By God, I believe they've killed him. Devil take you, evil scoundrels. He was a good guy. By God, this is awful, but the foolish are never wise, the poor aren't rich, the generous are never stingy, and no cuckoo is a sparrowhawk. I'd be happy if I could fuck my wife that well. (4350–61)[45]

Because the blows remind him of sex, they lead to a fantasy about what he'd do if he were free to marry a more desirable woman. His wife returns to the scene at this point with the usual insults and puts him to work: herself stepping outside the dramatic framework, she tells him to do what's written on his role (4386–87), and the following rubric indicates that they unbind Sebastian from the bench, dress him in a long robe, and provide him with a diadem.[46] We might suppose that the bench in question resembles those depicted in the Saint Apollonia and Saint Denis miniatures, given Diocletian's earlier instruction to bind Sebastian tightly and upside down (4255–56).[47] Similar instructions accompany the play's martyrdoms: Tiburcius is robed and diademed after his firewalking (f.5349), presumably by the Villain, who is later instructed to ad lib while laying out the corpse (f.5433), as he was after the first group of executions (f.4800).[48] The robes would handily conceal the various *feints* required to accomplish the torments and the killing. Perhaps the Villain dresses and accessorizes the living actor to indicate that he now represents an eternal soul and then removes from the gibbet the dummy that has taken the actor's place for execution.

The instruction to ad lib during this business suggests performance by a professional or at least accomplished actor. His scripted commentary continues as well and, as events progress, begins to include some serious observation. Upon Maximian's report to Diocletian that the bodies of Marcus and Marcellianus have been left to the wolves (4986), for example, the Villain comments at length on the poison of anger:

> One who eats poison swells up, but when the poison is too strong a man doesn't deflate until he's dead. This is very good to know. That's how the emperor must have eaten, because he'd like to deflate but can't, in good faith, because he has too narrow a throat. He's eaten such a big piece of barley all in one gulp with no safety valve that it will burst his belly. Now, by our lady, I think bad things will come of this. We've reached a season where good people are being hurled down. I cry hot tears every time I think about not taking off when I knew I should. Haven't I often been reproached for being so defiled that I can't be one of these good people? But I still have the space and time to become a good man. (4994–5017)[49]

He seems afraid that he might be taken for a good person, which would put him in danger, yet he's also drawn to the notion that he can indeed become better. The Villain's transformation is not complete, of course—he doesn't exactly convert. But his raillery decreases to such an extent that his wife and Dame Margot take the lead in a long exchange about drinking, playing games, and scatological matters while Sebastian is being tied to the pillar and shot with arrows. The astonished Villain witnesses Sebastian's revival after this first death, and after the second, asks the audience for a Pater Nostre, offering in return for a robe or a hat to pray for the donor's soul his entire life (6510–15). This request comes just before the enraged emperors and their henchmen are dragged off to Hell.

Le Mystère de Saint Sébastien's Villain belongs to the quotidian world of the late-medieval French spectator, relegated to its socioeconomic and bodily lower bounds. He occupies this same region within the dramatic world as he quarrels with his wife or Sebastian's knights, drinks with the henchmen, and elaborates his sexual and scatological fantasies. We might compare him to the grotesque body in Rabelais' *Gargantua and Pantagruel* that Bakhtin celebrates as an emblem of medieval folk culture, an "unfinished" body, "not separated from the rest of the world," that "outgrows itself, transgresses its own limits." According to Bakhtin, this culture emphasizes "those parts of the body that are open to the outside world, that is, the parts through which the world enters the body or emerges from it, or through which the body itself goes out to meet the world."[50] In developing his argument about the regenerative power of laughter, Bakhtin makes assumptions about the folk life of the Middle Ages and Renaissance on the basis of the literature that had supplanted it. He claims that "no dogma, no authoritarianism, no narrow-minded seriousness can coexist with Rabelaisian images; these images are opposed to all that is finished and polished, to all pomposity, to every ready-made solution in the sphere of thought and world outlook."[51] Although the Villain fits this description, he exceeds his subalterity as he provides moral and metatheatrical commentary and manages the martyrs' physical transition from earthly life to eternal blessedness.

Bakhtin locates an oppositional force in both Rabelaisian images and carnival, which temporarily inverts and ultimately revitalizes official culture. This analysis makes particular sense in the context of a clearly defined official culture, such as that provided by the Stalinist regime within which he lived. The late-medieval Roman Catholic Church and the emerging fifteenth-century French nation may have provided similarly oppressive hierarchies. Yet the primary function for inversions and representations of chaos in late-medieval drama is to delineate and reaffirm order. The ultimate victory of stage martyrs over their pagan oppressors raises no challenge to the authority of the present Christian rulers, provided those rulers are understood to enjoy their power rightfully. For all that the Villain moves between the various story lines and character groupings in *Le Mystère de Saint Sébastien*, he remains a peasant. His scurrilous diatribes and fights provide a background against which the peaceful nature of the Christians can stand out, and his later commentary and stagehand tasks reinforce the victory within this dramatic framework of the spiritual hierarchy over the fleshly. *Le Mystère de Saint Sébastien* is not conciliatory: the devils lose, the tyrants are punished, and the Villain marks the margin. His proximity—in every sense—to the spectators encourages them to make sure that *they* don't get pushed outside the bounds of the Christian community, outside the protection of God, the Virgin Mary, and the saints.

The *Parisian Journal's* reports of chaotic suffering work in a similar manner to establish by contrast what is required for a well-ordered society, as we see with its progression from the Burgundian faction's ritualistic execution of traitorous nobility to the unceremonious drowning of English prisoners who can't come up with their ransom after Charles VII regains Paris. The final executions mentioned in the *Journal* (in 1449) are "beggars, thieves, and murderers...who confessed, by torture or otherwise, that they had stolen children; they had put out the eyes of one, cut off others' legs, of others again the feet, and done many other dreadful things" (369). This concern with fake maladies and with mutilating children in order to train them as beggars shows up in late-medieval legal records as well as chronicles.[52] Paris first began trying to control begging and vagabondage in the middle of the fourteenth century, when the Black Death created a labor shortage. Wages increased, and refusal to work became a problem. This empowerment of wage earners threatened feudal structures and created anxiety about public order. An ordinance of 1351, its provisions strengthened in 1354, mandated that individuals work or else leave Paris within three days.[53] The Hundred Years' War exacerbated the situation by moving more people to the margins of society, where they mixed with prostitutes and some kinds of beggars. Young men from lower classes fought as mercenaries and then subsisted as roving brigands between campaigns. As Bronislaw Geremek writes, "The parasitic life they led during the war taught them the habits of hardened old soldiers who lived 'at war with society.' War was no longer an occupation for knights alone; it was turning into a trade which absorbed...young people from poor backgrounds."[54] As the number of urban poor grew during the fourteenth and fifteenth centuries, law began to distinguish the false poor from the true, a category that included those who were crippled, sick, old, widowed, or orphaned.[55] The true poor had their place within society; the false had to be thrust outside; and the disabled, right on the margin, defined the borders of society.

I propose that saint plays' systematic inversions and grotesqueries defended against a frightening upheaval of categories during chaotic times of social transformation by reinscribing boundaries, not only presenting mirrored hierarchies of good and evil but also depicting the margins of society in order to shore up its center. In the face of a clearly defined and coherent evil, whether that be the English, the Armagnacs, the plague, the forces of Hell or scapegoats such as the Jews or Muslims, performative pain was structured to bring everyone—all Christians, all French, or all Parisians—together, since vulnerability was collective. In the face of similar upheavals now, we can find similar inversions and scapegoating. I have chosen to focus instead on theatre that blasts away familiar categories and finds dark laughter amid the chaos, because I find it to be more hopeful. For Sarah Kane as well as for the medieval Parisian, abjection is tied to the possibility of redemption, but the notions of what constitutes redemption are not much alike. Post-modernity gives us a dispersed and unpredictable evil, and Kane's plays give us the emotional tools to remain responsive, resourceful, and inhabiting the margins.

Conclusion

Pain is a complicated phenomenon, an integral component of human experience that we most often do our best to avoid or end, but sometimes paradoxically seek out. Organizing an elaborate response system in the face of potentially harmful stimuli, pain involves the central and peripheral nervous systems; circulatory, respiratory, and endocrine systems; our feelings and our thoughts. Pain is a message that cannot be separated from its communication network. Injury doesn't always hurt, and pain doesn't always signal tissue damage but sometimes self-generates or self-perpetuates. Pain engraves our memories more deeply, draws us closer together, and takes us out of ourselves. Pain transforms the contours of the self and of the social body. Intensely private, as is all experience, pain makes us reach out to others, generates urgent if always incommensurable messages as we seek relief or at least the comfort of recognition. Pain comes in myriad forms, from discomfort to agony, acute to chronic, localized to diffuse, obvious to mysterious. Some pains curl us inward to lick our wounds and heal, but others scream for attention. We dissimulate, and we display, minimize, and fake it. We react, and we read the pain of others. Pain is a performance that we interpret, both when it happens within ourselves and when we witness the pain of others.

The forms of interpretation are as varied as the performances. In sympathy, we extend ourselves to imagine the pain of another person. Some performances of pain trigger our preconscious empathic response, so that deep down we feel the pain as if it were our own. A squirm relocates our feelings in our own bodies. Sometimes empathy activates our conscious imaginations as well. A moral judgment that the suffering exceeds the bounds of justice transforms this response into pity. Repeated performances of such undeserved pain form communities of sentiment—the pain might be reiterated by one body over and over, across multiple allied bodies, real or mimed, through the arts or via news media. Even though we may witness the suffering face to face, the community of sentiment doesn't begin to coalesce until someone reperforms the pain by speaking it, writing it, displaying its image, or acting it out—all forms of public speech that constitute a politics of pity and contribute to a plan of action in response to the pain. And this entire conceptual structure depends upon the notion that freedom from pain is a human right—a notion inconceivable before nineteenth- and twentieth-century advances in anesthesia.

The remaining traces of medieval culture suggest different economies of pain, with the lives of martyrs as evidence that one could undergo severe trauma without hurting. The spiritual rectitude that made this possible not only brought one straight to Paradise after death but benefitted the Christian community as well, because saints remained involved with humanity and could intercede with God on behalf of those still alive. Although painless engagement with torment was not a viable goal for late-medieval Christians, the days of bloody martyrdom being far in the past, its persistence as a metaphysical possibility laid the groundwork for a relation to pain quite distinct from our own. To be free of pain because God protects you is not at all the same as being free from pain because you've been administered the proper anesthetic. The great persecutions took place from the second century through the fourth, but their stories continued to be revised and elaborated over the succeeding millennium. Although each martyr's torments were distinctive, they followed a pattern starting with flagellation in direct correspondence to the scourging of Christ. Subsequent events were more or less metaphorical: an attachment to some kind of apparatus and a piercing of the flesh to echo nailing to the Cross, boiling in water or oil for Christ's total immersion in pain or perhaps for his harrowing of Hell during the time on the Cross, enclosure in a furnace for the entombment. Decapitation was the usual ending of earthly life and beginning of the saint's reward in Heaven. Only the divine Christ-become-man could actually endure such agony; therefore, God necessarily protected the martyrs. This impassability enabled them to endure extreme heat, dismemberment, evisceration—the most horrible torments imaginable. In the contemporary late-medieval world, wholesale persecution of Christians having ended, holiness found other painful methodologies. Mystics suffered in the course of their ecstatic transports. Sometimes their ascetic practices caused pain in order to initiate rapture. They suffered for the sake of their own souls and on behalf of those in Purgatory. Penitential processions featured ritual flagellation for the spiritual benefit of the participants and for the sake of the community or even the world—as expiation to ward off plague, for example. If God sent pain and illness into the world, he could as easily remove it. One had to ask in a satisfactory manner, and performances of pain did just that whether the pain was real or simulated. Often they appealed through an intermediary, the Virgin or an appropriate saint.

Post-modern religious belief may, of course, allow for divine intervention in suffering, whether to alleviate it or inflict it, but any such belief must contend with the scientific worldview that shapes dominant Euro-American social structures. For those who presented and watched saint plays in fourteenth- and fifteenth-century France, affective spirituality was the controlling paradigm. The martyrs provided an extreme example of the compassion that remained not only viable but also obligatory for ordinary Christians in the later Middle Ages. To imitate Christ's passion would surely benefit the soul. The question was what form such imitation might best take, and the church's answers varied from time to time and place to place. Anxieties about those who might take it too far were closely bound to issues of social control, with the mystic presenting an uncontrolled individual as public spectacle; mass flagellant movements, the danger of organized public behavior beyond the control of church or state. By the time that the extant saint plays were being written down, official Christian doctrine favored a spiritual *imitatio Christi* with limited outward display. What went unquestioned was the basic utility of compassionate vision; that is, visually incorporating an image of Christ in pain or of the martyrs whose torments mirrored the Passion. The spectacle upon which one gazed impressed itself upon the inner senses, and the impression remained active within for continued spiritual benefit. Like a holy relic, a holy image continued to do work in the world. Images of quotidian suffering accrued no such benefit, however, and created no obligation to see and remember—not all suffering was spiritually useful. One was, in fact, free to laugh. The medieval conception of sympathy as a radical connection, correspondence, and resonance at all levels of being suggested that one ought to guard against monstrous visual experiences lest one partake of their nature.

Conceptually, the medieval body's borders were porous. Pneuma, the medium through which the eye made contact with images, was also taken into the body and transformed into the spirits—animal, natural, and vital—required to carry out essential life functions. We may understand certain substances such as oxygen and germs to pass into the body, to be transformed and to transform us, and to pass between people. Yet we conceive of experience as essentially private and contained within the individual body. This radical separateness calls forth a notion of empathy, required to foster relationship and responsibility. Even the still-controversial theory postulating mirror-neuron systems that link us to other people at a preconscious level places the relevant neurons securely within the individual skull. Perhaps we stand on the verge of a paradigm shift here—perhaps we will leave behind us the idea that we can never share the pain of another (or any other experience). We aren't there yet. In fact, the popular understanding of pain remains quite close to Descartes' bell rope pulled to signal injury, and that's the understanding that shapes most public performances of pain.

In modern and post-modern theatre, pain signals damage or disorder, often at the social level. Plays typically embed scenes of torture and execution within a narrative framework designed to position spectators on the side of the character who suffers, drawing us into a community of sentiment with respect to an issue of social justice. Perhaps in some other plays the suffering serves a different function. Certainly film and television deploy pain to produce the pleasures of thrill, horror, and schadenfreude—I look forward to other scholarship that will examine material outside the scope of this project. In the contemporary American theatre, though, whether extending ourselves in sympathy to imagine the pain of an onstage execution or involuntarily squirming to get some distance from empathic response to a simulated torture, we are most often being wooed to pity the character's suffering and to oppose the agent who inflicts it. A shifting cast of oppressors shoot, beat, hang, and behead Afghanis (*Beyond the Mirror*). A wrongful regime in South Africa imprisons and tortures John and Winston in order to maintain apartheid (*The Island*). The rogue lieutenant of a terrorist splinter group tortures, shoots, supervises the cutting up of corpses on a stage running with blood but is himself shot to death at close range, vitiating the entire self-perpetuating system of violent retribution (*The Lieutenant of Inishmore*). Casting an even wider accusatory net, a middle-aged journalist torments his disease-ridden body with gin and cigarettes, rapes his companion, is himself raped and mutilated, all in a hotel room torn apart by a bomb blast (*Blasted*). The cop who tortures Katurian and the one who shoots him in the head are scary, arbitrary, wrong; Katurian is wrong for strangling his addled brother, but we can see that others are ultimately responsible for his actions (*The Pillowman*). These representative post-modern plays stage a world in which no one should suffer but many do, and each one speaks out against a source of pain easily understood as a metaphor for political systems or social structures that cause suffering in the real world, seeking more or less urgently to turn us toward action. Even in the murkiest instances, theatre imposes some clarity upon experience.

Real-world agents work with similar rhetorics of pain, but multiple conflicting narratives almost always frame the performances. Mangled, burned, beheaded bodies displayed to frighten people into submission can just as easily serve as foci for vengeance or resistance. Thus different strategies come into play, none without drawbacks: al Qaeda operatives use Internet video channels to broadcast beheadings, whereas the United States keeps execution out of public view and under George W. Bush forbade the photography of coffins returned from Iraq. When a state tortures and kills, whether inside its own borders or in other lands, it displays the power to subjugate but at the same time exhibits vulnerability: why else would it need pain as a mechanism for control? And pain justifies more pain. I perform my pain, narrate the wounds of my ancestor or compatriot, display the suffering of a stranger with whom I side in order to show cause for the hurt that I inflict upon those responsible. I can choose alternatives to vengeance, performing the pain in order to denounce or accuse, sublimating it to produce a work of art and thus nourish a community of sentiment. Transforming the pain in this way rather than passing it along in an equivalent (eye for an eye) or exponential (a thousand deaths for that of my father) exchange has the advantage of producing less pain-ammunition to be turned back against me.

This generalized analysis pertains to pain inflicted by another person or persons, whether through active violence or passive deprivation of life's necessities. Voluntary suffering is quite a different matter, carrying overtones of sacrifice, transcendence, or both. When an actor simulates this sort of volitional pain in the theatre, the dramatic framework tends to position the act as resulting from some injustice, thus turning it into something related to interpersonal violence but not quite the same. Initially at a loss for an example of self-inflicted pain in contemporary theatre, I happened to see the Broadway revival of August Wilson's *Joe Turner's Come and Gone* (1984) while drafting this conclusion.[1] The accumulated pain of African American experience washes over this play relentlessly, from visions of the Middle Passage to forced servitude in the Jim-Crow South and inequity in the North, cutting its characters off from their heritage, one another, and themselves. At the end, the angry and damaged Herald Loomis (Chad L. Coleman) reclaims his own destiny through his body by reclaiming his own pain: he pulls out his knife, rips his shirt open, and cuts from the left shoulder down to the middle of the chest. Loomis frees himself of all that has been inflicted upon him and brings the play to an end as he leaves for a new road of his own choosing. That we rejoice for him at this moment does not diminish our outrage over past wrongs.

We do at times see an actor actually suffer on stage, due to accidental injury or intentional performance design such as Isabelle Huppert's painful immobility for *4.48 Psychose*, and we see this as a sort of heroic self-sacrifice for art. We look for and admire these signs of the actor's aesthetic-athletic prowess: they play a vital role in the performance connoisseur's pleasure, also operative when a body artist's pain is central to the art. Lacking the narrative scaffolding that a dramatic text would provide, conceptual performance art demands interpretation, and the presence of suffering lends an urgency to that demand. During the initial development of conceptual/body/performance art in the latter half of the twentieth century, artists challenged the anesthetic culture of modernity by freely choosing to suffer. Walter Benjamin argues in "The Work of Art in the Age of Mechanical Reproduction" that the modern world forces us to defend against overstimulation. As Susan Buck-Morss explains, Benjamin extends Freud's work on shell shock to the situation of the worker in the modern world and identifies modern culture as an anesthetic system designed to help the mind keep external stimuli from contact with internal memories—a contact that's essential to seeing and understanding what's going on around us.[2] This alienation from our own sensory experience transforms politics into an aesthetic system that encourages us to take pleasure "in viewing our own destruction."[3] Benjamin identifies this arrangement as typical of fascism but surviving it, and he calls for an alternative that is more difficult to achieve than simply politicizing art and producing propaganda: art must strive "to *undo* the alienation of the corporeal sensorium, to *restore the instinctual power of the human bodily senses for the sake of humanity's self-preservation*, and to do this, not by avoiding the new technologies, but by *passing through* them."[4] In response to the mystification-effect of anesthetic postwar culture, movements such as Viennese Actionism and Fluxus sought ways to immerse artists and audiences in immediate experience. Subsequently, individual artists such as Marina Abramović, Gina Pane, and Chris Burden sought to wrest control away from social structures that they perceived as oppressive in order both to self-define and to overcome isolation, and these aims persist in performances of the twenty-first century. In art as in everyday life, scars, piercings, and tattoos reclaim the body and communicate through these surface traces of pain.

These performances generally eschew the dramatic framework that enables spectators to make sense of suffering in the theatre. Often the artist provides an explicit statement of intent that takes the place of a story, provided that spectators have access and take the time to read it. Regardless of whether one finds the artist's statement adequate, to be a member of the audience for conceptual art typically entails "consuming" the concepts behind the events, which have a significant audience that does not always witness the event—does not, in fact, necessarily see photos or videos. Some post-modern body art—Gina Pane's language of wounds, for example—relies upon a preconscious emotional response and presumes quite problematically that its meaning is universally legible. Although we are probably safe in assuming an empathic response for most if not all spectators, there is no blank slate and no "meaning" without thought. Empathic pain is only one component of a complex response, and meaning remains open. Both Abramović and Ron Athey use pain to forge connections with others and to define the community within which their suffering has meaning. Abramović generalizes from her own experience and seeks a spiritual merging with all spectators willing to enter into what she understands as a shared energetic field. Her recent endurance events resemble contemporaneous feats by magician David Blaine and tumo-practitioner Wim Hof. But whereas these two men exhibit their extraordinary control over involuntary somatic functions such as body temperature, Abramović constructs her ordeals as mechanisms for transcending individuated corporeal boundaries, her conceptualization increasingly drawn from Buddhism. Most of Abramović's performances are not explicitly political, although they do answer Benjamin's demand for art to counteract anesthetic culture. As an alternative to the conception of the self located inside a human body and its nervous system, isolated from the environment, Buck-Morss proposes the concept of an open synaesthetic system "decentered from the classical subject, wherein external sense-perceptions come together with the internal images of memory and anticipation."[5] A confrontation with body art simultaneously activates one's sensorium, memories, and interpretative facility. In the effort to understand the pain that we see, we also bring into play our own memories of painful experience together with culturally disseminated images and ideas about pain. These discomfiting performances do not merely rely upon reflexive response; they create an opportunity to reformulate the place of pain in our shared world.

Yet the very ambiguity that creates this opportunity for new understanding also renders it always vulnerable to reinscription by structures of power: the mystic is redefined and burned as a witch, the flagellant as a heretic; the body artist is neutralized and marketed as an art commodity. Glamorous photographs of Marina Abramović in the *New York Times T Magazine* or her own exhibition catalogs are not so easily distinguished from the appropriation of *Relation in Space* for a *Vogue Italia* spread.[6] In contrast to Abramović's Buddhist spirituality, Athey remains more closely engaged with Christian concepts of sacrifice and communion, although he performs in opposition to hegemonic and homophobic Christianity. Many aspects of his work are wide open to interpretation, but their politics is not: his performances always reaffirm relatedness within queer communities, always position his pain within these overlapping communities rather than positioning himself as a heroic individual or his experience as universal, making it clear that he speaks neither for nor to everyone. As a result, his work retains a greater capacity to disturb and seems unlikely ever to achieve wide circulation within the art commodity market. Athey remains at the margins of the art world, particularly in his native United States—he receives more support and performs more often in Europe. In the dispersed public spheres of the twenty-first century, though, strong positions on the margin have increasing power as new centers. Athey's painful performances invite us into a delimited aesthetic framework within which we can tolerate abjection.

Sarah Kane's plays—or Martin McDonagh's for that matter—employ a similar logic of abjection. Ian suffers horribly in the course of *Blasted*, soliciting the spectator's empathy, but at the same time his behavior toward Cate, his crudeness and racism, his abrogation of journalistic responsibility all block a sympathetic response—that is, they mitigate against imaginatively occupying his position, as do the extreme brutality of Kane's images and the collapse of categories that she engineers. Yet it is the imagination upon which they work. *Blasted* and Kane's other plays are not easily assimilated into the private realm of fantasy. Instead, they activate the collective, social imagination. In their very unmanageability, these performances resensitize us to the world around us, including its pain, a world that is so big, so complex, and so dispersed that our categories are no longer adequate. As the performing body in pain calls upon all of our emotional, cognitive, embodied resources within an aesthetic experience, we gain flexibility in responding to a real world in upheaval. We rehearse our survival, as did the audience-participants for late-medieval upheavals and their pain.

Although the general continuity of human bodily experience suggests many similarities, mentalities and social structures shaped the medieval pain experience in some ways that remain influential in the modern world and others that can seem quite unfamiliar. The suffering of saint plays affirms mirrored orders of good and evil, shoring up existing hierarchies and reinscribing boundaries by incorporating the margins of society. In *Le Geu Saint Denis,* the patron saint of France converts a bourgeois Parisian couple, receives communion from Jesus, and picks up his own head after it's cut off. Other Parisians make fun of the Christians and remain unconverted during the play's dramatic arc, yet they find themselves incapacitated when they try to attack Denis. The occupying Roman army is responsible for all torment and death, yet the play leaves them unpunished. *Le Geu Saint Denis* and its companion plays staged Paris as an indisputably French city, performing reconciliation and, by means of performance, helping to unify the nation.

Le Mystère de Saint Sébastien does punish the guilty and is thus less conciliatory than *Le Geu Saint Denis*. Although Western culture has continued to make a great deal of Saint Sebastian's body in pain and that of Saint Denis languishes in comparative obscurity, *Le Mystère de Saint Sébastien* actually spreads its pain among multiple bodies and focuses less on that of its eponymous martyr. This play's first day includes miraculous cures, two of them from crippling gout. These opportunities to perform pain followed by its relief thus place the suffering body at the spectacle's center even before the martyrdoms begin. Comforted and encouraged by angels, Sebastian guides the other martyrs through their hanging, stoning, fire-walking, and decapitation before his emblematic moment as archery target. The central importance of this martyrdom is not simply that he is shot through with arrows but that he survives this death to die again, pierced by lances. Angels take an active part here as they do in *Le Geu Saint Denis*. This play also features devils, who not only initiate the persecution of Christians but also chart its progress with their increasing frustration and finally drag the pagan wrongdoers off to a Hell full of insult and argument. As Elyse Dupras points out, the sounds of Hell contrast with the harmony of Heaven. The insults that the devils hurl at one another simply invert Christian values without establishing an alternative value system, excluding them from God's world without presenting their world as possibly viable.[7]

Le Mystère de Saint Sébastien is typical in this respect, and its hierarchical structure is more complex than that of *Le Geu Saint Denis*. Alongside the familiar presentation of Hell as the inverse of Heaven, the play uses Roman emperors, their henchmen, and the trio of the Villain, his wife, and tavernière Dame Margot to provide a contrasting parallel to the harmonious relations of Sebastian with his parents and teachers, his companions, and the Romans whom he converts to Christianity. The Villain disrupts this neat structure, though. He fights with his wife and anyone else whom he encounters, flirts with Margot, shares his raunchy fantasies with the audience, and drinks with the henchmen. But his commentary on the happenings in the play grows increasingly wholesome in moral tenor, to the point that he delivers a homily on anger as a poison. Furthermore, he's essential to the mechanics of staging this play, costuming each successive martyr to indicate the transition from mortal body to immortal soul and then removing the dummy corpse from the central killing ground so that there's clear space for the next martyrdom. Never thoroughly abandoning his role as vulgarian, the Villain connects the play's dramatic world to the lifeworld of its spectators through direct address and bad behavior. He crosses and thus defines the borders between life and art and between good and evil. By treading the margins of medieval Christian society, he shows the audience how to remain within the pale. Returning to the idea that a French town or confraternity might stage *Le Mystère de Saint Sébastien* to ward off plague, we might view the play as an appeal to the saint to intervene on behalf of the community staging it. It was crucial to bring everyone inside that community's boundaries, because plague by its very nature affects masses of people rather than individuals. One doesn't need a germ theory of contagion to perceive this. Just as illness or infirmity might strike an individual because of his sins, so might plague strike a city—afflicting the good Christians along with the bad.

The *Parisian Journal* describes life in a deeply divided city, and the text's many painful processions trace the contours of a violently changing community. While Charles VI lived, citizens walked together in bare feet both for the success of his military efforts on behalf of France and for his return to health and sanity. As rival factions brought the city into civil war during his madness and after his death, processions to the gallows defined the community's boundaries by expelling the traitor and also reintegrating him *post mortem*—providing he gave an adequate performance of remorse, that is. Performative shame and suffering obliterated the identity "traitor" even as they engraved it on the public memory, while recantation and contrition paved the way to the good death that could heal both the immortal soul and the social body. The form of the execution changed along with the nature of the crime being punished, and both reflect the pressures to which the city was subjected. The rhetorical function of the executions themselves cannot be fully sorted out from the rhetorical ends of the text within which they are inscribed. Yet the inscription of suffering throughout the *Journal* creates a vivid picture of its central position in the late-medieval social order.

Christianity provides an interpretive framework capable of encompassing all the markers of pain, from stigmata to plague sores and Sebastian's arrow wounds, and the active performance of suffering by mystics and penitents. This belief structure controls the significance of pain and provides a uniform decoding system quite distinct from the ambiguity of post-modern performances. Even though we can identify points in medieval culture at which a Bakhtinian loophole opens up, we can see the subsequent drawing shut of such openings. Thus the virgin martyr's body occupies a dialogical position within the saint play, silent and obedient as the church and society would have her but also a figure for the mystic who transgresses and exceeds those limits through her embodied imitation of the Passion. By the fifteenth century, this particular loophole was closing like a noose, changing the register for ecstatic transport from holy rapture to demonic possession. The latter might be deemed voluntary, whereas the former was less likely to be seen this way. In other words, the demoniac was in some way responsible for giving the demon control. But medieval mystics did not conceive of their suffering as a conscious choice, in the manner of post-modern body artists; instead, they understood rapture to be thrust upon them by Christ. Dyan Elliott points out that *raptus* derives from *rapire*, meaning to carry off by force—a word that can also mean rape.[8] Medieval performances of pain did communicate, but their primary audience was understood to be outside the worldly sphere: both the mystic's rapture and the flagellation of a penitential procession communicated with God, either directly or through saintly intercessors. Of course, these performances did communicate to other human beings as well. We can analyze their social function in terms familiar from the modern world, and I have done so throughout this book alongside my attempts to adopt a late-medieval perspective.

The performances central to *Performing Bodies in Pain* all give pain at least a partially positive valence. In a spiritual register, pain enables the medieval Christian mystic to merge with God or the saint play's spectator to incorporate through compassionate vision some species of the divine. The post-modern mystic uses pain to merge with humanity or some post-Christian sense of a larger spirit. In an instrumental register, the medieval flagellant uses his pain to get the attention of a saint or the Virgin and, through this intercessor, of God. A confraternity or community represents a martyr's torments for the same purpose. The post-modern theatre simulates pain to draw attention to a social injustice, eliciting an emotional engagement in order to form a community of sentiment and foment a politics of pity. Both the simulated pain of theatre and the real pain of body art can also galvanize others on the margin of or excluded from the mainstream, thus providing central focus for a new community. To affirm pain, usually coded as negative, seems an especially appropriate tool. Yet because that which forms by inverting current hierarchies is particularly susceptible to being neutralized by reversion, this last tactic is questionable in the long term unless it also results in a politics.

So can we do without pain as a source of identity? The multiplication of ideopathic pain syndromes accompanying advances in analgesics would suggest that we can't eliminate pain. But Fakir Musafar offers a lesson even to those who don't care to take things as far as he does: pain is an intense sensation that does not have to be aversive if it's expected and prepared for. We can figure out how to tolerate some of it and use the available means to alleviate what we can't tolerate. And I suspect that pain, so deeply integrated within our neurological makeup, will remain central to memory and thus to identity. Perhaps this is susceptible to some degree of control by recalibrating the connection between pain and fear. The episodic memory that contributes to reflective consciousness and the sense of a self seems to depend upon how much we think about an event rather than how much physical pain it entails. But *Performing Bodies in Pain* has been more concerned with group identity than with the individual one, and here my answer must be equivocal. Yes, I think that we could stop using pain to cement social bonds, and I believe that it is morally desirable to do so. But I don't think this is likely to happen. Pain is too dramatic, too familiar, and too readily available.

Notes

INTRODUCTION

1. As noted by Malcom Vale, "Aristocratic Violence: Trial by Battle in the Later Middle Ages," in *Violence in Medieval Society*, ed. Richard W. Kaeuper (Rochester: Boydell Press, 2000), 159.
2. Norbert Elias, *The Civilising Process, Vol. II: Power and Civility* (New York: Pantheon, 1982), 72, discussed by Richard W. Kaeuper, "Chivalry and the 'Civilizing Process,'" in *Violence in Medieval Society*, 21.
3. See Carolyn Dinshaw, *Getting Medieval: Sexualities and Communities, Pre- and Postmodern* (Durham: Duke University Press, 1999).
4. Marc Lacey, "Somalia Talks Are Stormy, But They Still Inch Ahead," *New York Times*, 19 January 2003, 1.8.
5. Charles Onyango-Obbo, "Poor in Money, but Even Poorer in Democracy," *New York Times*, 12 July 2003, A.11.
6. Thom Shanker, "Television Review; The Bad Old Days of Yugoslavia's Fallen Dictator," *New York Times*, 26 August 2003, E.7.
7. Dexter Filkins, "Aftereffects: Brutality; Iraqis Confront Memories in a Place of Torture," *New York Times*, 21 April 2003, A.1.
8. Jeffrey Gettleman, "4 from U.S. Killed in Ambush in Iraq; Mob Drags Bodies," *New York Times*, 1 April 2004, A.1.
9. Don Wycliff, "Gruesome Pictures from within the Gates of Hell," *Chicago Tribune*, 13 May 2004, 27.
10. Michael Getler, "The Images Are Getting Darker," *Washington Post*, 9 May 2004, B.6.
11. Louis Meixler, "Iraq Beheadings Appear to Inspire Copycats Elsewhere," *St. Louis Post Dispatch*, 7 November 2004, A.13; Thanassis Cambanis, "Tape Shows Beheading of US Engineer; Militants Vow to Kill 2 Others Held in Iraq," *Boston Globe*, 21 September 2004, A.1.
12. Wycliff, "Gruesome Pictures."
13. Susan Sontag, "Regarding the Torture of Others," *New York Times Magazine*, 23 May 2004, 27.
14. Frank Rich, "It Was the Porn That Made Them Do It," *New York Times*, 30 May 2004, 2.1, 16, quoting Charles Colson, "Watergate felon turned celebrity preacher."

15. Jane Mayer, "Outsourcing Torture," *New Yorker,* 14 and 21 February 2005, 106–23; Richard A. Serrano, "Group Says U.S. Sent Up to 150 to Possible Torture Sites," *Los Angeles Times,* 23 April 2005, A.4.
16. Anthony Kubiak, *Stages of Terror: Terrorism, Ideology, and Coercion as Theatre History* (Bloomington: Indiana University Press, 1991), 2, quoting Charles Krauthammer, "Terrorism and the Media: A Discussion," *Harper's,* October 1984, 47.
17. Caryle Murphy and Khalid Saffar, "Actors in the Insurgency Are Reluctant TV Stars; Terror Suspects Grilled, Mocked on Hit Iraqi Show," *Washington Post,* 5 April 2005, A.18.
18. *Guantánamo: "Honor Bound to Defend Freedom"* by Victoria Brittain and Gillian Slovo, dir. Nicolas Kent and Sacha Wares, The Culture Project at 45 Bleeker, New York, 19 August–19 December 2004.
19. "Teachers Disciplined for Showing Beheading," *New York Times,* 24 May 2004, A.21; "American Admits Beheading Was a Hoax," *New York Times,* 8 August 2004, 1.20.
20. For their most recent presentation of gate control theory, see Ronald Melzack and Patrick Wall, *The Challenge of Pain,* 2nd updated ed. (London: Penguin, 1996).
21. Patrick Wall, *Pain: The Science of Suffering* (New York: Columbia University Press, 2002), 33–43. Wall wrote this very readable volume to make his work accessible to a lay readership. For a concise summary of recent theory that requires a more thorough understanding of scientific terminology, see Joyce A. DeLeo, "Basic Science of Pain," *Journal of Bone & Joint Surgery* 88-A. Supp. 2 (2006): 58–62.
22. Ronald Melzack, "Introduction: The Pain Revolution," *Handbook of Pain Management* (Edinburgh: Churchill Livingston, 2003), 1–9. The precise areas are "somatosensory projection areas, the anterior cingulate cortex and other limbic system structures, the prefrontal and posterior parietal cortex, the insula, hypothalamus and midbrain periaquaductal grey area, portions of the thalamus, and extensive interconnecting pathways" (2, citing M. Ingvar and J-C. Hsieh, "The Image of Pain," in *Textbook of Pain,* 4th ed., ed. Ronald Melzack and Patrick Wall [Edinburgh: Churchill Livingston, 1999], 215–33).
23. Melzack, "Pain Revolution," 2–3.
24. Ronald Melzack, "Phantom Limbs," *Scientific American* 7.1 (1997): 84–85.
25. V.S. Ramachandran and Sandra Blakeslee, *Phantoms in the Brain: Probing the Mysteries of the Human Mind* (New York: William Morrow, 1998).
26. Melzack, "Phantom Limbs," 86.
27. Ibid., 87.
28. Ibid., 88.
29. Ibid., 90.
30. A.D. Craig, "Interoception: The Sense of the Physiological Condition of the Body," *Current Opinion in Neurobiology* 13 (2003): 500.

31. Ibid., 503.
32. Melzack, "Pain Revolution," 3.
33. Ibid.
34. Ibid., quoting the Committee of the Internal Association for the Study of Pain, 1979.
35. Ronald Melzack and Patrick Wall, *The Challenge of Pain*, 2nd ed. (New York: Basic Books, 1983), 56–63, with the 1975 version of the questionnaire at 62, citing Melzack and W.S. Torgerson, "On the Language of Pain," *Anesthesiology* 34 (1971): 50–59. The questionnaire is typically reproduced in books on pain; see, e.g., Bill Burns, Cathy Busby, and Kim Sawchuck, eds., *When Pain Strikes* (Minneapolis: University of Minnesota Press, 1999), 25; David B. Morris, *The Culture of Pain* (Berkeley: University of California Press, 1991), 17; Valerie Gray Hardcastle, *The Myth of Pain* (Cambridge, Mass.: Bradford/ MIT Press, 1999), 150.
36. Melzack and Wall, *Challenge of Pain*, 71, italics original.
37. Virginia Woolf, "On Being Ill," in *Collected Essays*, vol. 4 (New York: Harcourt, Brace & World, 1967), 194, quoted by Elaine Scarry, *The Body in Pain: The Making and Unmaking of the World* (New York: Oxford University Press, 1985), 4.
38. Scarry, *Body in Pain*, 5.
39. Woolf, "On Being Ill," 193.
40. Ibid.
41. See Scarry, *Body in Pain*, 51. Katherine J. Morris challenges the model that we have a different knowledge of our own pain than of someone else's, whereas our knowledge of injury is symmetrical. She suggests that a richer mind/body picture can eliminate both the asymmetry and the apparent inadequacies of natural language descriptions of pain phenomena. "Pain, Injury and First/Third-Person Asymmetry," *Philosophy and Phenomenological Research* 56.1 (1996): 125–36.
42. Valerie Gray Hardcastle provides a useful chart and summary of philosophical positions in *Myth of Pain*, 93–96.
43. Murat Aydede and Güven Güzeldere, "Some Foundational Problems in the Scientific Study of Pain," *Philosophy of Science* 69.3 (2002): S266–69.
44. Ibid., S271.
45. Melzack and Wall, *Challenge of Pain*, 57.
46. Jean Jackson, "Chronic Pain and the Tension between the Body as Subject and Object," in *Embodiment and Experience: The Existential Ground of Culture and Self*, ed. Thomas J. Csordas (Cambridge: Cambridge University Press, 1994), 217.
47. Arthur Kleinman, "Pain and Resistance: The Delegitimation and Relegitimation of Local Worlds," in *Pain as Human Experience: An Anthropological Perspective*, ed. Mary-Jo DelVecchio Good et al. (Berkeley: University of California Press, 1992), 177.

48. Arthur Kleinman, *The Illness Narratives: Suffering, Healing, and the Human Condition* (New York: Basic Books, 1988), xi–xii.
49. Didier Anzieu, *The Skin Ego*, trans. Chris Turner (New Haven: Yale University Press, 1989), 203–9.
50. Byron J. Good, "A Body in Pain—The Making of a World of Chronic Pain," in *Pain as Human Experience*, 31 (ellipsis original).
51. Good, "A Body in Pain," 35.
52. D.E. Bresler and R. Trubo, *Free Yourself from Pain* (New York: Simon & Schuster, 1979), quoted by Hardcastle, *Myth of Pain*, 9.
53. *Wit* by Margaret Edson, dir. Derek Anson Jones, with Kathleen Chalfant, Union Square Theatre, New York, 16 December 1998.
54. Esther Cohen, "Towards a History of European Physical Sensibility: Pain in the Later Middle Ages," *Science in Context* 8 (1995): 66–69. Also see Nancy G. Siraisi, *Medieval and Early Renaissance Medicine* (Chicago: University of Chicago Press, 1990); Guido Majno, *The Healing Hand: Man and Wound in the Ancient World* (Cambridge, Mass.: Harvard University Press, 1975).
55. Roselyne Rey, *The History of Pain*, trans. Louise Elliott Wallace, J.A. Cadden, and S.W. Cadden (Cambridge, Mass.: Harvard University Press, 1995), 27.
56. Stanley Finger, *Origins of Neuroscience: A History of Explorations into Brain Function* (New York: Oxford University Press, 1994), 148–9.
57. Rey, *History of Pain*, 122–4.
58. Finger, *Origins of Neuroscience*, 150; William Henry York, "Experience and Theory in Medical Practice during the Later Middle Ages: Valesco de Tarenta (Fl. 1382–1426) at the Court of Foix" (Ph.D. Diss., Johns Hopkins University, 2003), 199–202.
59. Rey, *History of Pain*, 108–10, 23.
60. York, "Experience and Theory," 2–7, citing Vivian Nutton, "Medicine in Medieval Western Europe, 1000–1500," in *The Western Medical Tradition: 800 B.C.–1800 A.D.*, ed. Lawrence I. Conrad, Michael Neve, Vivian Nutton, Roy Porter, and Andrew Wear (Cambridge: Cambridge University Press, 1995), 202–5.
61. Mary J. Carruthers, *The Book of Memory: A Study of Memory in Medieval Culture* (Cambridge: Cambridge University Press, 1990), 260.
62. For this very reason, *Performing Bodies in Pain* contains few citations to Michel Foucault's writings even though I consciously build upon his foundational work on pain and power. When Foucault invokes the medieval, he treats it as continuous with the ancien régime, describing gruesome torments that occurred during the seventeenth and eighteenth centuries, just prior to the period that most interests him; that is, the transition from public execution to other forms of punishment beginning in the eighteenth century.

1 FEELING TORTURE

1. *The Island* by Athol Fugard, John Kani, and Winston Ntshona, Brooklyn Academy of Music, Brooklyn, 5 April 2003.
2. Bernard James Seubert, ed., *Le Geu Saint Denis du Manuscrit 1131 de la Bibliothèque Sainte-Geneviève de Paris* (Geneva: Librairie Droz, 1974). Citations to this edition will be given by line number within the text. Unless otherwise attributed, translations are mine.
3. Athol Fugard, John Kani, and Winston Ntshona, *The Island* (1973), in *Statements* (New York: Theatre Communications Group, 1986), 47. The script names the characters "John" and "Winston." To distinguish, I use the last names "Kani" and "Ntshona" for the actors.
4. Bruce Weber, "The Spirit Triumphs in a South African Prison," *New York Times*, 3 April 2003, E.1.
5. Kenneth M. Prkachin, "The Consistency of Facial Expressions of Pain: A Comparison Across Modalities," in *What the Face Reveals: Basic and Applied Studies of Spontaneous Expression Using the Facial Action Coding System (FACS)*, ed. Paul Ekman and Erika L. Rosenberg (New York: Oxford University Press, 1997), 192.
6. Kenneth D. Craig, Susan A. Hyde, and Christopher J. Patrick, "Genuine, Suppressed, and Faked Facial Behavior during Exacerbation of Chronic Low Back Pain," in *What the Face Reveals*, 172–74.
7. Melzack and Wall, *Challenge of Pain*, 100.
8. For examples, see the essays in Good et al., *Pain as Human Experience*.
9. Gustav Jahoda, "Theodor Lipps and the Shift from 'Sympathy' to 'Empathy,'" *Journal of the History of the Behavioral Sciences* 41(2).3 (2005): 151–63.
10. Martha Craven Nussbaum, *Upheavals of Thought: The Intelligence of Emotions* (Cambridge: Cambridge University Press, 2001), 302, italics added.
11. Ibid., 327.
12. W.D. Hutchison et al., "Pain-Related Neurons in the Human Cingulate Cortex," *Nature Neuroscience* 2.5 (1999): 403–5.
13. Stephanie D. Preston and Frans B.M. de Waal, "Empathy: Its Ultimate and Proximate Bases," *Behavioral and Brain Sciences* 25 (2002): 4, italics original.
14. Ibid., 16–17.
15. Tania Singer et al., "Empathy for Pain Involves the Affective but Not Sensory Components of Pain," *Science* 303.5661 (2004): 1157–62.
16. India Morrison and Paul E. Downing, "Organization of Felt and Seen Pain Responses in Anterior Cingulate Cortex," *NeuroImage* 37 (2007): 642–51.
17. Jill Bennett, *Empathic Vision: Affect, Trauma, and Contemporary Art* (Stanford: Stanford University Press, 2005), 42. Bennett is an art historian, and Chesterman is her student.
18. Quoted ibid., 43.

19. *The Lieutenant of Inishmore* by Martin McDonagh, dir. Wilson Milam, Atlantic Theatre Company, New York, 10 March 2006.
20. Luc Boltanski, *Distant Suffering: Morality, Media, and Politics*, trans. Graham Burchell (Cambridge: Cambridge University Press, 1999), 8–13.
21. Ibid., 14–24.
22. Scarry, *Body in Pain*, 45–51.
23. See, e.g., Vivian Patraka, *Spectacular Suffering: Theatre, Fascism, and the Holocaust* (Bloomington: Indiana University Press, 1999); Diana Taylor, *Theatre of Crisis: Drama and Politics in Latin America* (Lexington: University of Kentucky Press, 1991). I have argued elsewhere that, by focusing spectator attention on the body of the actor (as distinct from the character) and by refusing to give the tyrant a body of his own, *The Island* allows spectators to derive pleasure from the actors' performance of pain without rendering that pleasure sadistic. "Antigone's Bodies: Performing Torture," *Modern Drama* 46.3 (2003): 381–403, also discussing Griselda Gambaro's *Antígona Furiosa*.
24. See Loren Kruger, *The Drama of South Africa: Plays, Pageants and Publics Since 1910* (London: Routledge, 1999), 156–61, for a discussion of *Sizwe Banzi Is Dead*.
25. Mary Benson, "Athol Fugard and 'One Little Corner of the World,'" *yale/theater* 4.1 (1973): 59–61; Dennis Walder, *Athol Fugard* (New York: Grove Press, 1985), 82. Walder says that Fugard was inspired by notes that Barney Simon and Mary Benson took at Grotowski's lectures in New York, and by the newly published *Towards a Poor Theatre*. See also Elenore Lester, "I Am in Despair About South Africa," *New York Times*, 1 December 1974, D.5.
26. For conditions on Robben Island, see also Nelson Mandela, *Long Walk to Freedom* (Boston: Little, Brown, 1994), 296–304, 333–444. Mandela was incarcerated on Robben Island for a fortnight in 1962, and then from 1964 until 1982. Interestingly enough, Mandela mentions playing Creon in one of the prisoners' annual Christmas-time theatricals (397). Unlike Ntshinga, he was apparently too important to be tortured, and another informant tells Fugard that the "big" boys were "strictly isolated from the other prisoners." Athol Fugard, *Notebooks: 1960–1977* (New York: Knopf, 1984), 145.
27. Fugard, *Notebooks*, 145.
28. Ibid., 151. Fugard first sketched out a play based on Ntshinga's experiences in 1970, just prior to his inspiration by Grotowski (185–86, 212). He committed to a collaboration with Kani and Ntshona in 1972, just five weeks before their performance date at The Space for the as-yet-unwritten play that became *Sizwe Banzi Is Dead* (201–2). For a brief reprise of the play's origin narrative, see Ron Jenkins, "'Antigone' as a Protest Tactic," *New York Times*, 30 March 2003, 2.6.
29. Fugard, *Notebooks*, 211.
30. Ibid., 151, 177.
31. Ibid., 153.

32. See, e.g., Robert Wahls, "Tony Around the World," *Sunday News*, 20 April 1975, 8; John Engstrom, "These Cries For Help," *London Observer*, 15 February 1981, 35.
33. Henry Kamm, "Freed Actors Resume War on Apartheid," *New York Times*, 27 October 1976, 5.
34. "'Art Is Life and Life Is Art': An Interview with John Kani and Winston Ntshona of the Serpent Players from South Africa," *UFAHAMU: Journal of the African Activist Association (Los Angeles)* 6.2 (1976): 14–15.
35. John F. Burns, "Transkei Sets Terms to Free Detained Actors," *New York Times*, 14 October 1976, L.3; "Two Black Actors to be Tried for Transkei Remarks," *New York Times*, 16 October 1976, 3; Jay Barney, "Ntshona and Kani Are Set Free," *Backstage*, 5 November 1976, 36; Kamm, "Freed Actors Resume War on Apartheid."
36. Boltanski, *Distant Suffering*, 30.
37. Nacunan Sáez, "Torture: A Discourse on Practice," in *Tattoo, Torture, Mutilation, and Adornment: The Denaturalization of the Body in Culture and Text*, ed. Frances E. Mascia-Lees and Patricia Sharpe (Albany: State University of New York Press, 1992), 129.
38. John Conroy, *Unspeakable Acts, Ordinary People: The Dynamics of Torture* (New York: Knopf, 2000), xi.
39. Ibid., ix.
40. Ibid.
41. Edward Peters, *Torture* (Philadelphia: University of Pennsylvania Press, 1996), 135–36; see also Albie Sachs, *Justice in South Africa* (Berkeley: University of California Press, 1973), 24–31.
42. For recent summaries and critique, see Andreas Gestrich, "The Public Sphere and the Habermas Debate," *German History* 24.3 (2006): 413–30; Ingrid Volkmer, "The Global Network Society and the Global Public Sphere," *development* 46.1 (2003): 9–16.
43. Arjun Appadurai, *Modernity at Large* (Minneapolis: University of Minnesota Press, 1996), 4.
44. Ibid., 7.
45. Ibid., 8.
46. Peter Lattman, "Justice Scalia Hearts Jack Bauer," *WSJ Law Blog*, 20 June 2007, http://blogs.wsj.com/law/2007/06/20/justice-scalia-hearts-jack-bauer/ (22 July 2008); "'Meet the Press' Transcript for Sept. 30, 2007," *MSNBC*, 30 September 2007, http://www.msnbc.msn.com/id/21065954/ (23 July 2008).
47. Dahlia Lithwick, "The Fiction Behind Torture Policy," *Newsweek*, 26 July 2008, http://www.newsweek.com/id/149009/page/1 (20 November 2009).
48. See Jane Mayer, "Whatever It Takes: The Politics of the Man Behind '24,'" *New Yorker*, 19 February 2007, http://www.newyorker.com/reporting/2007/02/19/070219fa_fact_mayer (22 July 2008).

49. Trans. Jody Enders, *The Medieval Theater of Cruelty: Rhetoric, Memory, Violence* (Ithaca: Cornell University Press, 1999), 125. "Doulz Jhesucrist, je vous rens graces / De cen qu'i vous plaist que les traces / De vostre sainte passion / Ont en mon corps impression" (text emended by Graham Runnalls in e-mail, 12 September 2002).
50. Trans. Enders, *Cruelty*, 173. "Bonnes gens, ne vous tristoiez / Se tourmenter vous me voiez, / Car par la paine temporele / Vient la joye perpetuele. / Prenez bon cuer et hardiece; / Souffrez tous maulz a grant leece."
51. "Frapez fort; ilz ne font que rire."
52. The first four plays (*Le Martire Saint Estiene, La Convercion Saint Pol, La Conversion Saint Denis* and *Le Martire Saint Pere et Saint Pol*) are included in Graham A. Runnalls, ed., *Le Cycle de Mystères des Premiers Martyrs: du Manuscrit 1131 de la Bibliothèque Sainte-Geneviève* (Geneva: Librairie Droz, 1976). For the sixth, see Clotilde Sennewaldt, ed., *Miracles de Madame Sainte Geneviève* (Frankfort a. Main: Moritz Dieterweg, 1937).
53. Runnalls, *Cycle des Premiers Martyrs*, 8, 26–29. As an example of the devices linking the plays as a cycle, Runnalls notes the appearance of some characters across plays: when Domitian is made Emperor to replace Nero at the end of the *Martyrdom of St. Peter and St. Paul*, the scene has little importance for that play but does set the stage for *The Conversion of St. Denis*, which follows (29).
54. For Seubert, linguistic considerations suggest a date of composition in the last part of the fourteenth century. He believes that this play was written slightly later than the others in MS 1131 (69–70). Runnalls thinks the plays were more likely composed in the first half of the fifteenth century, not long before the manuscript was copied. *Cycle des Premiers Martyrs*, 7, 10, 51–52. Lynette Muir notes that the *Miracles de Ste. Geneviève* from MS 1131 is very different from the martyr plays, and similar to *Le Mystère du Siège d'Orléans*, from the mid-fifteenth century. "The Saint Play in Medieval France," in *The Saint Play in Medieval Europe*, ed. Clifford Davidson (Kalamazoo: Medieval Institute, 1986), 133–37.
55. Runnalls considers a Sainte-Geneviève confraternity more probable than the Confraternity of the Passion. *Cycle des Premiers Martyrs*, 7, 14–16.
56. Graham A. Runnalls, "Drama and Community in Late Medieval Paris," in *Drama and Community: People and Plays in Medieval Europe*, ed. Alan Hindley (Turnhout, Belgium: Brepols, 1999), 18–33; Robert L.A. Clark, "French Confraternity Drama and Ritual," in *Drama and Community*, 34–56; Clark, "Charity and Drama: The Response of the Confraternity to the Problem of Urban Poverty," *Le Théâtre et la Cité dans l'Europe Médiéval: Fifteenth Century Studies* 13 (1988): 359–70.
57. Peter Meredith and John E. Tailby, eds., *The Staging of Religious Drama in Europe in the Later Middle Ages: Texts and Documents in English Translation* (Kalamazoo: Medieval Institute, 1983), 109.

58. Ibid., 104–5. The Mellurins also contracted to provide an earthquake and multiple fireworks, including some that would boil a seneschal in a cauldron "without heating the water in the best possible way" (109).
59. Ibid., 102, 110–11.
60. For the change in meaning during the eighteenth century, see Barbara Eckstein, *The Language of Fiction in a World of Pain: Reading Politics as Paradox* (Philadelphia: University of Pennsylvania Press, 1990), 32 (citing the *Oxford English Dictionary*).
61. Hans-Jurgen Diller, "Laughter in Medieval English Drama: A Critique of Modernizing and Historical Analyses," *Comparative Drama* 36.1, 2 (2002): 1–4. Diller says that "it would be desirable if historical research could always distinguish neatly between situations in which *somebody had to* laugh and situations in which *everybody was meant to* laugh" (1).
62. Muir, "Saint Play in Medieval France," 153.
63. *A Parisian Journal*, ed. and trans. Janet Shirley (Oxford: Clarendon, 1968), 205–6.
64. Mitchell B. Merback argues that, because crucifixion had been obsolete since the fifth century, "late medieval realist painters presented the sacred scene of the Crucifixion in terms of their own, but more importantly their *audience's* experiences with criminal justice rituals." *The Thief, the Cross, and the Wheel: Pain and the Spectacle of Punishment in Medieval and Renaissance Europe* (Chicago: University of Chicago Press, 1998), 21.
65. Elizabeth Lalou, "Les Tortures dans Les Mystères: Théâtre et Réalité," *Medieval English Theatre* 16 (1994): 43.
66. The treatment of martyrdom in *Le Geu Saint Denis* is different in many respects from Hrotsvit's. In particular, Denis explicitly asks God for protection from the torments that follow the initial beating, whereas Hrotsvit's virgins do not need to ask—they feel no pain at any point during their ordeal. See Marla Carlson, "Impassive Bodies: Hrotsvit Stages Martyrdom," *Theatre Journal* 50.4 (1998): 473–87.
67. Clifford Davidson, "Sacred Blood and the Late Medieval Stage," *Comparative Drama* 31.3 (1997): 436–58; "Suffering and the York Plays," *Philological Quarterly* 81.1 (2002): 1–32; Véronique Plesch, "Etalage Complaisant? The Torments of Christ in French Passion Plays," *Comparative Drama* 28.4 (1994): 458–86. Davidson catalogues the likely torments staged in lost English saint plays in "Violence and the Saint Play," *Studies in Philology* 98 (2001): 292–314.
68. Véronique Plesch, "Etalage Complaisant?" 460.
69. Ibid., 474.
70. Cohen, "Towards a History," 52–7. The conception of "living saints" developed around the same time. Until the late eleventh century, only those who had been martyred at least a century earlier were considered saints. See Aviad M. Kleinberg, *Prophets in Their Own Country: Living Saints and the Making*

of *Sainthood in the Later Middle Ages* (Chicago: University of Chicago Press, 1992), 21–25.
71. Cohen, "Towards a History," 57–61. Before this time, representations of Christ most often depicted him as the ruler of the world, and the few early images of the crucifixion that exist do not portray his suffering (58); see also Merback, *Thief, Cross, and Wheel*, 57–66; Nigel Spivey, "Christ and the Art of Agony," *History Today* 49.8 (1999): 16–23. Cohen introduces the term "philopassianism" for the late-medieval positive valuation of pain (51), but I have found it stylistically out of place in my own discussion.
72. Davidson, "Suffering and the York Plays," 20–21.
73. Merback, *Thief, Cross, and Wheel*, 45.
74. Thomas H. Bestul, *Texts of the Passion: Latin Devotional Texts and Medieval Society* (Philadelphia: University of Pennsylvania Press, 1996), 147, quoted in Enders, *Cruelty*, 187.
75. Merback, *Thief, Cross, and Wheel*, 47.
76. Suzannah Biernoff, *Sight and Embodiment in the Middle Ages* (New York: Palgrave Macmillan, 2002), 134.
77. Carruthers, *Book of Memory*, 54–57.
78. Biernoff, *Sight and Embodiment*, 87, 71, citing *De iride*. Also see David C. Lindberg, *Theories of Vision from Al-Kindi to Kepler* (Chicago: University of Chicago Press, 1976), 98, for Grosseteste's summary of the doctrine of species in *De lineis, angulis et figuris*.
79. Biernoff, *Sight and Embodiment*, 90–92.
80. Ibid., 95.
81. Roger Bacon, *Opus majus* 2:445–46 (5.1.4.2), quoted in Biernoff, *Sight and Embodiment*, 96.
82. Biernoff, *Sight and Embodiment*, 96–97.
83. Ibid., 81–82, citing Roger Bacon, *Opus majus*, 2:423 [5.1.1.3].
84. Ibid., 124–25.
85. Ibid., 82, citing Lectio 14 on Bk II par 417 of Thomas Aquinas's commentary on *De Anima*.
86. Simone Roux, *Paris in the Middle Ages*, trans. Jo Ann McNamara (Philadelphia: University of Pennsylvania Press, 2009), 50.
87. Ibid., 173.
88. David Nicholas, *Urban Europe, 1100–1700* (New York: Palgrave Macmillan, 2003), 152–53.
89. Ibid., 78–90.
90. Ibid., 2.
91. Ibid., 72.
92. Ibid., 121–29.
93. Ibid., 136–37.
94. Clark, "French Confraternity Drama," 35.

95. Carol Symes, *A Common Stage: Theater and Public Life in Medieval Arras* (Ithaca: Cornell University Press, 2007), 127, quoting Habermas, *The Structural Transformation of the Public Sphere*, 7, 14–17.
96. Ibid., 127–28. Symes notes that Habermas himself revised his view on the basis of his reading of Bakhtin's *Rabelais and His World*.

2 IMAGINING DEATH

1. *The Pillowman* by Martin McDonagh, dir. John Crowley, Booth Theatre, New York, videotaped by the New York Public Library's Theatre on Film and Tape Archive, 22 June 2005.
2. "*Lors saint Denis prenge sa teste entre sez mains et lez anges le meinent un pou avant en chantant: 'Gloria tibi domini...' puis le metent souz .i. couverteur et s'en revoisent*" (1041).
3. Michel Foucault, *Discipline and Punish: the Birth of the Prison*, trans. Alan Sheridan (New York: Vintage Books, 1977), 63.
4. *Parisian Journal*, trans. and ed. Shirley, cited parenthetically hereinafter. I shall refer to this memoir as "the *Journal*" or "*PJ*" and the author as "the Bourgeois," even though he was almost definitely a cleric. See the discussion in Colette Beaune's introduction to *Journal d'un Bourgeois de Paris de 1405–1449* (Paris: Livre de Poche, 1990), 1, 11–18.
5. Jahoda, "Shift from 'Sympathy' to 'Empathy,'" 152.
6. "Sympathy, n., 1.a.," *OED Online*, 2nd ed. (Oxford: Oxford University Press, 1989).
7. Finger, *Origins of Neuroscience*, 280. Galen mistakenly thought that these nerves came from the soft and impressionable brain, that they were involved in sensory perception, and that the harder fibers projecting from the spinal cord provided motor power to the viscera.
8. For a historical overview of the period, see Jacques Le Goff, "*Résistances et Progrès de l'État monarchique (XIVe–XVe Siècle)*, in *L'État et les Pouvoirs*, vol. 2 of *Histoire de la France*, ed. Robert Descimon, et al. (Paris: Seuil, 1989), 127–80. Also see C.T. Allmand, *The Hundred Years War: England and France at War, c. 1300–c. 1450* (Cambridge: Cambridge University Press, 1988), esp. 141–44, for a discussion of France and nationhood. See also David Nicholas, *The Evolution of the Medieval World: Society, Government and Thought in Europe, 312–1500* (London: Longman, 1992), 399–499; J.R.S. Phillips, *The Medieval Expansion of Europe*, 2nd ed. (Oxford: Clarendon Press, 1998); Susan Reynolds, "The Historiography of the Medieval State," in *Companion to Historiography*, ed. Michael Bentley (London: Routledge, 1997), 117–38; Claude Gauvard, "Le Royaume de France au XVe Siècle," in *Art et Société en France au XVe Siècle*, ed. Christiane Prigent (Paris: Maisonneuve et Larose, 1999), 21–30.

9. Petrus Cornelis (Pieter) Spierenburg, *The Spectacle of Suffering: Executions and the Evolution of Repression* (Cambridge: Cambridge University Press, 1984), 200–207.
10. For the transition from trial by ordeal to torture, see Esther Cohen, *The Crossroads of Justice: Law and Culture in Late Medieval France* (Leiden: E.J. Brill, 1993), 55–56; Robert Bartlett, *Trial by Fire and Water: Medieval Judicial Ordeal* (Oxford: Clarendon Press, 1986); Peters, *Torture*. For the argument that "the real period of tortured bodies arrives" in the sixteenth century, see Robert Muchembled, *Le Temps des Supplices: de l'Obéissance sous les Rois Absolus, XVe–XVIIIe Siècle* (Paris: A. Colin, 1992), 28.
11. Cohen, *Crossroads*, 67–71; Spierenburg, *Spectacle*, 8.
12. Cohen, *Crossroads*, 157, 160, 191. Trevor Dean argues that executions were much more often decreed than carried out. *Crime in Medieval Europe, 1200–1550* (New York: Longman, 2001), esp. 25.
13. Merback, *Thief, Cross, and Wheel*, 132–37.
14. Cohen, *Crossroads*, 195–99.
15. Merback, *Thief, Cross, and Wheel*, 19–20.
16. Cohen, *Crossroads*, 152–53.
17. Merback, *Thief, Cross, and Wheel*, 146.
18. See Esther Cohen, "Symbols of Culpability and the Universal Language of Justice: The Ritual of Public Executions in Late Medieval Europe," *History of European Ideas* 11 (1989): 410; Merback, *Thief, Cross, and Wheel*, 138. Cities in Northern Europe had begun to welcome the king with dramatic pageantry in the late fourteenth century. See Gordon Kipling, *Enter the King: Theatre, Liturgy, and Ritual in the Medieval Civic Triumph* (Oxford: Clarendon Press, 1998), 6, 11.
19. For a detailed discussion, see Lawrence M. Bryant, *The King and the City in the Parisian Royal Entry Ceremony: Politics, Ritual and Art in the Renaissance* (Geneva: Librairie Droz, 1986). See also Bernard Guenée and Françoise Lehoux, *Les Entrées Royales Françaises de 1328 à 1515* (Paris: Centre National de la Recherche Scientifique, 1968). For the entry of Henry VI, see Guy Llewelyn Thompson, *Paris and Its People under English Rule: the Anglo-Burgundian Regime, 1420–1436* (Oxford: Clarendon, 1991), 199–205; Lawrence M. Bryant, "Configurations of the Community in Late Medieval Spectacles," in *City and Spectacle in Medieval Europe*, ed. Barbara A. Hanawalt and Kathryn L. Reyerson (Minneapolis: University of Minnesota Press, 1994), 3–33.
20. For the execution as a liminal ritual, see Cohen, *Crossroads*, 77–83. For the relation of the royal entry to coronation, see Bryant, *King and City*, 225. The Parisian entry occurred after the coronation, except in the case of Henry VI's dual regency; however, even that entry marked a change in the city's relationship to the new king. For variations in the ceremony during this period that show what sorts of issues were at stake, see Bryant, *King and City*; Kipling, *Enter the King*; and Thompson, *Paris and Its People*. See also Roy Strong,

Art and Power: Renaissance Festivals 1450–1650 (Woodbridge: Boydell Press, 1984), 3–19.
21. See, e.g., the execution in 1398 of two Augustinian monks who were brought to Paris to cure Charles VI but were accused of having bewitched him. During the procession, they were invested with and then stripped of all accoutrements of identity, beginning with the clerical. Cohen, *Crossroads*, 184–86. Cohen points out that the mutilations were carried out quickly and were not ritualized (166) and argues against reading prurience into the stripping of a prisoner (97).
22. Cohen, *Crossroads*, 187–90. See Jacques Hillairet, *Gibets, Piloris et Cachots de Vieux Paris* (Paris: Editions Minuit, 1956), 15–29, for places of execution in Paris.
23. Cohen, *Crossroads*, 183; Merback, *Thief, Cross, and Wheel*, 132–37.
24. Cohen, *Crossroads*, 193–95. See *PJ* 245 for an example. Miraculous rescues from execution also provide evidence of a persistent belief in immanent justice. See Michael Goodich, ed., *Other Middle Ages: Witnesses at the Margins of Medieval Society* (Philadelphia: University of Pennsylvania Press, 1998), 42–57.
25. Enders, *Cruelty*, 190.
26. See Le Goff, *L'État et Les Pouvoirs*, 149. For the establishment of stable bureaucratic apparatus, see Gauvard, "Le Royaume de France au XVe Siècle."
27. Meredith and Tailby, *Staging of Religious Drama*, 110–12, 103.
28. Patrick J. Geary, *Living with the Dead in the Middle Ages* (Ithaca: Cornell University Press, 1994), 202.
29. Ibid., 95, 102, 111.
30. Runnalls, *Cycle des Premiers Martyrs*, 32–33.
31. Colette Beaune, *The Birth of an Ideology: Myths and Symbols of Nation in Late Medieval France*, trans. Susan Ross Huston, ed. Fredric L. Cheyette (Berkeley: University of California Press, 1991), 23–39. In 1120, e.g., Abelard was forced to retract his criticism.
32. Beaune, *Birth of an Ideology*, 21. Dagobert (623–39), Charles Martel (714–41), Charlemagne (751–814), Charles the Bold (843–7), and Philip Augustus (1180–1223) all had such visions. Beaune provides a detailed analysis of the relation of Saint Denis to the Capetian kings, including their physical and spiritual health (35–36), visions (36–44), and royal death rites (44–46).
33. Runnalls, *Cycle des Premiers Martyrs*, 25–26.
34. Martin, *Légende de Saint Denis*, 18–20.
35. Beaune, *Birth of an Ideology*, 33.
36. Jelle Koopmans, *Le Théâtre Des Exclus Au Moyen Age: Hérétiques, Sorcières Et Marginaux* (Paris: Imago, 1997), 27–28.
37. Brigitte Cazelles, "Introduction," in *Images of Sainthood in Medieval Europe*, ed. Renate Blumenfeld-Kosinski and Timea Szell (Ithaca: Cornell University Press, 1991), 2.

38. Runnalls, *Cycle des Premiers Martyrs*, 46–50.
39. "Sire, il presche .i. Dieu a Paris / Qui fait tous les monts et les vauls. / Il va a cheval sans chevauls. / Il fait; it defait tout ensemble. / Il vit, il meurt; il sue, il tremble. / Il pleure, il rit; il vueille et dort. / Il est jeune et viex; foible et fort. / Il fait d'un coq une poulete. / Il jeue des ars de Toulete. / Ou je ne scay que ce puet estre." The MS has "monls" in line 389, for which Seubert reads "monts," and "les ars de Toulete" makes use of Toledo's reputation as a center of sorcery.
40. "Humebrouet: Or ça viellart de pute afaire / Vien jargoullier au commissaire. / Tu yras ja a Pierrelate. / Denis: Jhesucrist qui fut a Pilate / Mené pour nous, seigneurs, vous sauve!" [Pierrelaye is a town near Pontoise.]
41. "Mauvais tirans, mauvais paiens, / Pour quoy tuez lez crestïens / Qui ont bonne loy, vraie et saine? / Mais la vostre est mauvaise et vaine, / Fausse, desloyal et dampnable."
42. These four also appear in the *Martyrdom of Saint Peter and Saint Paul*. Runnalls, *Cycle des Premiers Martyrs*, 28. For names such as these as a melange of carnivalesque alimentary themes and stereotypes of social "types" considered to be dangerous, see Koopmans, *Théâtre des Exclus*, 109–14. Koopmans identifies a "lopin" as a morsel of meat (111).
43. Martin, *Légende de Saint Denis*, 75.
44. Beaune, *Birth of an Ideology*, 19, 8.
45. Edward J. Gallagher, "Civic Patroness and Moral Guide: The Role of the Eponymous Heroine in the *Miracles De Sainte Geneviève* (c. 1420) from MS 1131 from the Bibliothèque Sainte-Geneviève, Paris," *Studia Neophilologica* 80.1 (2008), 31–34.
46. Koopmans, *Théâtre des Exclus*, 25–26, noting that during an outbreak of plague in 1545, "the inhabitants of Beaune... 'made a vow to play the *Mystère de Saint Sébastien*'; in 1564, 'to prevent and preserve the peasants and inhabitants of said Beaune from said infection of the plague,'" the inhabitants made a similar vow (quoting J. Chocheyras, *Le Théâtre Religieux en Savoie*, Geneva, 1971, 47–48).
47. Allmand, *Hundred Years Wars*, 39–40, gives as examples English victories and French defeats.
48. *Beyond the Mirror* by Exile Theatre of Kabul and Bond Street Theatre of New York, dir. Joanna Sherman and Mahmoud Shah Salimi, Theatre for the New City, New York, 4 December 2005.
49. *Assassins*, music and lyrics by Stephen Sondheim, book by John Weidman, dir. Joe Mantello, musical staging Jonathan Butterel, Roundabout Theatre Company at Studio 54, New York, videotaped by the New York Public Library's Theatre on Film and Tape Archive, 9 June 2004.
50. CBS documentary quoted in Wall, *Pain*, 7.
51. Wall, *Pain*, 1–11.
52. Ibid., 146–47.
53. Ibid., 143.

54. Nussbaum, *Upheavals of Thought*, 301. Nussbaum is actually defining compassion but considers sympathy to be much the same thing, differentiated only by degree—compassion being more intense. As discussed in the previous chapter, I reserve the term "compassion" for a medieval emotion distinct from either of these.
55. Adam Smith, *The Theory of the Moral Sentiments*, 9, quoted in Austin Sarat, "Killling Me Softly: Capital Punishment and the Technologies for Taking Life," *Pain, Death, and the Law*, ed. Sarat (Ann Arbor: University of Michigan Press, 2001), 43.
56. *Lieutenant of Inishmore*, Atlantic Theatre Company.
57. Sarat, "Killling Me Softly," 51–2.
58. Karl Shoemaker, "The Problem of Pain in Punishment: Historical Perspectives," in *Pain, Death, and the Law*, 15.
59. Sarat, "Killing Me Softly," 47. I believe that Sarat means by "pity" the same thing as I mean by "sympathy."
60. Jerry Markon and Timothy Dwyer, "Jurors Reject Death Penalty For Moussaoui," *Washington Post*, 4 May 2006, A.01.
61. "Video of Saddam Hussein Being Executed," *Google Video*, 30 December 2006, http://video.google.com/videoplay?docid=-7532034279766935521 (1 July 2008); Joshua Partlow, "Guard at Hanging Blamed for Covert Video of Hussein," *Washington Post*, 4 January 2007, A.14.
62. William Glaberson, "Arraigned, 9/11 Defendants Talk of Martyrdom," *New York Times*, 6 June 2008, A.01.
63. Sarat, "Killing Me Softly," 48.
64. Ibid., 57.
65. Lorne Dwight Conquergood, "Lethal Theatre: Performance, Punishment, and the Death Penalty," *Theatre Journal* 54.3 (2002): 352.
66. Susan Sontag, *Regarding the Pain of Others* (New York: Farrar, Strauss, and Giroux, 2003), 41.
67. Conquergood, "Lethal Theatre," 353, citing Joseph Roach, *Cities of the Dead* (New York: Columbia University Press, 1996). Interestingly enough, efforts to exonerate those wrongly convicted and condemned to death rely upon the same excremental materials that are used to form a physical effigy: that is, body fluids such as blood, semen, and saliva, along with hair and fingernail trimmings. These provide the DNA that can exonerate, and although the evidence is thoroughly physical, it is not visible to the naked eye.
68. Ibid., 361, quoting Frank Bruni and Jim Yardley, "Inmate Is Executed in Texas as 11th-Hour Appeals Fail," *New York Times*, 23 June 2000, A.18.
69. Ibid., 361.
70. Sarat, "Killing Me Softly," 64, citing *Provenzano v. Moore*, Case No. 95, 973, Corrected Opinion (September 24, 1999), Supreme Court of Florida, 43, 45, 51. Sarat includes the photos in his article.
71. Timothy V. Kaufman-Osborn, "Reviving the Late Liberal State: On Capital Punishment in an Age of Gender Confusion," *Signs* 24.4 (1999): 1123–24.

72. Martin McDonagh, *The Pillowman* (London: Faber and Faber, 2003), 10–13. Subsequent page references will be included parenthetically within the text.
73. For a more complete discussion of allegory, see Hana Worthen and W.B. Worthen, "*The Pillowman* and the Ethics of Allegory," *Modern Drama* 49.2 (2006): 155–73.
74. "Nick Berg Execution," *EncoderX*, n.d., http://encoderx.co.uk/nickberg/ (30 April 2006). This URL is no longer available, but the video can be found elsewhere on the Internet.
75. Frank Rich, "At Last, 9/11 Has Its Own Musical," *New York Times*, 2 May 2004, 2.1. The first production of *Assassins* opened at Playwrights Horizons in December 1990, at the start of the first Gulf War, and ran for 71 performances (*Lortel Archives: The Internet Off-Broadway Database*, http://www.lortel.org/LLA_archive/index.cfm [21 November 2009]). A Broadway production was planned for 2001, postponed as a result of 9/11, and finally opened in April 2004, running for 101 performances. Director Joe Mantello won a Tony award as did Michael Cerveris for his performance as John Wilkes Booth (*Internet Broadway Database*, http://ibdb.com [21 November 2009]).
76. Conquergood, "Lethal Theatre," 343, 352. He points out that Robert Bork argued in a 1976 brief that "capital punishment 'serves a vital social function as society's expression of moral outrage'" (359).
77. Boltanski discusses literary evidence for the development of interiority beginning in the sixteenth century: the novel, the essay, and autobiography were new forms making use of a split between an acting self and an observing consciousness. *Distant Suffering*, 44.

3 ENDURING ECSTASY

1. Marina Abramović, *Seven Easy Pieces* at the Solomon R. Guggenheim Museum, New York, 9–15 November 2005.
2. The miniature by Jean Fouquet is now in the Musée Condé, Chantilly. For a color reproduction, see Jean Fouquet, *The Hours of Etienne Chevalier*, ed. Charles Sterling and Claude Schaefer, trans. Marianne Sinclair (New York: Braziller, 1971), plate 45. The miniature is also reproduced and discussed in Lionello Puppi, *Torment in Art: Pain, Violence, and Martyrdom*, trans. Jeremy Scott (New York: Rizzoli, 1991), plate 5, 76–77.
3. M.M. Bakhtin, *Problems in Dostoevsky's Poetics*, ed. and trans. Caryl Emerson (Minneapolis: University of Minnesota Press, 1984), 185.
4. Jerome Kroll and Bernard Bachrach, *The Mystic Mind: The Psychology of Medieval Mystics and Ascetics* (New York: Routledge, 2005), 40–42.
5. Ariel Glucklich, *Sacred Pain: Hurting the Body for the Sake of the Soul* (New York: Oxford University Press, 2001), 207.
6. Janet A. Kaplan, "Deeper and Deeper: Interview with Marina Abramović," *Art Journal* 58.2 (1999): 14.

7. I was not aware at the time that the boots, also used for *The Room with the Ocean View* (2002) and *How to Explain Pictures to a Dead Hare* (2005), and the stick were both remnants of *The Lovers* (1988). Nancy Spector, "Marina Abramović Interviewed," in *7 Easy Pieces* (Milan: Edizioni Charta, 2007), 16–17.
8. Tom Marioni, "Marina Abramović; Now Playing the Artist," *New York Times*, 13 November 2005, 8.
9. Beatrix Ruf and Hans-Peter von Däniken, "Marina Abramović in Conversation," in *Marina Abramović: Double Edge*, ed. Ruf and Markus Landert (Sulgen, Switzerland: Verlag Niggli, 1996), 43.
10. There have been performances at the Hebbel Theater in Berlin (1993) and the Singel Theater in Antwerp (1995). For texts and extensive photos, see Marina Abramović, *Marina Abramović: Artist Body: Performances 1969–1998* (Milano: Edizioni Charta, 1998), 388–95. Abramović has performed Biography at Edge '92, Madrid; Kunsthalle, Vienna; and Documenta 9, Kassel (all 1992); the Greer Carson theatre, Santa Fe (1995); and the Groninger Schouwburg, Groningen (1996). Another theatrical work, *Delusional* (1995), explores Abramović's Balkan background, which took on a different valence with the conflicts in the region during the 1990s.
11. Ruf, "Abramović in Conversation," 31.
12. See Thomas McEvilley, "Stages of Energy: Performance Art Ground Zero?" in *Artist Body*, 46; RoseLee Goldberg, "Here and Now," in *Objects, Performance, Video, and Sound*, ed. Chrissie Iles (Oxford: Museum of Modern Art, 1995), 17.
13. See Antonin Artaud, *The Theatre and Its Double*, trans. Mary Caroline Richards (New York: Grove Press, 1958).
14. Jerzy Grotowski, *Towards a Poor Theatre* (New York: Simon and Schuster, 1968), 16, 23.
15. Abramović, *Artist Body*, 106–27.
16. See Beatrix Ruf, "Wei wu Wei—Short Circuit, Pause, Paradox," in *Double Edge*, 69. See also Bojana Pejić, "Being-in-the-Body: On the Spiritual in Marina Abramović's Art," in *Marina Abramović*, ed. Friedrich Meschede (Stuttgart: Edition Cantz, 1993), 25–38. Erika Fischer-Lichte provides a rich list of possible symbolic readings of the piece's various elements: "Performance Art—Experiencing Liminality," in *7 Easy Pieces*, 35–36.
17. See Kristine Stiles, "Between Water and Stone: Fluxus Performance: A Metaphysics of Acts," in *In the Spirit of Fluxus*, ed. Janet Jenkins (Minneapolis: Walker Art Center, 1993), 82. See also Kathy O'Dell, "Fluxus Feminus," *TDR* 41.1 (1997): 43–60; Paul Schimmel, "Leap Into the Void: Performance and the Object," in *Out of Actions: Between Performance and the Object 1949–1979*, ed. Russell Ferguson (New York: Thames and Hudson, 1998), 33–36; RoseLee Goldberg, *Performance: Live Art Since the 60s* (London: Thames and Hudson, 1998), 94–95, 128–29; Amelia Jones, *Body Art/Performing the Subject* (Minneapolis: University of

Minnesota Press, 1998), 86–90. One must remember that male action artists also engaged in conversations with prior art practices. Inspired by Klein and the Actionists, e.g., California artist Paul McCarthy painted with body parts in *Face Painting* (1972) and *Penis Painting* (1974).
18. Carolee Schneemann, *More Than Meat Joy: Complete Performance Works and Selected Writings* (New Paltz, N.Y.: Documentext, 1979), 194.
19. Ibid., 234–39.
20. Hélène Cixous, "The Laugh of the Medusa" (1975), in *New French Feminisms*, ed. Elaine Marks and Isabelle de Courtivron (New York: Schocken, 1980), 259–60.
21. See Luce Irigaray, *Speculum de l'Autre Femme* (Paris: Minuit, 1974), trans. Gillian C. Gill as *Speculum of the Other Woman* (Ithaca: Cornell University Press, 1985).
22. Roswitha Mueller, *Valie Export: Fragments of the Imagination* (Bloomington: Indiana University Press, 1994), 34–35. *Eros/ion* was performed at the "experimenta 4" in Frankfurt, the "arts lab" in London, and the "electric cinema" in Amsterdam. Sources are inconsistent in the capitalization of her name. I cite works as published but refer to the artist in accordance with her photographic renaming performance of 1968, in which she held a pack of cigarettes with the label VALIE EXPORT.
23. Artist's statement in "Endurance Art," *Performing Arts Journal* 18.3 (1996): 66. Basing her interpretation upon e-mail messages from EXPORT in 1999, Kristine Stiles interprets the artist's references to "the same material" with respect to *Eros/ion* as a comparison between the artist's body and glass, and sees a message about identity construction in keeping with the aesthetic action of this woman born as Waltraud Lehner, then married as Höllinger, "exporting" from her "outside" a new identity. "Corpora Vilia, VALIE EXPORT's Body," in *Ob/De+Con(Struction)*, ed. Robert Fleck (Philadelphia: Moore College of Art and Design, 1999), 22–26.
24. Mueller, *Valie Export*, 35. Mueller also points out that the glass was very thin and inflicted only minor injuries because the artist's body tended to push it sideways, whereas Stiles understands "without bleeding to death" as a reference to serious damage.
25. Helena Kontová, "The Wound as a Sign: an Encounter with Gina Pane," trans. Michael Moore, *Flash Art* 92–93 (October–November 1979): 38.
26. Effie Stephano and Gina Pane, "Performance of Concern," *Art and Artists* 8 (April 1973): 22.
27. See Catherine Elwes, "Floating Femininity: A Look at Performance Art by Women," in *Women's Images of Men*, ed. Sarah Kent and Jacqueline Morreau (London: Writers and Readers, 1985), 164; Jeanie Forte, "Women's Performance Art: Feminism and Postmodernism," *Theatre Journal* 40 (1988): 219, 226. See also Lucy Lippard, "The Pains and Pleasures of Rebirth: Women's Body Art," *Art in America* 64, May–June 1976, 73–80; Moira Roth, *The Amazing Decade: Women in Performance Art, 1970–1980*

(Los Angeles: Astro Artz, 1983); Jeanie Forte, "Focus on the Body: Pain, Praxis and Pleasure in Feminist Performance," in *Critical Theory and Performance*, ed. Janelle Reinelt and Joseph Roach (Ann Arbor: University of Michigan Press, 1985), 251–69.
28. Stephano and Pane, "Performance of Concern," 24–26.
29. Quoted in the program for *Seven Easy Pieces*.
30. See, e.g., Ruf, "Abramović in Conversation," 11–47.
31. *Artist Body*, 158–61.
32. Spector, "Abramović Interviewed," 28.
33. Judith Becker, "Music, Trancing, and the Absence of Pain," in *Pain and Its Transformations: The Interface of Biology and Culture*, ed. Sarah Coakley and Kay Kaufman Shelemay (Cambridge, Mass.: Harvard University Press, 2007), 167–68.
34. Marie-Elisabeth Faymonville, Mélanie Boly, and Steven Laureys, "Functional Neuroanatomy of the Hypnotic State," *Journal of Physiology-Paris* 99.4–6 (2006): 463–64.
35. Mélanie Boly, Marie-Elisabeth Faymonville, Brent A. Vogt, Pierre Maquet, and Steven Laureys, "Hypnotic Regulation of Consciousness and the Pain Neuromatrix," in *Hypnosis and Conscious States: The Cognitive Neuroscience Perspective*, ed. Graham A. Jamieson (Oxford: Oxford University Press, 2007), 22–23.
36. Wolfgang H.R. Miltner and Thomas Weiss, "Cortical Mechanisms of Hypnotic Pain Control," in *Hypnosis and Conscious States*, 53–59.
37. Ruf, "Abramović in Conversation," 37–39.
38. Ibid., 25.
39. Course description from the Hamburg Art Academy, quoted in Goldberg, "Here and Now," 18. See also Marina Abramović, *Student Body* (Milan: Edizioni Charta, 2003).
40. Hans Ulrich Obrist, "Talking with Marina Abramović on the Bullett Train to Kitakyushu, somewhere in Japan," in *Artist Body*, 45. She was describing an event that she wanted to stage in the Wall Street area for "150 people who are the major brains of this century" for which no image of any kind would be produced. For about an hour, an Indian holy man of her acquaintance would sit encased in a cube of water, and she would lie on a cross made of ice.
41. *Summa Theologiae, Second Part of the Second Part*, Question 91, trans. English Dominicans (London: Burns, Oates, and Washbourne, 1912–36; repr. New York: Benziger 1947–48; repr. New York: Christian Classics, 1981), *IntelLex*, http://www.library.nlx.com.offcampus.lib.washington.edu (24 December 2007).
42. *The House with the Ocean View* by Marina Abramović, Sean Kelly Gallery, New York, 15–26 November 2002.
43. Steven Henry Madoff, "Reflecting on an Ordeal That Was Also Art," *New York Times*, 23 November 2002, E.5.

44. For a thoughtful account over several days and interviews with a different spectator on each, see James Wescott, "Marina Abramović's *The House with the Ocean View*: The View of the House from Some Drops in the Ocean," *TDR* 47.3 (2003): 129–36. Also see Marina Abramović, *Marina Abramović: The House with the Ocean View* (Milano: Charta, 2003).
45. "Marina Abramović by Laurie Anderson," *Bomb Magazine* 84, 2003, www.bombsite.com/abramovic/abromovic3.html (7 January 2006).
46. In a recent bout of critical sparring, Gordon Kipling argues that the picture shows a Roman martyrdom being reenacted in a Roman theatre, and that the theatricality of this devotional image serves a homiletic purpose. In reply, Graham Runnalls defends the widespread use of the image as evidence of a medieval theatre in the round. Three essays were published in *Medieval English Theatre* 19 (1997): Gordon Kipling, "Theatre as Subject and Object in Fouquet's 'Martyrdom of St. Apollonia,'" 26–80; Graham Runnalls, "Jean Fouquet's 'Martyrdom of St. Apollonia' and the Medieval French Stage," 81–100; and Kipling, "Fouquet, St. Apollonia, and the Motives of the Miniaturist's Art: A Reply to Graham Runnalls," 101–20. Kipling and Runnalls include extensive citations to the debate. Although no dramatic manuscript survives, Runnalls has discovered a *Mystère de Sainte Apolline* listed in the catalogue of a late-fifteenth-century bookseller in Tours. See Graham A. Runnalls, "The Catalogue of the Tours Book-Seller and Late Medieval French Drama," *Le Moyen Français* 11 (1982): 127, reprinted in *Etudes sur les Mystères* (Paris: Champion, 1998), chapter 18; "The Catalogue of the Tours Bookseller and Antoine Vérard," *Pluteus* 2 (1984): 163–74. Although their articles are thorough and their arguments persuasive, to my mind the question of the miniature's real-world referent remains unresolved.
47. Meredith and Tailby, *Staging of Religious Drama*, 127.
48. Jocelyn Wogan-Browne, "Saints' Lives and the Female Reader," *Forum for Modern Language Studies* 27 (1991): 314–15.
49. Leslie Abend Callahan, "The Torture of Saint Apollonia: Deconstructing Fouquet's Martyrdom Stage," *Studies in Iconography* 16 (1994): 119–38.
50. Based at the University of Toronto's Victoria College, this international scholarly project has been engaged since 1975 in the study and transcription of "all surviving documentary evidence of drama, minstrelsy, and public ceremonial in England before 1642"—parish registers and account books as well as manuscripts. Abigail Ann Young and Gord Oxley, "What Is REED?" *Records of Early English Drama*, 2006, http://www.reed.utoronto.ca/index.html (13 November 2009).
51. Louis Petit de Julleville, *Histoire Du Théâtre En France: Les Mystères*, vol. 2 (Paris: Hachette, 1880).
52. Graham A. Runnalls, "Le Corpus Du Théâtre Religieux Français Du Moyen Âge," *French Medieval Drama Database Project*, July 2004, http://toisondor.byu.edu/fmddp/corpus.html (3 July 2009).

53. Sarah Kay, "The Sublime Body of the Martyr," in *Violence in Medieval Society*, ed. Richard W. Kaeuper (Rochester: Boydell Press, 2000), 3–5.
54. Brigitte Cazelles, "Bodies on Stage and the Production of Meaning," *Yale French Studies* 86 (1994): 64–65. Cazelles notes that Apollonia's eyes are closed, and thus her gaze does not invite the viewer's identification. Other scholars have objected that the eyes appear to be open. To me, they seem to be at half mast.
55. Ibid. To explain the means by which ideology interpellates individuals, Louis Althusser uses the example of a police officer calling out, "Hey, you there!" in the street. Upon hearing this call, an individual recognizes that the call is addressed to her and turns around—thus becoming a subject within ideology. "Ideology and Ideological State Apparatuses (Notes toward an Investigation) (*January–April 1969*)," in *Lenin and Philosophy*, ed. Ben Brewster (London: NLB, 1971), 162–64.
56. Fouquet, *Hours of Etienne Chevalier*, plates 2, 23.
57. Nerida Newbigin, "Agata, Apollonia and Other Martyred Virgins: Did Florentines Really See These Plays Performed?" *European Medieval Drama* 1 (1997): 89, 95; Lalou, "Tortures dans Les Mystères," 44.
58. Wogan-Browne, "Saints' Lives," 316.
59. See the summary in Lynda Hart, *Between the Body and the Flesh: Performing Sadomasochism (Between Men—Between Women)* (New York: Columbia University Press, 1998), 17.
60. Wogan-Browne, "Saints' Lives," 316–23.
61. Craig Taylor, *Debating the Hundred Years War: Pour Ce Que Plusieurs (La Loy Salicque) and a Declaration of the Trew and Dewe Title of Henry VIII* (Cambridge: Cambridge University Press, 2006), 18–19; Nicholas, *Evolution of Medieval World*, 446–48.
62. Goff, *L'État et les Pouvoirs*, 133.
63. Roux, *Paris in the Middle Ages*, 156.
64. Danielle Jacquart and Claude Thomasset, *Sexuality and Medicine in the Middle Ages*, trans. Matthew Adamson (Princeton: Princeton University Press, 1988), 48–50, use the term *spiritus animalis*, which appears to refer to post-Galenic theory. Julius Rocca, *Galen on the Brain: Anatomical Knowledge and Physiological Speculation in the Second Century AD* (Leiden: Brill, 2003), 59–66, refers only to *psychic pneuma*.
65. Rocca points out that the human brain contains no retiform plexus: Galen based his theory upon the brains of oxen that he dissected. *Galen on the Brain*, 202–9.
66. Jacquart and Thomasset, *Sexuality and Medicine*, 48–50. For foundational work in this area, see Joan Cadden, *Meanings of Sex Difference in the Middle Ages: Medicine, Science, and Culture* (Cambridge: Cambridge University Press, 1993); Thomas Laqueur, *Making Sex: Body and Gender from the Greeks to Freud* (Cambridge, Mass.: Harvard University Press, 1990).

67. Jacquart and Thomasset, *Sexuality and Medicine*, 75, citing *Les Admirable secrets de magie du Grand Albert et du petit Albert* (Paris, n.d.), which translates a passage from *De Secretis Mulierum* (MS Paris, Bibliothèque nationale, Latin 7138, fol. 2 r. 9v).
68. Dyan Elliott, *Proving Woman: Female Spirituality and Inquisitional Culture in the Later Middle Ages* (Princeton: Princeton University Press, 2004), 205.
69. Biernoff, *Sight and Embodiment*, 28–29.
70. Ibid., 30.
71. Ibid., 27.
72. Karma Lochrie, "The Language of Transgression: Body, Flesh, and Word in Mystical Discourse," in *Speaking Two Languages: Traditional Disciplines and Contemporary Theory in Medieval Studies*, ed. Allen J. Frantzen (Albany: State University of New York Press, 1991), 117–18, 120–23. Lochrie reworks this discussion in *Margery Kempe and Translations of the Flesh* (Philadelphia: University of Pennsylvania Press, 1991), 19–27, retaining the basic argument.
73. Lochrie, "Language of Transgression," 127.
74. Jo Ann McNamara, "The Need to Give: Suffering and Female Sanctity in the Middle Ages," in *Images of Sainthood in Medieval Europe*, ed. Renate Blumenfeld-Kosinski and Timea Szell (Ithaca: Cornell University Press, 1991), 199–221. See also Lochrie, "Language of Transgression," 117.
75. Caroline Walker Bynum, *Holy Feast and Holy Fast: The Religious Significance of Food to Medieval Women* (Berkeley: University of California Press, 1986; NetLibrary, 1987), 17, 21.
76. Ibid., 120–22.
77. Elliott, *Proving Woman*, 78, citing Jacques Le Goff, *The Birth of Purgatory*, trans. Arthur Goldhammer (Chicago: University of Chicago Press, 1984).
78. Kroll and Bachrach, *Mystic Mind*, 124.
79. Ibid., 116–17.
80. Caroline Walker Bynum, "Women Mystics and Eucharistic Devotion in the Thirteenth Century," in *Fragmentation and Redemption* (New York: Zone Books, 1991), 131–34, orig. pub. *Women's Studies* 11 (1984): 179–214. See also Talal Asad, "Notes on Body, Pain and Truth in Medieval Christian Ritual," *Economy and Society* 12.3 (1983): 311, citing Michel Foucault's discussion of texts by Cassian (ca. 360–435), "Le combat de la chasteté," *Communications* 35 (1982): 15–25.
81. Kroll and Bachrach, *Mystic Mind*, 126.
82. Elliott, *Proving Woman*, 48.
83. Ibid., 50–59.
84. Nancy Caciola, "Mystics, Demoniacs, and the Physiology of Spirit Possession in Medieval Europe," *Comparative Studies in Society and History* 42.2 (2000): 285.

85. Ibid., 280–85.
86. Elliott, *Proving Woman*, 70.
87. Ibid., 182.
88. Ibid., 183.
89. Ibid., 52, 64, citing James of Vitry, *Vita B. Mariae Oigniacensis, AA SS*, June, 5:552, trans. Margot King, *The Life of Marie d'Oignies* (Saskatoon, Saskatchewan: Peregrina, 1986).
90. Ibid., 184, citing Kleinberg, *Prophets in Their Own Country*, 121–25.
91. Caciola, "Mystics, Demoniacs," 270, 279.
92. Wogan-Browne, "Saints' Lives," 315; Martha Easton, "Saint Agatha and the Sanctification of Sexual Violence," *Studies in Iconography* 16 (1994): 106–8; McNamara, "Need to Give," 218.
93. Elliott, *Proving Woman*, 212–16, 249, 265–68.
94. Ibid., 265.
95. Ibid., 270. Elliot points out that this diagnosis "was in no way implicit in the discourse that he had inherited."
96. Caciola, "Mystics, Demoniacs," 296.
97. Callahan, "The Torture of Saint Apollonia," 127–33.
98. Kristine Stiles, "Inside/Outside: 'Balancing between a Dusthole and Eternity,'" in *Body and the East: From the 1960s to the Present*, ed. Zdenka Badovinac (Cambridge, Mass.: MIT Press, 1998), 29.
99. Ibid.
100. Jones, *Body Art*, 14, italics original.
101. Ibid., 5.
102. For a concise and clear summary of the issues, see Jones, *Body Art*, 22–29 and her chapter on Wilke, 151–95.

4 WHIPPING UP COMMUNITY

1. Ron Athey and Juliana Snapper, material based on *Judas Cradle*, a SCOUT literary performance, Participant Inc, New York, 17 November 2005.
2. Giovanni del Biondo's Saint Sebastian triptych, tempera on panel ca. 1375, is now in Florence's Museo dell'Opera del Duomo.
3. Tom Liesegang, "Perforating Saint," *Fallen Angels Digest*, 7 November 2007, http://www.fadmag.com/items/athey/athey.html (12 July 2008).
4. See "The Golden Legend: The Life of Sebastian" (1275), trans. William Caxton, *Internet Medieval Sourcebook*, Paul Haskell, 2002, http://www.catholic-forum.com/saints/golden155.htm (28 May 2008).
5. Nigel Spivey, *Enduring Creation: Art, Pain, and Fortitude* (Berkeley: University of California Press, 2001), 92–94.
6. Louise Marshall, "Manipulating the Sacred: Image and Plague in Renaissance Italy," *Renaissance Quarterly* 47.3 (1994): 496.

7. Sheila Barker, "The Making of a Plague Saint: Saint Sebastian's Imagery and Cult before the Counter-Reformation," in *Piety and Plague: From Byzantium to the Baroque*, ed. Franco Mormando and Thomas Worcester (Kirksville, Mo.: Truman State University Press, 2007), 93–95.
8. Ibid., 91–92, 97.
9. Ibid., 99–102.
10. Marshall, "Manipulating the Sacred," 485–500; Spivey, *Enduring Creation*, 92.
11. Barker, "Making of a Plague Saint," 106–7.
12. Patrick Vandermeersch, *La Chair de la Passion: Une Histoire de Foi: La Flagellation* (Paris: Le Cerf, 2002), 81–89. For a study that supports Vandermeersch but focuses primarily upon Germany and is thus largely outside the scope of this project, see Niklaus Largier, *In Praise of the Whip*, trans. Graham Harman (New York: Zone Books, 2007).
13. Ibid., 85–86, 88.
14. Ibid., 111–14; for Damien, 46–54.
15. Jacquart and Thomasset, *Sexuality and Medicine*, 150, citing *De Bono*, ed. H. Kühle, *Alberti Magni Opera Omnia*, vol. 28 (Münster: Aschendorff, 1951), 160–63.
16. *Expositio supra Librum Canonis Avicenne* (Lyon: Jean Trechsel, 1498), bk III, fen 20, tr. 1, ch. 36, quoted by Jacquart and Thomasset, *Sexuality and Medicine*, 158.
17. Mitchell B. Merback, "Living Image of Pity: Mimetic Violence, Peacemaking and Salvific Spectacle in the Flagellant Processions of the Later Middle Ages," in *Images of Medieval Sanctity: Essays in Honour of Gary Dickson*, ed. Debra Higgs Strickland (Leiden: E.J. Brill, 2007), 162, italics original.
18. Ibid., 163.
19. Vandermeersch, *Chair de la Passion*, 119–22.
20. Barker, "Making of a Plague Saint," 106–7.
21. Marshall, "Manipulating the Sacred," 496.
22. Barker, "Making of a Plague Saint," 122–27.
23. Spivey, *Enduring Creation*, 90.
24. Robert Mills, *Suspended Animation: Pain, Pleasure, and Punishment in Medieval Culture* (London: Reaktion, 2005), 159–60.
25. Richard J. Bodnar, Kathryn Commons, and Donald W. Pfaff, *Central Neural States Relating Sex and Pain* (Baltimore: Johns Hopkins University Press, 2002), 1.
26. Joel Kaye, *Economy and Nature in the Fourteenth Century: Money, Market Exchange, and the Emergence of Scientific Thought* (Cambridge: Cambridge University Press, 1998), 15–17.
27. Jacques Le Goff, *Your Money or Your Life: Economy and Religion in the Middle Ages*, trans. Patricia Ranum (New York: Zone Books, 1988), 25–50.
28. Ibid., 51.

29. Odd Langholm, *The Merchant in the Confessional: Trade and Price in the Pre-Reformation Penitential Handbooks* (Leiden: Brill, 2003), 8–9.
30. Barbara H. Rosenwein and Lester K. Little, "Social Meaning in the Monastic and Mendicant Spiritualities," *Past and Present* 63 (1974): 23–28.
31. See Gary Dickson, "Encounters in Medieval Revivalism: Monks, Friars, and Popular Enthusiasts," *Church History* 68.2 (1999): 265–93.
32. Vandermeersch, *Chair de la Passion*, 135–42, citing Crouzet, *Les Guerrieres de Dieu* (1990).
33. Barker, "Making of a Plague Saint," 117, italics original.
34. Vandermeersch, *Chair de la Passion*, 135–36, 200–202.
35. For the diversity of participants, see Vandermeersch, *Chair de la Passion*, 84. For the exclusionary description, Norman Cohn, *The Pursuit of the Millennium* (New York: Oxford University Press, 1970), 133–34.
36. Merback, "Living Image of Pity," 154.
37. Lisa Silverman, *Tortured Subjects: Pain, Truth, and the Body in Early Modern France* (Chicago: University of Chicago Press, 2001), 128–29.
38. Ruth Mazo Karras, *Sexuality in Medieval Europe: Doing Unto Others* (New York: Routledge, 2005), 55.
39. See David Román, *Acts of Intervention: Performance, Gay Culture, and AIDS* (Bloomington: Indiana University Press, 1998), 149–53; Stephanie Cash, "Ron Athey at P.S. 122," *Art in America*, February 1995, 99–101; John Edward McGrath, "Trusting in Rubber: Performing Boundaries during the AIDS Epidemic," *TDR* 39.2 (1995): 21–39; Patrick Cambell and Helen Spackman, "With/out An-aesthetic: The Terrible Beauty of Franko B.," *TDR* 42.4 (1998): 56–67.
40. Unless otherwise identified, Athey's statements and details about his life and work are cited from *Hallelujah! Ron Athey: A Story of Deliverance*, VHS, dir. Catherine Gund Saalfield (1998; USA: Artistic License, 1998). See also Ron Athey, "Gifts of the Spirit," in *Unnatural Disasters: Recent Writings from the Golden State*, ed. Nicole Panter (San Diego: Incommunicado, 1996), 70–80.
41. Dominic Johnson, "Perverse Martyrologies: An Interview with Ron Athey," *Contemporary Theatre Review* 18.4 (2008): 505.
42. Amelia Jones, "Holy Body: Erotic Ethics in Ron Athey and Juliana Snapper's *Judas Cradle*," *TDR* 50.1 (2006): 162, italics original.
43. Jones, "Holy Body," 163–65, citing Wayne Koestenbaum, *The Queen's Throat: Opera, Homosexuality, and the Mystery of Desire* (New York: Vintage Books, 1993).
44. Kateri Butler, "The Art Issue; Ron Athey; in Extremis and in My Life," *Los Angeles Times*, 28 January 2007, I.26.
45. Dominic Johnson, E-mail, 16 May 2008. Athey mentions the connection in passing but does not elaborate in an otherwise illuminating interview with Johnson, "Perverse Martyrologies." For other brief essays with photos, see RoseLee Goldberg, *PERFORMA* (New York: Performa, 2007);

Dominic Johnson, ed., *Encounters: Manuel Vason, Performance, Photography, Collaboration* (Bristol: Arnolfini, 2007). Also see the PERFORMA 05 festival Web site at http://05.performa-arts.org/about (22 November 2009); T. Nikki Cesare and Jenn Joy, "Performa/(Re)Performa," *TDR* 50.1 (2006): 170–77.

46. In addition to Gund Saalfield's *Hallelujah!, Bizarre Rituals: Dances Sacred and Profane,* VHS, dir. Dan Jury and Mark Jury (1987; USA: Gorgon Video, 1993); *Sick: The Life and Death of Bob Flanagan, Super-Masochist,* VHS, dir. Kirby Dick (1997; USA: Lions Gate Films, 1997).
47. Johnson, "Perverse Martyrologies," 512. Athey provides a useful "brief assholeography" of his own work at 507.
48. Allan Kaprow, "The Legacy of Jackson Pollack," *Art News,* October 1958, 24–26, 55–77.
49. See Schimmel, "Leap Into the Void," 17. For a full discussion of Pollock, see Jones, "The 'Pollockian Performative,'" in *Body Art,* 53–102.
50. Jones, *Body Art,* 80.
51. RoseLee Goldberg, *Performance Art: Futurism to the Present,* revised ed. (New York: Thames and Hudson, 2001), 149. Also see Kristine Stiles, "Uncorrupted Joy: International Art Actions," in *Out of Actions,* 290–96; *Brus, Muehl, Nitsch, Schwarzkogler: Writings of the Vienna Actionists,* ed. Malcolm Green (London: Atlas Press, 1999), for the work and death of Viennese Actionist Rudolf Shwarzkogler. An earlier version of this chapter includes a discussion of the Actionists, who unlike Burden created work that was overtly and polymorphously sexual: Marla Carlson, "Whipping up Community: Reworking the Medieval Passion Play, from Ron Athey to Mel Gibson," in *The Renaissance of Medieval Theatre,* ed. Véronique Dominguez (Academia Bruylant/Université Catholique de Louvain, 2009), 219–38.
52. Jones, *Body Art,* 82.
53. David Savran, *Taking It Like a Man: White Masculinity, Masochism, and Contemporary American Culture* (Princeton: Princeton University Press, 1998), 5.
54. Schimmel, "Leap into the Void," 94. For all of Burden's work, see esp. Chris Burden, *A Twenty-Year Survey* (Newport Harbor, CA: Newport Harbor Museum of Art, 1988).
55. Chris Burden, *Chris Burden 71–73* (Los Angeles: Chris Burden, 1974), 24.
56. Chris Burden, *Documentation of Selected Works, 1971–74,* VHS (1971–75; New York: Electronic Arts Intermix, 1975).
57. Kathy O'Dell, *Contract with the Skin: Masochism, Performance Art, and the 1970s* (Minneapolis: University of Minnesota Press, 1998), 2. Most central to her analysis are Theodor Reik, "Masochism in Modern Man," in *Of Love and Lust: On the Psychoanalysis of Romantic and Sexual Emotions* (1949; reprint New York: Farrar, Straus & Giroux, 1984), 206–54; Gilles Deleuze, *Masochism, Coldness, and Cruelty* (New York: Zone, 1989). Many of the relevant psychoanalytic texts are now conveniently collected in Margaret Ann

Fitzpatrick Hanly, ed., *Essential Papers on Masochism* (New York: New York University Press, 1995).
58. See Victor E. Taylor, "Contracting Masochism," in *One Hundred Years of Masochism: Literary Texts, Social and Cultural Contexts*, ed. Michael C. Finke and Carl Niekerk (Amsterdam: Rodopi, 2000), 64; Estela V. Welldon, *Sadomasochism* (Cambridge: Icon, 2002).
59. O'Dell, *Contract with the Skin*, 2.
60. Amelia Jones, "Survey," in *The Artist's Body*, ed. Tracey Warr (London: Phaidon, 2000), 32.
61. Paul Schimmel, "Just the Facts," in Chris Burden, *A Twenty-Year Survey*, 17–18.
62. Christopher Bedford, "This Boy's Toys: Chris Burden's *Bridges and Bullets*," *Angle: A Journal of Arts + Culture* 1.8 (October 2003), http://www.anglemagazine.org/articles/This_Boys_Toys_Chris_Burden_2132.asp (10 April 2005; no longer available); also see David Colman, "Art and the Zen of Garden Trains," *New York Times*, 25 January 2004, ST.7.
63. Savran, *Taking It Like a Man*, 229. Savran points out that the top's masculinity is reinforced because he dominates; the bottom's, because he "can take it like a man."
64. Also see Daniel Harris, "The Death of Kink: Five Stages in the Metamorphosis of the Modern Dungeon," in *The Rise and Fall of Gay Culture* (New York: Hyperion, 1997), 179–202. I thank Chris Sieving for the reminder about *Scorpio Rising*.
65. Melzack and Wall, *Challenge of Pain*, 169–73. Endorphins are "endogenous morphine-like substances." Enkephalins are "opioid substances 'in the brain.'"
66. See, e.g., Geoffrey Mains, *Urban Aboriginals: A Celebration of Leathersexuality* (San Francisco: Gay Sunshine Press, 1984); Carol Truscott, "S/M: Some Questions and a Few Answers," in *Leatherfolk: Radical Sex, People, Politics, and Practice*, 3rd ed., ed. Mark Thompson (Los Angeles: Daedalus, 2004), 21.
67. Leo Bersani, *Homos* (Cambridge, Mass.: Harvard University Press, 1995), 94.
68. See Gilles Deleuze, *Masochism, Coldness, and Cruelty*, orig. pub. *Le Froid et le Cruel*, in *Presentation de Sacher-Masoch* (Paris: Editions de Minuit, 1967).
69. See Taylor, "Contracting Masochism," 62, quoting Deleuze, 134.
70. See, e.g., Anne McClintock, "Maid to Order: Commercial S/M and Gender Power," in *Dirty Looks: Women, Pornography, Power*, ed. Pamela Church Gibson and Roma Gibson (London: British Film Institute, 1993), 207–31.
71. Bersani, *Homos*, 89–90. Lynda Hart attributes the emphasis on power to the long history of denial within psychoanalytic theory that masochists actually desire pain. *Between the Body and the Flesh*, 134.
72. See Savran, *Taking It Like a Man*, 218, citing *Sex Exposed: Sexuality and the Pornography Debate*, ed. Lynne Segal and Mary McIntosh (New Brunswick, N.J.: Rutgers University Press, 1993), and Gayle Rubin, "The Leather

Menace: Comments on Politics and S/M, in *Coming to Power: Writings and Graphics on Lesbian S/M*, ed. SAMOIS (Boston: Alyson, 1981, rev. ed. 1987), 194–229.
73. Dana Kennedy, "S&M Enters The Mainstream," *San Francisco Chronicle*, 21 December 1992, D.3.
74. "I Was a Middle-Aged Suburban Dominatrix," *Redbook*, August 1994, 64–65, 73.
75. Alex Duval Smith, "Game for a lash? One minute Madonna was in rubber and the next a spanking good time was being had in suburban bedrooms everywhere. So why has S&M moved into the mainstream so fast? We visit the Europerve ball in Amsterdam and find that the Brits are undisputed kings of kinkiness," *Guardian*, 16 December 1994.
76. Kennedy, "S&M Enters The Mainstream," quoting Dr. Barry Lubetkin, clinical director of the Institute for Behavior Therapy in New York.
77. Bersani, *Homos*, 87.
78. Savran, *Taking It Like a Man*, 33.
79. Ibid., 37.
80. Philippe Liotard, "The Body Jigsaw," *UNESCO Courier*, July/August 2001, 22. As Margo DeMello points out, the discourse of the modern primitive movement denies the working-class history of tattooing in the United States. *Bodies of Inscription: A Cultural History of the Modern Tattoo Community* (Durham: Duke University Press, 2000), 182–83.
81. Talal Asad, *Formations of the Secular: Christianity, Islam, Modernity* (Stanford: Stanford University Press, 2003), 111–12.
82. See "About Fakir Musafar: Father of the Modern Primitive Movement," *Fakir.org 2009/2010*, http://www.fakir.org/aboutfakir/index.html (22 November 2009); *Modern Primitives: An Investigation of Contemporary Adornment and Ritual*, ed. Andrea Juno and V. Vale (San Francisco: Re/Search Press, 1989).
83. Rebecca McClean Novick, "Skin Deep: Interview with Fakir Musafar," *Lycaeum*, 1992, http://www.lycaeum.org/~maverick/mus-int.htm (21 November 2009).
84. Fakir Musafar, "Body Play," in Armando R. Favazza, *Bodies under Siege: Self-Mutilation and Body Modification in Culture and Psychiatry*, 2nd ed. (Baltimore: Johns Hopkins University Press, 1996), 326–27; *Modern Primitives*.
85. Gloria Brame, "Interview with Fakir Musafar," *The Internet Companion to Different Loving: The World of Sexual Domination and Submission*, 2001, http://gloriabrame.com/diflove/fakir.html (10 April 2005).
86. Fakir Musafar, "Body Play," in Favazza, 327.
87. Diane Sussman, "Fakir Musafar: A Theory Full of Holes," *Palo Alto Online*, 29 March 1995, http://www.paloaltoonline.com/weekly/morgue/news/1995_Mar_29.PEOPLE29.html (21 November 2009).
88. Novick, "Skin Deep."
89. Fakir Musafar, "Body Play," in Favazza, 313–17.

90. Reissued, Andrea Juno and V. Vale, eds., *Bob Flanagan: Supermasochist* (New York: Juno Books, 2000).
91. Dennis Cooper, "Flanagan's Wake," *Artforum* 34.8 (1996): 77.
92. See Bob Flanagan, "Pain Journal," in *When Pain Strikes*, ed. Bill Burns et al., 163–75.
93. Linda S. Kauffman, *Bad Girls and Sick Boys: Fantasies in Contemporary Art and Culture* (Berkeley: University of California Press, 1998), 37.
94. Cooper, "Flanagan's Wake," 77.
95. Santa Monica Museum (1992); New Museum, New York (1994); Boston School of the Arts (1995).
96. Kauffman, *Bad Girls and Sick Boys*, 33.
97. Jones, *Body Art*, 231.
98. Kauffman, *Bad Girls and Sick Boys*, 37.
99. C. Carr, "The Rite Stuff," *Village Voice*, 15 December 1998, 81.
100. See, e.g., Marilee Strong, *A Bright Red Scream: Self-Mutilation and the Language of Pain* (New York: Viking, 1998), 36–47; Jennifer Egan, "The Thin Red Line," *New York Times Magazine*, 27 July 1997, 20–25ff.
101. Favazza, *Bodies under Siege*, 148.
102. Anzieu, *Skin Ego*, 205–6. See also Barent W. Walsh and Paul M. Rosen, *Self-Mutilation: Theory, Research, and Treatment* (New York: Guilford, 1988).
103. Favazza, *Bodies under Siege*, 222, 287.
104. Fakir Musafar, "Body Play: State of Grace or Sickness? Part II: The New Culture Matures," *BMEZINE.COM*, 14 August 2003, http://www.bmezine.com/news/fakir/ 20030814.html (14 April 2005).
105. Victoria Pitts, *In the Flesh: The Cultural Politics of Body Modification* (New York: Palgrave Macmillan, 2003), 105, 114, italics original.
106. Kaja Silverman, *Male Subjectivity at the Margins* (New York: Routledge, 1992), 206, cited in Pitts, *In the Flesh*, 100.
107. Pitts, *In the Flesh*, 105.
108. Ibid., 114–15.
109. See the "History" section of Athey's Web site, 7 July 2005, http://www.ronathey.com (31 January 2008).
110. For a detailed discussion, see Johnson, "Perverse Martyrologies," 507.
111. Johnson, "Perverse Martyrologies," 506.
112. Peter J. Boyer, "The Jesus War: A Reporter at Large," *New Yorker* 79.26, 15 September 2003, 58.
113. Daniel J. Wakin, "A Season of Faith and a Film: Gibson's Movie Goes to Church," *New York Times*, 9 April 2004, B.1.
114. *South Park*, Episode 804, "The Passion of the Jew" by Matt Stone and Trey Parker, dir. Stone, 31 March 2004, *Comedy Central*, http://www.southparkstudios.com/episodes/103880 (22 November 2009).
115. Terry Eagleton, "Spiritual Rock Star," *London Review of Books*, 3 February 2005, 19–20.

116. "Salvifici Doloris," quoted in Christopher Dickey and Rod Norland, "'Precious' Suffering," *Newsweek*, 28 February 2005, 24.
117. Quoted in Dickey and Norland, "'Precious' Suffering."
118. See Sylvia Poggioli, "Ailing Pope to Sit out Easter Ceremony," *Morning Edition*, 25 March 2005, http://www.npr.org/templates/story/story.php?storyId=4560705 (25 April 2005).

5 CONTAINING CHAOS

1. *Blasted* by Sarah Kane, dir. Sarah Benson, with Reed Birney, Marin Ireland, Louis Cancelmi, Soho Rep., New York, 30 October 2008.
2. Léonard R. Mills, ed., *Le Mystère de Saint Sébastien* (Geneva: Librairie Droz, 1965). Parenthetical line citations refer to this edition.
3. Mark Johnson, *The Body in the Mind: The Bodily Basis of Meaning, Imagination, and Reason* (Chicago: University of Chicago Press, 1987), 21–23, 34–40.
4. Julia Kristeva, *Powers of Horror: An Essay on Abjection*, trans. Leon S. Roudiez (New York: Columbia University Press, 1982), 4.
5. Ibid., 2.
6. Ibid., 3, italics original.
7. Ibid., 5, italics original.
8. Ibid., 8, italics original.
9. Ibid., 9, brackets and italics original.
10. Sarah Kane, *Blasted* in *Complete Plays* (London: Methuen, 2001), 24. All further references to Kane's plays will be cited from this source parenthetically within the text.
11. Sean Carney, "The Tragedy of History in Sarah Kane's *Blasted*," *Theatre Survey* 46.2 (2005): 284.
12. Heidi Stephenson and Natasha Langridge, *Rage and Reason: Women Playwrights on Playwriting* (London: Methuen, 1997), 133.
13. See, e.g., Tom Sellar, "Truth and Dare: Sarah Kane's *Blasted*," *Theater* 27.1 (1996): 32, citing the observation of Carl Miller in the *Independent* that one would expect "a group of men in comfortable shoes" to respond unfavorably to this play. Kane makes the same point in Stephenson and Langridge, *Rage and Reason*, 130.
14. Annabelle Singer, "Don't Want to Be This: The Elusive Sarah Kane," *TDR* 48.2 (2004): 145.
15. Sellar, "Truth and Dare," 31. The most notorious feature of *Saved* is the stoning to death of a baby by a group of young men, including the baby's father. The "baby" is presumed to occupy the carriage onstage but is not visible during this incident.
16. Sarah Kane, "Brief Encounter," platform, Royal Holloway College, London, 3 November 1998, quoted in Graham Saunders, *"Love Me or Kill Me": Sarah*

Kane and the Theatre of Extremes (Manchester: Manchester University Press, 2002), 39.
17. Sarah Kane, "Brief Encounter," quoted in Graham Saunders, "'Out Vile Jelly': Sarah Kane's 'Blasted' and Shakespeare's 'King Lear,'" *New Theatre Quarterly* 20.1 (2004): 70.
18. Carney, "Tragedy of History." Alyson Campbell, "Experiencing Kane: An Affective Analysis of Sarah Kane's 'Experiential' Theatre in Performance," *Australasian Drama Studies* 46 (2005): 80–97.
19. Interview, quoted in Saunders, *Love Me or Kill Me*, 66.
20. Conversation with Nils Tabert, 16 July 2000, in ibid., 138.
21. Campbell, "Experiencing Kane," 85.
22. *4.48 Psychose* by Sarah Kane, dir. Claude Régy, trans. Michael Bugdahn, subtitles Mike Sens/MWT, with Isabelle Huppert, Brooklyn Academy of Music, Brooklyn, 29 October 2005.
23. Carney, "Tragedy of History," 289. Interestingly enough, the initial critical response was a refusal to interpret.
24. Quoted in Saunders, *Love Me or Kill Me*, 59, 64. Also quoted in Carney, "Tragedy of History," 289.
25. Carney, "Tragedy of History," 278.
26. Ibid., 283.
27. Matthew D. Lieberman and Naomi I. Eisenberger, "Conflict and Habit: A Social Cognitive Neuroscience Approach to the Self," in *On Building, Defending, and Regulating the Self: A Psychological Perspective*, ed. Abraham Tesser, Joanne V. Wood, and Diederik A. Stapel (New York: Psychology Press, 2005), 77–83.
28. Ibid., 82–83.
29. Ibid., 84.
30. Ariel Watson, "Performing Mental Illness: Anxious Metatheatre and the Therapy Trope" (paper presented at the American Society for Theatre Research, Chicago, 17 November 2006).
31. Interview with Tabert, quoted in Saunders, *Love Me or Kill Me*, 78.
32. Kristeva, *Powers of Horror*, 8.
33. *Phaedra's Love* by Sarah Kane, dir. Ianthe Demos, One Year Lease at Cherry Lane Theatre Studio, New York, 17 December 2005.
34. Interview with Tabert, quoted in Saunders, *Love Me or Kill Me*, 114.
35. Robert Mills points out the racial stereotypes of an altarpiece by Master Franke that shows Saint Barbara as an upper class and emphatically white woman tormented by a "motley crew: all shabby clothes, distorted features and brutish gestures—one even exposes his buttocks to view." *Suspended Animation*, 138.
36. Koopmans, *Théâtre des exclus*, 21–28, 164.
37. Véronique Plesch, "Killed by Words: Grotesque Verbal Violence and Tragic Atonement in French Passion Plays," *Comparative Drama* 33.1 (1999): 47. She

argues that in farce, the grotesque produces a joyful alienation; that is, a relief that one is not like what one sees on stage.

38. Véronique Plesch, "Etalage Complaisant? The Torments of Christ in French Passion Plays," *Comparative Drama* 28.4 (1994): 484 n.82, quoting Carruthers, *Book of Memory*, 245.
39. *Oxford English Dictionary*, Compact Edition.
40. Wolfgang Kayser, *The Grotesque in Art and Literature*, trans. Ulrich Weisstein (New York: McGraw-Hill, 1966; orig. pub. Indiana University Press, 1963), 21, 185.
41. Elyse Dupras puts its date at around 1446. *Diables Et Saints: Rôle Des Diables Dans Les Mystères Hagiographiques Français* (Geneva: Droz, 2006), 15.
42. Diocletian finishes instructing the henchmen at line 4270. The binding and beating follow, likely continuing while the Villain responds (4350–75) and then completes a brief scene with his wife (4376–91).
43. Mikhail M. Bakhtin, *Rabelais and His World*, trans. Hélène Iswolsky (Cambridge, Mass.: MIT Press, 1968), 8.
44. "Ce n'est que pechié et ordure, / corte joye, longue tristesse."
45. "Par noustre damme, c'est mal fet. / Par Dieu, je croy qu'il l'ont tüé. / Au dyable souyés vous donné, / larons de mauveyse fassom. / Il estoit ung beau compagniom. / Par Dieu, ce a esté grant dommage, / mes les foul ne sont jamés sage, / ny les pouvres ne sont pas riches, / les larges ne sont jamés siches, / ne nul coquut n'est esparvier. / Se je puisse ausi bien feytoyer / ma femme, je fusse bien eyse." My particular thanks to Catherine Jones for help with this translation and for explaining "no cuckoo is a sparrowhawk" as an adage meaning that no one can escape his condition.
46. "La Femme: Alés feyre vous parchimin, / ou je te ferey villanie. / *(deligent eum de scamno et induant eum longa veste et ponant ei dyadematn).*" Thanks to Steven Smith and Robert L.A. Clark for helping me with this passage.
47. "Le me liés fort et just tout au revers."
48. The first rubric reads *"stultus loquitur et interim ponatur corpus,"* and the second is identical except for referring to him as *"fatuus."*
49. "Qui mange venin tantoust enfle; / mes, quant le venin est trop fort, / l'om ne desamffle jusqu'on est mort. / Ceci est tresbom a sçavoir. / L'empereur si en doit avoir / mangé, car desamfler ce veust; / mes, en bonne foys, il ne peut, / car il ha trop petite gorge. / Mes si mangoit ung boeceau d'orge / tout a ung cop, sen le vanter, / garde n'aroit de desamfler, / mes creveroit par my la pance. / Or, par noustre damme, je pance / qu'il en y ara de mal venus. / Bonnes gens seront rües jus / en ceste sceysom qu'est venue. / Par Dieu, aucunes foys j'en plure / des chaus yeulx quant je m'en advise, / non hostant quant bien je m'avise. / Souvant ne m'est pas reprouché / que je souye trop entaché / d'estre de celle bonnes gens, / j'ey assés espace et temps / pour devenir encour bonns homme."
50. Bakhtin, *Rabelais*, 26.

51. Ibid., 3.
52. Bronislaw Geremek, *The Margins of Society in Late Medieval Paris*, trans. Jean Birrell (Cambridge: Cambridge University Press, 1987), 192–201. See also Lalou, "Les Tortures dans les Mystères," 37–50.
53. Geremek, *Margins of Society*, 21–33.
54. Ibid., 126.
55. Ibid., 169; also see Nicholas, *Urban Europe*, 150–51.

CONCLUSION

1. *Joe Turner's Come and Gone* by August Wilson, dir. Bartlett Sher, Lincoln Center Theater at the Belasco Theatre, New York, 3 June 2009.
2. Susan Buck-Morss, "Aesthetics and Anaesthetics: Walter Benjamin's Artwork Essay Reconsidered," *October* 62 (1992), 16–18.
3. Ibid., 4.
4. Ibid., 5, italics original.
5. Ibid., 13.
6. Madhu Puri, "The Originals: Give Them an Envelope Clutch, and They'll Push It," *New York Times*, 26 February 2006, n.p.; *Relation in Space* adapted by Steven Meisel in *Vogue Italia*, November 1998, reproduced alongside Marina Abramović /Ulay *Relation in Space* in *7 Easy Pieces*, 8.
7. Dupras, *Diables et Saints*, 65–69, 84–85.
8. Dyan Elliott, "The Physiology of Rapture and Female Spirituality," in *Medieval Theology and the Natural Body*, ed. Peter Biller and A.J. Minnis (Rochester, N.Y.: York Medieval Press, 1997), 142.

Bibliography

Abramović, Marina. *The House with the Ocean View*. Milano: Charta, 2003.
———. *The House with the Ocean View*. Sean Kelly Gallery: New York. 15–26 November 2002.
———. *Marina Abramović: Artist Body: Performances 1969–1998*. Milano: Edizioni Charta, 1998.
———. *Marina Abramović: Seven Easy Pieces*. Solomon R. Guggenheim Museum: New York. 9–15 November 2005.
———. *Student Body*. Milan: Edizioni Charta, 2003.
Allmand, C.T. *The Hundred Years War: England and France at War, C. 1300–C. 1450*. Cambridge: Cambridge University Press, 1988.
Althusser, Louis. "Ideology and Ideological State Apparatuses (Notes toward an Investigation) (*January–April 1969*)." In *Lenin and Philosophy*, 121–73. London: NLB, 1971.
"American Admits Beheading Was a Hoax." *New York Times*, 8 August 2004, 1.20.
Anderson, Laurie. "Marina Abramović by Laurie Anderson." *Bomb Magazine*, Summer 2003, www.bombsite.com/abramovic/abromovic3.html (7 January 2005).
Anzieu, Didier. *The Skin Ego*. Translated by Chris Turner. New Haven: Yale University Press, 1989.
Appadurai, Arjun. *Modernity at Large*. Minneapolis: University of Minnesota Press, 1996.
Artaud, Antonin. *The Theatre and Its Double*. Translated by Mary Caroline Richards. New York: Grove Press, 1958.
Asad, Talal. *Formations of the Secular: Christianity, Islam, Modernity*. Stanford: Stanford University Press, 2003.
———. "Notes on Body, Pain and Truth in Medieval Christian Ritual." *Economy and Society* 12, no. 3 (1983): 287–327.
Athey, Ron. "Gifts of the Spirit." In *Unnatural Disasters: Recent Writings from the Golden State*, edited by Nicole Panter, 70–80. San Diego: Incommunicado, 1996.
———. *Hallelujah! Ron Athey: A Story of Deliverance*. VHS. Directed by Catherine Gund Saalfield. 1998; USA: Artistic License, 1998.

Athey, Ron, and Juliana Snapper. Material based on *Judas Cradle*, a SCOUT literary performance. Participant: New York. 17 November 2005.
Aydede, Murat, and Güven Güzeldere. "Some Foundational Problems in the Scientific Study of Pain." *Philosophy of Science* 69, no. 3, Supplement: Proceedings of the 2000 Biennial Meeting of the Philosophy of Science Association. Part II: Symposia Papers (2002): S265–83.
Bakhtin, Mikhail M. *Problems in Dostoevsky's Poetics*. Translated by Caryl Emerson. Minneapolis: University of Minnesota Press, 1984.
———. *Rabelais and His World*. Translated by Hélène Iswolsky. Cambridge, Mass.: MIT Press, 1968.
Barker, Sheila. "The Making of a Plague Saint: Saint Sebastian's Imagery and Cult before the Counter-Reformation." In *Piety and Plague: From Byzantium to the Baroque*, edited by Franco Mormando and Thomas Worcester, 90–131. Kirksville, Mo.: Truman State University Press, 2007.
Barney, Jay. "Ntshona and Kani Are Set Free." *Backstage*, 5 November 1976, 36.
Bartlett, Robert. *Trial by Fire and Water: Medieval Judicial Ordeal*. Oxford: Clarendon Press, 1986.
Beaune, Colette. *The Birth of an Ideology: Myths and Symbols of Nation in Late Medieval France*. Translated by Susan Ross Huston and edited by Fredric L. Cheyette. Berkeley: University of California Press, 1991.
———, ed. *Journal d'un Bourgeois de Paris de 1405–1449* (orig. ed. Alexandre Tuety, 1881). Paris: Livre de Poche, 1990.
Becker, Judith. "Music, Trancing, and the Absence of Pain." In *Pain and Its Transformations: The Interface of Biology and Culture*, edited by Sarah Coakley and Kay Kaufman Shelemay, 166–94. Cambridge, Mass.: Harvard University Press, 2007.
Bennett, Jill. *Empathic Vision: Affect, Trauma, and Contemporary Art*. Stanford: Stanford University Press, 2005.
Benson, Mary. "Athol Fugard and 'One Little Corner of the World.'" *yale/theater* 4, no. 1 (1973): 60.
Bersani, Leo. *Homos*. Cambridge, Mass.: Harvard University Press, 1995.
Biernoff, Suzannah. *Sight and Embodiment in the Middle Ages*. New York: Palgrave Macmillan, 2002.
Bodnar, Richard J., Kathryn Commons, and Donald W. Pfaff. *Central Neural States Relating Sex and Pain*. Baltimore: Johns Hopkins University Press, 2002.
Boltanski, Luc. *Distant Suffering: Morality, Media, and Politics*. Translated by Graham Burchell. Cambridge: Cambridge University Press, 1999.
Boly, Mélanie, Marie-Elisabeth Faymonville, Brent A. Vogt, Pierre Maquet, and Steven Laureys. "Hypnotic Regulation of Consciousness and the Pain Neuromatrix." In *Hypnosis and Conscious States: The Cognitive Neuroscience Perspective*, edited by Graham A. Jamieson, 15–27. Oxford: Oxford University Press, 2007.

Boyer, Peter J. "The Jesus War: A Reporter at Large." *New Yorker*, 15 September 2003, 58+.

Brittain, Victoria, and Gillian Slovo. *Guantánamo: "Honor Bound to Defend Freedom."* Dir. Nicolas Kent and Sacha Wares. The Culture Project at 45 Bleeker: New York. 19 August–19 December 2004.

Brus, Muehl, Nitsch, Schwarzkogler: Writings of the Vienna Actionists. Edited and translated by Malcolm Green in collaboration with the artists. London: Atlas Press, 1999.

Bryant, Lawrence M. "Configurations of the Community in Late Medieval Spectacles." In *City and Spectacle in Medieval Europe*, edited by Barbara A. Hanawalt and Kathryn L. Reyerson, 3–33. Minneapolis: University of Minnesota Press, 1994.

———. *The King and the City in the Parisian Royal Entry Ceremony: Politics, Ritual and Art in the Renaissance.* Geneva: Librairie Droz, 1986.

Buck-Morss, Susan. "Aesthetics and Anaesthetics: Walter Benjamin's Artwork Essay Reconsidered." *October* 62 (1992): 3–41.

Burden, Chris. *Chris Burden 71–73.* Los Angeles: Chris Burden, 1974.

———. *Documentation of Selected Works, 1971–74.* VHS. 1971–75; New York: Electronic Arts Intermix, 1975.

———. *A Twenty-Year Survey.* Newport Harbor, Calif.: Newport Harbor Museum of Art, 1988.

Burns, Bill, Cathy Busby, and Kim Sawchuck, eds. *When Pain Strikes.* Minneapolis: University of Minnesota Press, 1999.

Burns, John F. "Transkei Sets Terms to Free Detained Actors." *New York Times*, 14 October 1976, L.3.

Butler, Kateri. "The Art Issue; Ron Athey; in Extremis and in My Life." *Los Angeles Times*, 28 January 2007, I.26.

Bynum, Caroline Walker. *Fragmentation and Redemption: Essays on Gender and the Human Body in Medieval Religion.* New York: Zone Books, 1991.

———. *Holy Feast and Holy Fast: The Religious Significance of Food to Medieval Women.* Berkeley: University of California Press, 1986; NetLibrary, 1987.

Caciola, Nancy. "Mystics, Demoniacs, and the Physiology of Spirit Possession in Medieval Europe." *Comparative Studies in Society and History* 42, no. 2 (2000): 268–306.

Cadden, Joan. *Meanings of Sex Difference in the Middle Ages: Medicine, Science, and Culture.* Cambridge: Cambridge University Press, 1993.

Callahan, Leslie Abend. "The Torture of Saint Apollonia: Deconstructing Fouquet's Martyrdom Stage." *Studies in Iconography* 16 (1994): 119–38.

Campbell, Alyson. "Experiencing Kane: An Affective Analysis of Sarah Kane's 'Experiential' Theatre in Performance." *Australasian Drama Studies* 46 (2005): 80–97.

Cambell, Patrick, and Helen Spackman. "With/out an-Aesthetic: The Terrible Beauty of Franko B." *TDR* 42, no. 4 (1998): 56–67.

Carlson, Marla. "Antigone's Bodies: Performing Torture." *Modern Drama* 46, no. 3 (2003): 381–403.

———. "Impassive Bodies: Hrotsvit Stages Martyrdom." *Theatre Journal* 50, no. 4 (1998): 473–87.

———. "Whipping up Community: Reworking the Medieval Passion Play, from Ron Athey to Mel Gibson." In *The Renaissance of Medieval Theatre*, edited by Véronique Dominguez, 219–38. Louvain: Academia Bruylant/Université Catholique de Louvain, 2009.

Carney, Sean. "The Tragedy of History in Sarah Kane's *Blasted*." *Theatre Survey* 46, no. 2 (2005): 275–96.

Carr, C. "The Rite Stuff." *Village Voice*, 15 December 1998, 81.

Carruthers, Mary J. *The Book of Memory: A Study of Memory in Medieval Culture*. Cambridge: Cambridge University Press, 1990.

Cash, Stephanie. "Ron Athey at P.S. 122." *Art in America*, February 1995, 99–101.

Cazelles, Brigitte. "Bodies on Stage and the Production of Meaning." *Yale French Studies* 86 (1994): 56–74.

———. "Introduction." In *Images of Sainthood in Medieval Europe*, edited by Renate Blumenfeld-Kosinski and Timea Szell, 1–20. Ithaca: Cornell University Press, 1991.

Cesare, T. Nikki, and Jenn Joy. "Performa/(Re)Performa." *TDR* 50, no. 1 (2006): 170–77.

Cixous, Helene. "The Laugh of the Medusa" (1975). In *New French Feminisms*, edited by Elaine Marks and Isabelle de Courtivron, 245–64. New York: Schocken, 1980.

Clark, Robert L.A. "Charity and Drama: The Response of the Confraternity to the Problem of Urban Poverty." *Le Théâtre et la Cité dans l'Europe Médiéval: Fifteenth Century Studies* 13 (1988): 359–70.

———. "French Confraternity Drama and Ritual." In *Drama and Community: People and Plays in Medieval Europe*, edited by Alan Hindley, 34–56. Turnhout, Belgium: Brepols, 1999.

Cohen, Esther. *The Crossroads of Justice: Law and Culture in Late Medieval France*. Leiden: E.J. Brill, 1993.

———. "Symbols of Culpability and the Universal Language of Justice: The Rituals of Public Executions in Late Medieval Europe." *History of European Ideas* 11 (1989): 407–16.

———. "Towards a History of European Physical Sensibility: Pain in the Later Middle Ages." *Science in Context* 8 (1995): 47–74.

Cohn, Norman. *The Pursuit of the Millenium*. London: Oxford University Press, 1970.

Colman, David. "Art and the Zen of Garden Trains." *New York Times*, 25 January 2004, ST.7.

Conquergood, Lorne Dwight. "Lethal Theatre: Performance, Punishment, and the Death Penalty." *Theatre Journal* 54, no. 3 (2002): 339–67.

Conroy, John. *Unspeakable Acts, Ordinary People: The Dynamics of Torture.* New York: Knopf, 2000.
Cooper, Dennis. "Flanagan's Wake." *Artforum* 34, no. 8 (1996): 75–77.
Craig, A.D. "Interoception: The Sense of the Physiological Condition of the Body." *Current Opinion in Neurobiology* 13 (2003): 500–5.
Craig, Kenneth D., Susan A. Hyde, and Christopher J. Patrick. "Genuine, Suppressed, and Faked Facial Behavior during Exacerbation of Chronic Low Back Pain." In *What the Face Reveals: Basic and Applied Studies of Spontaneous Expression Using the Facial Action Coding System (FACS),* edited by Paul Ekman and Erika L. Rosenberg, 161–77. New York: Oxford University Press, 1997.
Davidson, Clifford. "Sacred Blood and the Late Medieval Stage." *Comparative Drama* 31, no. 3 (1997): 436–58.
———. "Suffering and the York Plays." *Philological Quarterly* 81, no. 1 (2002): 1–32.
———. "Violence and the Saint Play." *Studies in Philology* 98 (2001): 292–314.
Dean, Trevor. *Crime in Medieval Europe, 1200–1550.* New York: Longman, 2001.
DeLeo, Joyce A. "Basic Science of Pain." *Journal of Bone & Joint Surgery* 88-A, Supp. 2 (2006): 58–62.
Deleuze, Gilles. *Masochism, Coldness, and Cruelty.* New York: Zone, 1989.
DeMello, Margo. *Bodies of Inscription: A Cultural History of the Modern Tattoo Community.* Durham: Duke University Press, 2000.
Dickey, Christopher, and Rod Norland. "'Precious' Suffering." *Newsweek,* 28 February 2005, 24–9.
Dickson, Gary. "Encounters in Medieval Revivalism: Monks, Friars, and Popular Enthusiasts." *Church History* 68, no. 2 (1999): 265–93.
Diller, Hans-Jurgen. "Laughter in Medieval English Drama: A Critique of Modernizing and Historical Analyses." *Comparative Drama* 36, nos. 1, 2 (2002): 1–19.
Dinshaw, Carolyn. *Getting Medieval: Sexualities and Communities, Pre- and Postmodern.* Durham: Duke University Press, 1999.
Dupras, Elyse. *Diables et Saints: Rôle des Diables dans les Mystères Hagiographiques Françaises.* Geneva: Droz, 2006.
Eagleton, Terry. "Spiritual Rock Star." *London Review of Books,* 3 February 2005, 19–20.
Easton, Martha. "Saint Agatha and the Sanctification of Sexual Violence." *Studies in Iconography* 16 (1994): 83–118.
Eckstein, Barbara J. *The Language of Fiction in a World of Pain: Reading Politics as Paradox.* Philadelphia: University of Pennsylvania Press, 1990.
Edson, Margaret. *Wit.* Dir. Derek Anson Jones. Perf. Kathleen Chalfant. Union Square Theatre: New York. 16 December 1998.
Egan, Jennifer. "The Thin Red Line." *New York Times Magazine,* 27 July 1997, 20–25ff.

Elliott, Dyan. "The Physiology of Rapture and Female Spirituality." In *Medieval Theology and the Natural Body*, edited by Peter Biller and A.J. Minnis, 141–74. Rochester, N.Y.: York Medieval Press, 1997.

———. *Proving Woman: Female Spirituality and Inquisitional Culture in the Later Middle Ages*. Princeton: Princeton University Press, 2004.

Elwes, Catherine. "Floating Femininity: A Look at Performance Art by Women." In *Women's Images of Men*, edited by Sarah Kent and Jacqueline Morreau. London: Writers and Readers, 1985.

Enders, Jody. *The Medieval Theater of Cruelty: Rhetoric, Memory, Violence*. Ithaca: Cornell University Press, 1999.

Engstrom, John. "These Cries for Help." *London Observer*, 15 February 1981, 35.

Exile Theatre of Kabul and Bond Street Theatre of New York. *Beyond the Mirror*. Dir. Joanna Sherman and Mahmoud Shah Salimi. Theatre for the New City: New York. 4 December 2005.

EXPORT, VALIE. "'Artist Statement' in 'Endurance Art.'" *Performing Arts Journal* 18, no. 3 (1996): 66–70.

Favazza, Armando R. *Bodies under Siege: Self-Mutilation and Body Modification in Culture and Psychiatry*. 2nd ed. Baltimore: Johns Hopkins University Press, 1996.

Faymonville, Marie-Elisabeth, Mélanie Boly, and Steven Laureys. "Functional Neuroanatomy of the Hypnotic State." *Journal of Physiology-Paris* 99, nos. 4–6 (2006): 463–69.

Filkins, Dexter. "Aftereffects: Brutality; Iraqis Confront Memories in a Place of Torture." *New York Times*, 21 April 2003, A.1.

Finger, Stanley. *Origins of Neuroscience: A History of Explorations into Brain Function*. New York: Oxford University Press, 1994.

Fischer-Licthe, Erika. "Performance Art—Experiencing Liminality." In *Marina Abramović: Seven Easy Pieces*, 33–45. Milan: Edizioni Charta, 2007.

Flanagan, Bob. "Pain Journal." In *When Pain Strikes*, edited by Bill Burns, Cathy Busby, and Kim Sawchuck, 163–75. Minneapolis: University of Minnesota Press, 1999.

———. *Sick: The Life and Death of Bob Flanagan, Super-Masochist*. VHS. Directed by Kirby Dick. 1997; USA: Lions Gate Films, 1997.

Flanagan, Bob, and Sheree Rose. *Visiting Hours*. Santa Monica Museum (1992); New Museum, New York (1994); Boston School of the Arts (1995).

Forte, Jeanie. "Focus on the Body: Pain, Praxis and Pleasure in Feminist Performance." In *Critical Theory and Performance*, edited by Janelle Reinelt and Joseph Roach, 248–62. Ann Arbor: University of Michigan Press, 1985.

———. "Women's Performance Art: Feminism and Postmodernism." In *Performing Feminisms*, edited by Sue-Ellen Case, 251–69. Baltimore: Johns Hopkins University Press, 1990.

Foucault, Michel. *Discipline and Punish: The Birth of the Prison*. Translated by Alan Sheridan. New York: Vintage Books, 1977.

Fouquet, Jean. *The Hours of Etienne Chevalier*. Translated by Marianne Sinclair, edited by Claude Schaefer and Charles Sterling. New York: Braziller, 1971.
Fugard, Athol. *Notebooks: 1960–1977*. New York: Knopf, 1984.
Fugard, Athol, John Kani, and Winston Ntshona. *The Island*. Brooklyn Academy of Music: New York. 5 April 2003.
———. *The Island* (1973). In *Statements*, 46–77. New York: Theatre Communications Group, 1986.
Gallagher, Edward J. "Civic Patroness and Moral Guide: The Role of the Eponymous Heroine in the *Miracles De Sainte Geneviève* (c. 1420) from MS 1131 from the Bibliothèque Sainte-Geneviève, Paris." *Studia Neophilologica* 80, no. 1 (2008): 30–42.
Gauvard, Claude. "Le Royaume de France au XVe Siècle." In *Art et Société en France au XVe Siècle*, edited by Christiane Prigent, 21–30. Paris: Maisonneuve et Larose, 1999.
Geary, Patrick J. *Living with the Dead in the Middle Ages*. Ithaca: Cornell University Pres, 1994.
Geremek, Bronislaw. *The Margins of Society in Late Medieval Paris*. Translated by Jean Birrell. Cambridge: Cambridge University Press, 1987.
Gestrich, Andreas. "The Public Sphere and the Habermas Debate." *German History* 24, no. 3 (2006): 413–30.
Getler, Michael. "The Images Are Getting Darker." *Washington Post*, 9 May 2004, B.6.
Gettleman, Jeffrey. "4 from U.S. Killed in Ambush in Iraq; Mob Drags Bodies." *New York Times*, 1 April 2004, A.1.
Glaberson, William. "Arraigned, 9/11 Defendants Talk of Martyrdom." *New York Times*, 6 June 2008, A.1.
Glucklich, Ariel. *Sacred Pain: Hurting the Body for the Sake of the Soul*. New York: Oxford University Press, 2001.
Goldberg, RoseLee. *PERFORMA*. New York: Performa, 2007.
———. *Performance: Live Art Since the 60s*. London: Thames and Hudson, 1998.
———. *Performance Art: Futurism to the Present*. Revised ed. New York: Thames and Hudson, 2001.
Good, Byron. "A Body in Pain—The Making of a World of Chronic Pain." In *Pain as Human Experience: An Anthropological Perspective*, edited by Mary-Jo DelVecchio Good, Paul Brodwin, Byron Good, and Arthur Kleinman, 29–48. Berkeley: University of California Press, 1992.
Good, Mary-Jo DelVecchio, Paul Brodwin, Byron Good, and Arthur Kleinman, eds. *Pain as Human Experience: An Anthropological Perspective*. Berkeley: University of California Press, 1992.
Goodich, Michael, ed. *Other Middle Ages: Witnesses at the Margins of Medieval Society*. Philadelphia: University of Pennsylvania Press, 1998.
Grotowski, Jerzy. *Towards a Poor Theatre*. New York: Simon and Schuster, 1968.

Guenée, Bernard, and Françoise Lehoux. *Les Entrées Royales Françaises de 1328 à 1515.* Paris: Centre National de la Recherche Scientifique, 1968.
Hanly, Margaret Ann Fitzpatrick, ed. *Essential Papers on Masochism.* New York: New York University Press, 1995.
Hardcastle, Valerie Gray. *The Myth of Pain.* Cambridge, Mass.: Bradford/MIT Press, 1999.
Harris, Daniel. "The Death of Kink: Five Stages in the Metamorphosis of the Modern Dungeon." In *The Rise and Fall of Gay Culture*, 179–202. New York: Hyperion, 1997.
Hart, Lynda. *Between the Body and the Flesh: Performing Sadomasochism (Between Men—Between Women).* New York: Columbia University Press, 1998.
Herman, Edward, and Gerry O'Sullivan. *The "Terrorism" Industry.* New York: Pantheon, 1989.
Hutchison, W.D., K.D. Davis, A.M. Lozano, R.R. Tasker, and J.O. Dostrovsky. "Pain-Related Neurons in the Human Cingulate Cortex." *nature neuroscience* 2, no. 5 (1999): 403–5.
"I Was a Middle-Aged Suburban Dominatrix." *Redbook*, August 1994, 64–5, 73.
Iles, Chrissie, ed. *Marina Abramović: Objects, Performance, Video, and Sound.* Oxford: Museum of Modern Art, 1995.
Irigaray, Luce. *Speculum of the Other Woman.* Translated by Gillian C. Gill. Ithaca: Cornell University Press, 1985.
Jackson, Jean. "Chronic Pain and the Tension between the Body as Subject and Object." In *Embodiment and Experience: The Existential Ground of Culture and Self*, edited by Thomas J. Csordas, 201–28. Cambridge: Cambridge University Press, 1994.
Jacquart, Danielle, and Claude Thomasset. *Sexuality and Medicine in the Middle Ages.* Translated by Matthew Adamson. Princeton: Princeton University Press, 1988.
Jahoda, Gustav. "Theodor Lipps and the Shift from 'Sympathy' to 'Empathy.'" *Journal of the History of the Behavioral Sciences* 41(2), no. 3 (2005): 151–63.
Jenkins, Ron. "'Antigone' as a Protest Tactic." *New York Times*, 30 March 2003, 2.6.
Johnson, Dominic, ed. *Encounters: Manuel Vason, Performance, Photography, Collaboration.* Bristol: Arnolfini, 2007.
———. "Perverse Martyrologies: An Interview with Ron Athey." *Contemporary Theatre Review* 18, no. 4 (2008): 503–13.
Johnson, Mark. *The Body in the Mind: The Bodily Basis of Meaning, Imagination, and Reason.* Chicago: University of Chicago Press, 1987.
Jones, Amelia. *Body Art/Performing the Subject.* Minneapolis: University of Minnesota Press, 1998.
———. "Holy Body: Erotic Ethics in Ron Athey and Juliana Snapper's *Judas Cradle*." *TDR* 50, no. 1 (2006): 159–69.
Juno, Andrea, and V. Vale, eds. *Bob Flanagan: Supermasochist.* New York: Juno Books, 2000.
———. *Modern Primitives: An Investigation of Contemporary Adornment and Ritual.* San Francisco: Re/Search Press, 1989.

Kaeuper, Richard W. "Chivalry and the 'Civilizing Process.'" In *Violence in Medieval Society*, edited by Richard W. Kaeuper, 21–35. Rochester: Boydell Press, 2000.
Kamm, Henry. "Freed Actors Resume War on Apartheid." *New York Times*, 27 October 1976, 5.
Kane, Sarah. *Blasted*. Dir. Sarah Benson. Perf. Reed Birney, Marin Ireland, Louis Cancelmi. Soho Rep.: New York. 30 October 2008.
———. *Complete Plays*. London: Methuen, 2001.
———. *Phaedra's Love*. Dir. Ianthe Demos. One Year Lease, Cherry Lane Theatre Studio: New York. 17 December 2005.
———. *4.48 Psychose*. Dir. Claude Régy. Perf. Isabelle Huppert. Brooklyn Academy of Music: Brooklyn. 29 October 2005.
Kani, John, and Winston Ntshona. "'Art Is Life and Life Is Art': An Interview with John Kani and Winston Ntshona of the Serpent Players from South Africa." *UFAHAMU: Journal of the African Activist Association, Los Angeles* 6, no. 2 (1976): 5–26.
Kaplan, Janet A. "Deeper and Deeper: Interview with Marina Abramović." *Art Journal* 58, no. 2 (1999): 7–19.
Kaprow, Allan. "The Legacy of Jackson Pollack." *Art News*, October 1958, 24–6, 55–77.
Karras, Ruth Mazo. *Sexuality in Medieval Europe: Doing Unto Others*. New York: Routledge, 2005.
Kauffman, Linda S. *Bad Girls and Sick Boys: Fantasies in Contemporary Art and Culture*. Berkeley: University of California Press, 1998.
Kaufman-Osborn, Timothy V. "Reviving the Late Liberal State: On Capital Punishment in an Age of Gender Confusion." *Signs* 24, no. 4 (1999): 1119–29.
Kay, Sarah. "The Sublime Body of the Martyr." In *Violence in Medieval Society*, edited by Richard W. Kaeuper, 3–20. Rochester: Boydell Press, 2000.
Kaye, Joel. *Economy and Nature in the Fourteenth Century: Money, Market Exchange, and the Emergence of Scientific Thought*. Cambridge: Cambridge University Press, 1998.
Kayser, Wolfgang. *The Grotesque in Art and Literature*. Translated by Ulrich Weisstein. New York: McGraw-Hill, 1966.
Kennedy, Dana. "S&M Enters the Mainstream." *San Francisco Chronicle*, 21 December 1992, D.3.
Kipling, Gordon. *Enter the King: Theatre, Liturgy, and Ritual in the Medieval Civic Triumph*. Oxford: Clarendon Press, 1998.
———. "Fouquet, St. Apollonia, and the Motives of the Miniaturist's Art: A Reply to Graham Runnalls." *Medieval English Theatre* 19 (1997): 101–20.
———. "Theatre as Subject and Object in Fouquet's 'Martyrdom of St. Apollonia.'" *Medieval English Theatre* 19 (1997): 26–80.
Kleinberg, Aviad M. *Prophets in Their Own Country: Living Saints and the Making of Sainthood in the Later Middle Ages*. Chicago: University of Chicago Press, 1992.

Kleinman, Arthur. *The Illness Narratives: Suffering, Healing, and the Human Condition.* New York: Basic Books, 1988.

———. "Pain and Resistance: The Delegitimation and Relegitimation of Local Worlds." In *Pain as Human Experience: An Anthropological Perspective,* edited by Mary-Jo Good, et al., 169–97. Berkeley: University of California Press, 1992.

Kontová, Helena. "The Wound as a Sign: An Encounter with Gina Pane." Translated by Michael Moore. *Flash Art* 92–93 (October–November 1979): 36–38.

Koopmans, Jelle. *Le Théâtre des Exclus au Moyen Age: Hérétiques, Sorcières et Marginaux.* Paris: Imago, 1997.

Kristeva, Julia. *Powers of Horror: An Essay on Abjection.* Translated by Leon S. Roudiez. New York: Columbia University Press, 1982.

Kroll, Jerome, and Bernard Bachrach. *The Mystic Mind: The Psychology of Medieval Mystics and Ascetics.* New York: Routledge, 2005.

Kruger, Loren. *The Drama of South Africa: Plays, Pageants and Publics since 1910.* London: Routledge, 1999.

Kubiak, Anthony. *Stages of Terror: Terrorism, Ideology, and Coercion as Theatre History.* Bloomington: Indiana University Press, 1991.

Lacey, Marc. "Somalia Talks Are Stormy, but They Still Inch Ahead." *New York Times,* 19 January 2003, 1.8.

Lalou, Elizabeth. "Les Tortures dans les Mystères: Théâtre et Réalité." *Medieval English Theatre* 16 (1994): 37–50.

Langholm, Odd. *The Merchant in the Confessional: Trade and Price in the Pre-Reformation Penitential Handbooks.* Leiden: Brill, 2003.

Laqueur, Thomas. *Making Sex: Body and Gender from the Greeks to Freud.* Cambridge, Mass.: Harvard University Press, 1990.

Largier, Niklaus. *In Praise of the Whip.* Translated by Graham Harman. New York: Zone Books, 2007.

Le Goff, Jacques. *"Résistances et Progrès de l'État Monarchique (XIVe–XVe Siècle).* In *L'État Et Les Pouvoirs,* 127–80. *Histoire de la France,* edited by Robert Descimon, Alain Guéry, Jacques Le Goff, Pierre Lévêque, and Pierre Rosanvallon, vol. 2. Paris: Seuil, 1989.

———. *Your Money or Your Life: Economy and Religion in the Middle Ages.* Translated by Patricia Ranum. New York: Zone Books, 1988.

Lester, Elenore. "I Am in Despair About South Africa." *New York Times,* 1 December 1974, D.5.

Lieberman, Matthew D., and Naomi I. Eisenberger. "Conflict and Habit: A Social Cognitive Neuroscience Approach to the Self." In *On Building, Defending, and Regulating the Self: A Psychological Perspective,* edited by Abraham Tesser, Joanne V. Wood, and Diederik A. Stapel, 77–102. New York: Psychology Press, 2005.

Lindberg, David C. *Theories of Vision from Al-Kindi to Kepler.* Chicago: University of Chicago Press, 1976.

Liotard, Philippe. "The Body Jigsaw." *UNESCO Courier*, July/August 2001, 22–25.

Lippard, Lucy. "The Pains and Pleasures of Rebirth: Women's Body Art." *Art in America*, May–June 1976, 73–80.

Lochrie, Karma. "The Language of Transgression: Body, Flesh, and Word in Mystical Discourse." In *Speaking Two Languages: Traditional Disciplines and Contemporary Theory in Medieval Studies*, edited by Allen J. Frantzen, 115–40. Albany: State University of New York Press, 1991.

———. *Margery Kempe and Translations of the Flesh*. Philadelphia: University of Pennsylvania Press, 1991.

Madoff, Steven Henry. "Reflecting on an Ordeal That Was Also Art." *New York Times*, 23 November 2002, E.5.

Mains, Geoffrey. *Urban Aboriginals: A Celebration of Leathersexuality*. San Francisco: Gay Sunshine Press, 1984.

Majno, Guido. *The Healing Hand: Man and Wound in the Ancient World*. Cambridge, Mass.: Harvard University Press, 1975.

Mandela, Nelson. *Long Walk to Freedom*. Boston: Little, Brown & Company, 1994.

Marioni, Tom. "Marina Abramović; Now Playing the Artist." *New York Times*, 13 November 2005, 8.

Markon, Jerry, and Timothy Dwyer. "Jurors Reject Death Penalty for Moussaoui." *Washington Post*, 4 May 2006, A.1.

Marshall, Louise. "Manipulating the Sacred: Image and Plague in Renaissance Italy." *Renaissance Quarterly* 47, no. 3 (1994): 485–532.

Martin, Henry, ed. *Légende de Saint Denis: Reproduction des Miniatures du Manuscrit Original Présenté en 1317 au Roi Philippe le Long*. Paris: Champion, 1908.

Mayer, Jane. "Outsourcing Torture." *New Yorker*, 14 and 21 February 2005, 106–23.

———. "Whatever It Takes: The Politics of the Man Behind '24.'" *New Yorker*, 19 February 2007, http://www.newyorker.com/reporting/2007/02/19/070219fa_fact_mayer (22 July 2008).

McClintock, Anne. "Maid to Order: Commercial S/M and Gender Power." In *Dirty Looks: Women, Pornography, Power*, edited by Pamela Church Gibson and Roma Gibson, 207–31. London: British Film Institute, 1993.

McDonagh, Martin. *The Lieutenant of Inishmore*. Dir. Wilson Milam. Atlantic Theatre Company: New York. 10 March 2006.

———. *The Pillowman*. Dir. John Crowley. Booth Theatre: New York, videotaped by The New York Public Library's Theatre on Film and Tape Archive, 22 June 2005.

———. *The Pillowman*. London: Faber and Faber, 2003.

McGrath, John Edward. "Trusting in Rubber: Performing Boundaries during the AIDS Epidemic." *TDR* 39, no. 2 (1995): 21–39.

McNamara, Jo Ann. "The Need to Give: Suffering and Female Sanctity in the Middle Ages." In *Images of Sainthood in Medieval Europe*, edited by Renate Blumenfeld-Kosinski and Timea Szell, 199–221. Ithaca: Cornell University Press, 1991.

Meixler, Louis. "Iraq Beheadings Appear to Inspire Copycats Elsewhere." *St. Louis Post-Dispatch*, 7 November 2004, A.13.

Melzack, Ronald. "Introduction: The Pain Revolution." In *Handbook of Pain Management*, 1–9. Edinburgh: Churchill Livingston, 2003.

———. "Phantom Limbs." *Scientific American, Special Issue "The Mind"* 7, no. 1 (1997): 84–91.

Melzack, Ronald, and Patrick Wall. *The Challenge of Pain*. 2nd ed. New York: Basic Books, 1983; 2nd updated ed. London: Penguin, 1996.

Merback, Mitchell B. "Living Image of Pity: Mimetic Violence, Peacemaking and Salvific Spectacle in the Flagellant Processions of the Later Middle Ages." In *Images of Medieval Sanctity: Essays in Honour of Gary Dickson*, edited by Debra Higgs Strickland, 135–80. Leiden: E.J. Brill, 2007.

———. *The Thief, the Cross, and the Wheel: Pain and the Spectacle of Punishment in Medieval and Renaissance Europe*. Chicago: University of Chicago Press, 1998.

Meredith, Peter, and John E. Tailby, eds. *The Staging of Religious Drama in Europe in the Later Middle Ages: Texts and Documents in English Translation*. Kalamazoo: Medieval Institute Publications, 1983.

Mills, Léonard R., ed. *Le Mystère de Saint Sébastien*. Geneva: Librairie Droz, 1965.

Mills, Robert. *Suspended Animation: Pain, Pleasure, and Punishment in Medieval Culture*. London: Reaktion, 2005.

Miltner, Wolfgang H.R., and Thomas Weiss. "Cortical Mechanisms of Hypnotic Pain Control." In *Hypnosis and Conscious States: The Cognitive Neuroscience Perspective*, edited by Graham A. Jamieson, 51–66. Oxford: Oxford University Press, 2007.

Morris, David B. *The Culture of Pain*. Berkeley: University of California Press, 1991.

Morris, Katherine J. "Pain, Injury and First/Third-Person Asymmetry." *Philosophy and Phenomenological Research* 56, no. 1 (1996): 125–36.

Morrison, India, and Paul E. Downing. "Organization of Felt and Seen Pain Responses in Anterior Cingulate Cortex." *NeuroImage* 37 (2007): 642–51.

Muchembled, Robert. *Le Temps des Supplices: De L'Obéissance sous les Rois Absolus, XVe–XVIIIe Siècle*. Paris: A. Colin, 1992.

Mueller, Roswitha. *Valie Export: Fragments of the Imagination*. Bloomington: Indiana University Press, 1994.

Muir, Lynette. "The Saint Play in Medieval France." In *The Saint Play in Medieval Europe*, edited by Clifford Davidson, 123–80. Kalamazoo: Medieval Institute, 1986.

Murphy, Caryle, and Khalid Saffar. "Actors in the Insurgency Are Reluctant TV Stars; Terror Suspects Grilled, Mocked on Hit Iraqi Show." *Washington Post*, 5 April 2005, A.18.

Musafar, Fakir. *Dances Sacred and Profane.* VHS. Dir. by Dan Jury and Mark Jury. 1987; USA: Gorgon Video, 1993.

Newbigin, Nerida. "Agata, Apollonia and Other Martyred Virgins: Did Florentines Really See These Plays Performed?" *European Medieval Drama* 1 (1997): 175–97.

Nicholas, David. *The Evolution of the Medieval World: Society, Government and Thought in Europe, 312–1500.* London: Longman, 1992.

———. *Urban Europe, 1100–1700.* New York: Palgrave Macmillan, 2003.

Nussbaum, Martha Craven. *Upheavals of Thought: The Intelligence of Emotions.* Cambridge: Cambridge University Press, 2001.

O'Dell, Kathy. *Contract with the Skin: Masochism, Performance Art, and the 1970s.* Minneapolis: University of Minnesota Press, 1998.

———. "Fluxus Feminus." *TDR* 41, no. 1 (1997): 43–60.

Onyango-Obbo, Charles. "Poor in Money, but Even Poorer in Democracy." *New York Times*, 12 July 2003, A.11.

Partlow, Joshua. "Guard at Hanging Blamed for Covert Video of Hussein." *Washington Post*, 4 January 2007, A.14.

Patraka, Vivian. *Spectacular Suffering: Theatre, Fascism, and the Holocaust.* Bloomington: Indiana University Press, 1999.

Pejic, Bojana. "Being-in-the-Body: On the Spiritual in Marina Abramović's Art." In *Marina Abramović*, edited by Friedrich Meschede, 25–38. Stuttgart: Edition Cantz, 1993.

Peters, Edward. *Torture.* Expanded ed. Philadelphia: University of Pennsylvania Press, 1996.

Petit de Julleville, Louis. *Histoire du Théâtre en France: Les Mystères.* Vol. 2. Paris: Hachette, 1880.

Phillips, J.R.S. *The Medieval Expansion of Europe.* 2nd ed. Oxford: Clarendon Press, 1998.

Pitts, Victoria. *In the Flesh: The Cultural Politics of Body Modification.* New York: Palgrave Macmillan, 2003.

Plesch, Véronique. "Etalage Complaisant? The Torments of Christ in French Passion Plays." *Comparative Drama* 28, no. 4 (1994): 460–85.

———. "Killed by Words: Grotesque Verbal Violence and Tragic Atonement in French Passion Plays." *Comparative Drama* 33, no. 1 (1999): 22–53.

Preston, Stephanie D., and Frans B.M. de Waal. "Empathy: Its Ultimate and Proximate Bases." *Behavioral and Brain Sciences* 25 (2002): 1–72.

Prkachin, Kenneth M. "The Consistency of Facial Expressions of Pain: A Comparison across Modalities." In *What the Face Reveals: Basic and Applied Studies of Spontaneous Expression Using the Facial Action Coding System (FACS)*, edited by Paul Ekman and Erika L. Rosenberg, 181–97. New York: Oxford University Press, 1997.

Puppi, Lionello. *Torment in Art: Pain, Violence, and Martyrdom.* Translated by Jeremy Scott. New York: Rizzoli, 1991.
Puri, Madhu. "The Originals." *New York Times*, 26 February 2006.
Ramachandran, V.S., and Sandra Blakeslee. *Phantoms in the Brain: Probing the Mysteries of the Human Mind.* New York: William Morrow, 1998.
Reik, Theodor. "Masochism in Modern Man." In *Of Love and Lust: On the Psychoanalysis of Romantic and Sexual Emotions*, 206–54. New York: Farrar, Straus & Giroux, 1949; reprint 1984.
Rey, Roselyne. *The History of Pain.* Translated by Louise Elliott Wallace, J.A. Cadden and S.W. Cadden. Cambridge, Mass.: Harvard University Press, 1995.
Reynolds, Susan. "The Historiography of the Medieval State." In *Companion to Historiography*, edited by Michael Bentley, 117–38. London: Routledge, 1997.
Rich, Frank. "At Last, 9/11 Has Its Own Musical." *New York Times*, 2 May 2004, 2.1.
———. "It Was the Porn That Made Them Do It." *New York Times*, 30 May 2004, 2.1, 16.
Rocca, Julius. *Galen on the Brain: Anatomical Knowledge and Physiological Speculation in the Second Century AD.* Leiden: Brill, 2003.
Román, David. *Acts of Intervention: Performance, Gay Culture, and AIDS.* Bloomington: Indiana University Press, 1998.
Rosenwein, Barbara H., and Lester K. Little. "Social Meaning in the Monastic and Mendicant Spiritualities." *Past and Present* 63 (1974): 4–32.
Roth, Moira. *The Amazing Decade: Women in Performance Art, 1970–1980.* Los Angeles: Astro Artz, 1983.
Roux, Simone. *Paris in the Middle Ages.* Translated by Jo Ann McNamara. Philadelphia: University of Pennsylvania Press, 2009.
Ruf, Beatrix, and Markus Landert. *Marina Abramović: Double Edge: Kunstmuseum Des Kantons Thurgau, Kartause Ittingen, 8 Oktober 1995–28 April 1996.* Sulgen (Switzerland): Verlag Niggli, 1996.
Runnalls, Graham A. "The Catalogue of the Tours Book-Seller and Antoine Vérard." *Pluteus* 2 (1984): 163–74.
———. "The Catalogue of the Tours Book-Seller and Late Medieval French Drama." In *Etudes Sur Les Mystères*, Chapter 18. Paris: Champion, 1998.
———, ed. *Le Cycle de Mystères des Premiers Martyrs: Du Manuscrit 1131 de la Bibliotheque Sainte-Geneviève.* Geneva: Droz, 1976.
———. "Drama and Community in Late Medieval Paris." In *Drama and Community: People and Plays in Medieval Europe*, edited by Alan Hindley, 18–33. Turnhout, Belgium: Brepols, 1999.
———. "Jean Fouquet's 'Martyrdom of St. Apollonia' and the Medieval French Stage." *Medieval English Theatre* 19 (1997): 81–100.
Sachs, Albie. *Justice in South Africa.* Berkeley: University of California Press, 1973.

Sáez, Nacunan. "Torture: A Discourse on Practice." In *Tattoo, Torture, Mutilation, and Adornment: The Denaturalization of the Body in Culture and Text*, edited by Frances E. Mascia-Lees and Patricia Sharpe, 126–44. Albany: State University of New York Press, 1992.

Sarat, Austin. "Killling Me Softly: Capital Punishment and the Technologies for Taking Life." In *Pain, Death, and the Law*, edited by Austin Sarat, 43–70. Ann Arbor: University of Michigan Press, 2001.

Saunders, Graham. *"Love Me or Kill Me": Sarah Kane and the Theatre of Extremes*. Manchester: Manchester University Press, 2002.

———. "'Out Vile Jelly': Sarah Kane's 'Blasted' and Shakespeare's 'King Lear.'" *Theatre Quarterly* 20, no. 1 (2004): 69–78.

Savran, David. *Taking It Like a Man: White Masculinity, Masochism, and Contemporary American Culture*. Princeton: Princeton University Press, 1998.

Scarry, Elaine. *The Body in Pain: The Making and Unmaking of the World*. New York: Oxford University Press, 1985.

Schimmel, Paul. "Leap into the Void: Performance and the Object." In *Out of Actions: Between Performance and the Object 1949–1979*, edited by Russell Ferguson, 17–120. New York: Thames and Hudson, 1998.

Schneemann, Carolee. *More Than Meat Joy: Complete Performance Works and Selected Writings*. Edited by Bruce McPherson. New Paltz, N.Y.: Documentext, 1979.

Sellar, Tom. "Truth and Dare: Sarah Kane's *Blasted*." *Theater* 27, no. 1 (1996): 29–34.

Sennewaldt, Clotilde, ed. *Miracles De Madame Sainte Geneviève*. Frankfort a. main: Moritz Dieterweg, 1937.

Serrano, Richard A. "Group Says U.S. Sent up to 150 to Possible Torture Sites." *Los Angeles Times*, 23 April 2005, A.4.

Seubert, Bernard James, ed. *Le Geu Saint Denis du Manuscrit 1131 de la Bibliothèque Sainte-Geneviève de Paris*. Geneva: Librairie Droz, 1974.

Shanker, Thom. "Television Review; The Bad Old Days of Yugoslavia's Fallen Dictator." *New York Times*, 26 August 2003, E.7.

Shirley, Janet, ed. and trans. *A Parisian Journal*. Oxford: Clarendon, 1968.

Shoemaker, Karl. "The Problem of Pain in Punishment: Historical Perspectives." In *Pain, Death, and the Law*, edited by Austin Sarat, 15–41. Ann Arbor: University of Michigan Press, 2001.

Silverman, Lisa. *Tortured Subjects: Pain, Truth, and the Body in Early Modern France*. Chicago: University of Chicago Press, 2001.

Singer, Annabelle. "Don't Want to Be This: The Elusive Sarah Kane." *TDR* 48, no. 2 (2004): 139–71.

Singer, Tania, Ben Seymour, John O'Doherty, Holger Kaube, Raymond J. Dolan, and Chris D. Firth. "Empathy for Pain Involves the Affective but Not Sensory Components of Pain." *Science* 303, no. 5661 (2004): 1157–62.

Siraisi, Nancy G. *Medieval and Early Renaissance Medicine*. Chicago: University of Chicago Press, 1990.

Smith, Alex Duval. "Game for a Lash? One Minute Madonna Was in Rubber and the Next a Spanking Good Time Was Being Had in Suburban Bedrooms Everywhere. So Why Has S&M Moved into the Mainstream So Fast? We Visit the Europerve Ball in Amsterdam and Find That the Brits Are Undisputed Kings of Kinkiness." *Guardian*, 16 December 1994.

Sondheim, Stephen. *Assassins*. Book by John Weidman. Dir. Joe Mantello. Musical staging by Jonathan Butterel. Roundabout Theatre Company, Studio 54: New York, videotaped by the New York Public Library's Theatre on Film and Tape Archive, 9 June 2004.

Sontag, Susan. *Regarding the Pain of Others*. New York: Farrar, Strauss, and Giroux, 2003.

———. "Regarding the Torture of Others." *New York Times Magazine*, 23 May 2004, 25–29, 42.

Spector, Nancy. "Marina Abramović Interviewed." In *Marina Abramović: Seven Easy Pieces*, 13–31. Milan: Edizioni Charta, 2007.

Spierenburg, Petrus Cornelis (Pieter). *The Spectacle of Suffering: Executions and the Evolution of Repression*. Cambridge: Cambridge University Press, 1984.

Spivey, Nigel. "Christ and the Art of Agony." *History Today* 49, no. 8 (1999): 16–23.

———. *Enduring Creation: Art, Pain, and Fortitude*. Berkeley: University of California Press, 2001.

Stephano, Effie, and Gina Pane. "Performance of Concern." *Art and Artists* 8 (April 1973): 20–27.

Stephenson, Heidi, and Natasha Langridge. *Rage and Reason: Women Playwrights on Playwriting*. London: Methuen, 1997.

Stiles, Kristine. "Between Water and Stone: Fluxus Performance: A Metaphysics of Acts." In *In the Spirit of Fluxus*, edited by Janet Jenkins, 64–95. Minneapolis: Walker Art Center, 1993

———. "Corpora Vilia, VALIE EXPORT's Body." In *Ob/De+Con(Struction)*, edited by Robert Fleck, 16–33. Philadelphia: Moore College of Art and Design, 1999.

———. "Inside/Outside: 'Balancing between a Dusthole and Eternity.'" In *Body and the East: From the 1960s to the Present*, edited by Zdenka Badovinac, 19–30. Cambridge, Mass.: MIT Press, 1998.

———. "Uncorrupted Joy: International Art Actions." In *Out of Actions: Between Performance and the Object 1949–1979*, edited by Russell Ferguson, 227–329. New York: Thames and Hudson, 1998.

Strong, Marilee. *A Bright Red Scream: Self-Mutilation and the Language of Pain*. New York: Viking, 1998.

Strong, Roy. *Art and Power: Renaissance Festivals 1450–1650*. Woodbridge: Boydell Press, 1984.

Symes, Carol. *A Common Stage: Theater and Public Life in Medieval Arras*. Ithaca: Cornell University Press, 2007.

Taylor, Craig. *Debating the Hundred Years War: Pour ce que Plusieurs (La Loy Salicque) and a Declaration of the Trew and Dewe Title of Henry VIII*. Cambridge: Cambridge University Press, 2006.

Taylor, Diana. *Theatre of Crisis: Drama and Politics in Latin America*. Lexington: University of Kentucky Press, 1991.

Taylor, Victor E. "Contracting Masochism." In *One Hundred Years of Masochism: Literary Texts, Social and Cultural Contexts*, edited by Michael C. Finke and Carl Niekerk, 53–69. Amsterdam: Rodopi, 2000.

"Teachers Disciplined for Showing Beheading." *New York Times*, 24 May 2004, A.21.

Thompson, Guy Llewelyn. *Paris and Its People under English Rule: The Anglo-Burgundian Regime, 1420–1436*. Oxford: Clarendon, 1991.

Truscott, Carol. "S/M: Some Questions and a Few Answers." In *Leatherfolk: Radical Sex, People, Politics, and Practice*, 3rd ed., edited by Mark Thompson, 15–36. Los Angeles: Daedalus, 2004.

"Two Black Actors to Be Tried for Transkei Remarks." *New York Times*, 16 October 1976, 3.

Vale, Malcom. "Aristocratic Violence: Trial by Battle in the Later Middle Ages." In *Violence in Medieval Society*, edited by Richard W. Kaeuper, 159–81. Rochester: Boydell Press, 2000.

Vandermeersch, Patrick. *La Chair de la Passion: Une Histoire de la Foi: La Flagellation*. Paris: Le Cerf, 2002.

Volkmer, Ingrid. "The Global Network Society and the Global Public Sphere." *development* 46, no. 1 (2003): 9–16.

Wahls, Robert. "Tony around the World." *Sunday News*, 20 April 1975, 8.

Wakin, Daniel J. "A Season of Faith and a Film: Gibson's Movie Goes to Church." *New York Times*, 9 April 2004, B.1.

Walder, Dennis. *Athol Fugard*. New York: Grove Press, 1985.

Wall, Patrick. *Pain: The Science of Suffering*. New York: Columbia University Press, 2002.

Walsh, Barent W., and Paul M. Rosen. *Self-Mutilation: Theory, Research, and Treatment*. New York: Guilford, 1988.

Warr, Tracey, ed. *The Artist's Body*. London: Phaidon, 2000.

Watson, Ariel. "Performing Mental Illness: Anxious Metatheatre and the Therapy Trope." Paper presented at the American Society for Theatre Research, Chicago, 17 November 2006.

Weber, Bruce. "The Spirit Triumphs in a South African Prison." *New York Times*, 3 April 2003, E.1.

Welldon, Estela V. *Sadomasochism*. Cambridge: Icon, 2002.

Wescott, James. "Marina Abramović's *The House with the Ocean View*: The View of the House from Some Drops in the Ocean." *TDR* 47, no. 3 (2003): 129–36.

Wilson, August. *Joe Turner's Come and Gone*. Dir. Bartlett Sher. Perf. Chad L. Coleman. Lincoln Center Theater at the Belasco Theatre: New York. 3 June 2009.

Wogan-Browne, Jocelyn. "Saints' Lives and the Female Reader." *Forum for Modern Language Studies* 27 (1991): 314–32.
Woolf, Virginia. "On Being Ill" (1930). In *Collected Essays*, 193–203. New York: Harcourt, Brace & World, 1967.
Worthen, Hana, and W.B. Worthen. "*The Pillowman* and the Ethics of Allegory." *Modern Drama* 49, no. 2 (2006): 155–73.
Wycliff, Don. "Gruesome Pictures from within the Gates of Hell." *Chicago Tribune*, 13 May 2004, 27.
York, William Henry. "Experience and Theory in Medical Practice during the Later Middle Ages: Valesco de Tarenta (Fl. 1382–1426) at the Court of Foix." Ph.D. Diss., Johns Hopkins University, 2003.

Index

Note: Italicized page numbers reference figures.

24 (television series), 38
4.48 Psychosis (Kane), 140, 142–44, 159
9/11, 7, 69, 75

abjection, 11, 132–34, 154
  mysticism and, 97
  in work of Sarah Kane, 139–43
Abramović, Marina, 10, 80–90, 115, 161
  Art Must Be Beautiful. Artist Must Be Beautiful, 83
  Biography, 82
  Entering the Other Side, 89
  Expansion in Space, 86
  feminist theory in work of, 83–89
  Freeing the Body, 83
  Freeing the Memory, 83
  Freeing the Voice, 83
  House with the Ocean View, The, 88, 89
  Lips of Thomas, The, 10, *77*, 80, 81, 82, 83, 84, 85, 86, 88, 90
  Lovers, The/Great Wall Walk, 87
  Nightsea Crossing, 86
  Role Exchange, 83
  Seven Easy Pieces, 80, 85, 89, 90, 101
Abu Ghraib, 4, 5, 37, 114, 129
Acconci, Vito, 81
Action Pants: Genital Panic (EXPORT), 81
Afghanistan, 37, 114
Al Jazeera, 3
Al Qaeda, 158

Anger, Kenneth, 119
Antigone (Sophocles), 29
  quoted in *The Island*, 29–30, 34
Anzieu, Didier, 18, 125
Apollonia, Saint, 20, 90–93, 151
Appadurai, Arjun, 38
Aristotle, 21, 44
  De Anima, 43
  Art Must Be Beautiful. Artist Must Be Beautiful (Abramović), 83
Artaud, Antonin, 22, 144
  Theatre of Cruelty, 83
Asad, Talal, 121
Assassins (Sondheim), 67
  2004 revival, 75
Athey, Ron, 10, 105, 113–16, 124–27, 130, 161
  Deliverance, 114, 127
  Four Scenes from a Harsh Life, 113
  Incorruptible Flesh (Perpetual Wound), 129
  Judas Cradle, 10, *103*, 114, 127, 129
  Martyrs and Saints, 114, 124
  Saint Sebastian influences, 114
  Solar Anus, 114, 127
Augustine, Saint, 96
Autumn of the Middle Ages, The (Huizinga), 2
Avicenna, 21, 109
Aydede, Murat, 17

Bachrach, Bernard, 80, 97–98
Bacon, Roger, 44–45

Bakhtin, M.M., 79, 100, 149, 152, 164
Barker, Sheila, 106, 107, 110, 112
Basic Instinct (film), 120
Bataille, George, 114
Beaune, Colette, 62, 65
Beauty Queen of Leenane, The (McDonagh), 73
Becker, Judith, 87
Beckett, Samuel, 140
  Happy Days, 90
Bed Piece (Burden), 117
Benjamin, Walter, 160, 161
Berg, Nicholas, 4, 74
Bernard of Clairvaux, 96
Bersani, Leo, 119, 120, 121
Beuys, Joseph, 81, 85
Beyond the Mirror, 1, 66–67, 158
Bidgood, James
  Pink Narcissus, 114
Biernoff, Suzannah, 43–45, 96
Bin Laden, Osama, 67
Biography (Abramović), 82
Birney, Reed, *131*, 134
Black Death, 6, 22, 51, 153
Blaine, David, 161
Blasted (Kane), 11, *131*, 133–41, 142–43, 158, 162
Blessing, Jennifer, 80
Bodnar, Richard, 110
body art, 10, 12, 79, 82–86, 100–101, 105, 113–27, *See also* pain, self-inflicted
  gender issues, 83–90, 113–27
Body in Pain, The (Scarry), 16
body modification, 121–22, 125–27
Body Pressure (Naumann), 81, 89
Boltanski, Luc, 8, 27, 33–38, *See also* communities of sentiment; politics of pity
  Distant Suffering, 8
Boly, Mélanie, 87
Bond, Edward, 136
  Saved, 136

Boyer, Peter, 127
Brando, Marlon, 116, 119, 128
Brook, Peter, 27
Brooklyn Academy of Music, 1, 27
Buck-Morss, Susan, 160, 161
Burden, Chris, 81, 82, 116, 117–18, 123, 129, 160
  Bed Piece, 117
  Shoot, 117, 118
  Trans-fixed, 81
Burgundy, Duke of, 51–52
Bush, George W., 4, 6, 37, 158
  administration, 4, 38, 115
Butler, Judith, 119
Butler, Kateri, 114
Bynum, Carolyn Walker, 97

Caciola, Nancy, 99
Callahan, Leslie Abend, 91, 100
Campbell, Alyson, 137, 139
Campbell, Joseph, 122
Cancelmi, Louis, *131*, 137
capital punishment, 68–71
Carney, Sean, 135, 137, 140
Carruthers, Mary, 145
Cazelles, Brigitte, 63, 92
Charles IV, 51
Charles V, 51
Charles VI, 40, 51, 52, 54, 55, 62, 107, 164
Charles VII, 40, 52, 55, 60, 93, 153
Charles of Anjou, 99
Chesterman, Sarah, 32
Civilizing Process, The (Elias), 2
Cixous, Hélène, 84
Clark, Robert L.A., 47
Cleansed (Kane), 138
Clement, Pope, 63
Clemente, Chiara, 115
Clinton, Bill, 38
Club Fuck, 124
cognitive studies, 67–68, 132–33
Cohen, Esther, 52, 53, 57

Index   221

communities of sentiment, 2, 38–39, 46–48, 155–57, *See also* Boltanski, Luc
compassion, 8, 9, 27, 41–43, 48, 100–101, 110, 128–29, 157, 165, *See also* empathy; pity; politics of pity; sympathy
Conditioning, The (Pane), 81, 85
Confessions of a Mask (Mishima), 105
Conquergood, Dwight, 69–70, 75
Conroy, John, 36
Contemporary Arts Center (Cincinnati), 120
Contra sectum flagellantium (Gerson), 109
Contraction (Pane), 85
Cooper, Dennis, 123, 124
Cosmopolitan, 120
Craig, A.D., 15
Crave (Kane), 139
Cripple of Inishman, The (McDonagh), 73
Crisco, 1, *104*
Crudup, Billy, *49*, 66
cultural theory, 32–39, 50, 118–22, 159–62
Cut Piece (Ono), 83
cutting, 1, 125–26

Dances Sacred and Profane (film), 122
Davidson, Clifford, 42
De Anima (Aristotle), 43
de Waal, Frans, 31
Dead Man Walking School Project, 67
Dean, James, 116
decapitation, 1, 61–62, 65, 74, 147, 156, 163
Deleuze, Gilles, 119
Deliverance (Athey), 114, 127
Democritus, 21
Denis, Saint, 9, *26*, 40, *49*, *50*, 61, 62, 141, 147, 151, 162
  head as relic, 61–62
des Essarts, Pierre, 54, 58–60

Descartes, Réné, 11, 13, 158
Despars, Jacques, 109
Dick, Kirby
  Sick: The Life and Death of Bob Flanagan, Super-Masochist, 123, 124
Diller, Hans-Jurgen, 41
Distant Suffering (Boltanski), 8
Dupras, Elyse, 163
Duru, Welcome, 35

Eagleton, Terry, 128
Edson, Margaret
  Wit, 19–20
Edward II, 94
Edward III, 51, 94
Eisenberger, Naomi, 142
Elias, Norbert
  Civilizing Process, The, 2
Elliott, Dyan, 96–100, 165
Ellis, Perry, 120
empathy, 8, 27, 30–32, 33, 41, 45–46, 72, 121, 134, 155–58, 162, *See also* compassion; pity; politics of pity; sympathy
Enders, Jody, 58, 59
endorphins, 12, 119
England, Lynndie, 4
Entering the Other Side (Abramović), 89
Erasistratus, 22
Eros/ion (EXPORT), 84
execution, 4, 9, 22, 50–61
  in medieval Paris, 52–60
  of Saint Denis, 62
  of saints, 42
  staged
    in *Pillowman, The* (McDonagh), 66–67
  medieval, 60
  state-sponsored, 68–71
Expansion in Space (Abramović), 86
EXPORT, VALIE, 81, 84
  Action Pants: Genital Panic, 81
  Eros/ion, 84

Fakir Musafar, 115, 121–22, 124, 125, 127, 129, 165, See also *Dances Sacred and Profane*; *Modern Primitives*
Favazza, Armando, 126
Faymonville, Marie-Elisabeth, 87
feminist theory, 10, 83–85, 91–93, 100–101
Finley, Karen, 101
flagellants, 107–109, 110, 111–13, 130
flagellation
  erotic, 112–13
  gender and, 108–109, 111–13
Flanagan, Bob, 115, 121, 122–24, 125
  Pain Journal, 123
  You Always Hurt the One You Love, 123
  Visiting Hours, 123
Foucault, Michel, 50, 119
Fouquet, Jean, 79, 90, 91, 100
  Martyrdom of Saint Apollonia, The, 78, 90
Four Scenes from a Harsh Life (Athey), 113
Francis of Assisi, 43, 111
Freeing the Body (Abramović), 83
Freeing the Memory (Abramović), 83
Freeing the Voice (Abramović), 83
Fugard, Athol, 27, 34, See also *Island, The*; *Sizwe Banzi is Dead*

Galen, 21, 22, 95–96
  humors, theory of, 50–51
Gargantua and Pantagruel (Rabelais), 152
Gatewood, Charles, 122
Gaultier, Jean-Paul, 120
Geary, Patrick, 61
gender
  asceticism and, 96–98
  body art and, 83–90, 113–28
  feminism and, 77–101
  flagellation and, 108–109, 111–13

homosexuality and, 117–22, 124–27
martyrdom and, 90–8
masculinity and, 103–30
medieval economics and, 94–95
medieval medicine and, 95–96
mysticism and, 79–80, 91–94
S/M and, 118–24
saint plays and, 91–94
in work of Bob Flanagan, 122–24
in work of Marina Abramović, 83–90
in work of Ron Athey, 105, 124–27
Gerson, Jean, 99
  Contra sectum flagellantium, 109
Geu Saint Denis, Le, 6, 9, *26*, 39–42, 48, *50*, 61–66, 72, 76, 144, 148, 149, 162–63
  humor, 63–66
  vertical hierarchies, 62–66
Gibson, Mel, 127–29
  Mad Max (film), 127
  Passion of the Christ, The (film), 127
  Road Warrior (film), 127
Giovanni del Biondo, 105, 106
  Martyrdom of Saint Sebastian and Scenes from His Life, *104*
Glucklich, Ariel, 80
Goldberg, RoseLee, 114
Goldblum, Jeff, *49*, 71
Golden Legend (Jacobus de Voragine), 91, 105, 106
Good, Byron, 19
Grosseteste, Robert, 44
grotesque, the, 149–53
  in *Mystère de Saint Sébastien, Le*, 10, 132, 144–46, 149–53
Grotowski, Jerzy, 34, 83, 88
Guantánamo, 37, 69, 114
Guantánamo (play), 5
Guggenheim Museum, 1, 82, 86, 90, 115
Güzeldere, Güven, 17

Habermas, Jürgen, 37, 47
Hallelujah! Ron Athey: A Story of Deliverance (Saalfield), 113, 121
Happy Days (Beckett), 90
Hebb, Donald O., 14
Helms, Jesse, 119
Henry V, 52, 53
Henry VI, 52, 53
Herophilus, 22
Hof, Wim, 161
House with the Ocean View, The (Abramović), 88, 89
How to Explain Pictures to a Dead Hare (Beuys), 81, 85
Huizinga, Johannes
 Autumn of the Middle Ages, The, 2
Human Rights Watch, 5
humor
 in *Blasted* (Kane), 11, 132, 140–41
 medieval, 41–42, 63–66, 149–53
 in *Phaedra's Love* (Kane), 143–44
 in work of Bob Flanagan, 123
humors, 50–51, 95–96
Hundred Years' War, 1, 3, 6, 8, 40, 51, 66, 93, 94, 153
Huppert, Isabelle, 1, 140, 159
Hussein, Saddam, 3, 69

imitatio Christi, 6, 39, 42–43, 45, 60–61, 108, 157, 161
 gender differentiation, 96
Innocent III, Pope, 62
Interior Scroll (Schneemann), 84
International Association for the Study of Pain, 17
Iraq, 4, 5, 69, 74, 114, 159
Ireland, Marin, *131*, 134
Irigaray, Luce, 84
Island, The (Fugard, Kani, Ntshona), 9, 25, 27–30, 32–33, 158
 Antigone (Sophocles) quotation, 29–30
Ivanek, Zeljko, *49*, 72

Jackson, Jean, 18
Jacobus de Voragine, 105
Jesurun, John, 114
Joan of Arc, 52, 99
Joe Turner's Come and Gone (Wilson), 159
John Paul II, Pope, 128–29
Johnson, Dominic, 115, 127
Johnson, Mark, 132
Jones, Amelia, 100, 114, 116, 118
jouissance, 133–34, 141–42, 165–66
Judas Cradle (Athey), 10, *103*, 114, 127
Juno, Andrea
 Modern Primitives, 122
Jury, Dan and Mark
 Dances Sacred and Profane (film), 122

Kane, Sarah, 132–44, 154, 162
 4.48 Psychosis, 140, 142–44, 159
 Blasted, 11, *131*, 133–41, 142–43, 158, 162
 Cleansed, 138
 Crave, 139
 humor in dramatic works, 142–44
 Phaedra's Love, 138, 143–44
Kani, John, 9, *25*, 27–30, See also *Island, The*; *Sizwe Banzi is Dead*
Kaprow, Allan, 116
Karras, Ruth, 113
Kauffman, Linda, 123
Kaufman-Osborn, Timothy, 71
Kay, Sarah, 92
Kayser, Wolfgang, 145
Klein, Yves, 84, 116
Kleinman, Arthur, 18
Koestenbaum, Wayne, 114
Koopmans, Jelle, 62, 66, 145
Krauthammer, Charles, 5
Kristeva, Julia, 133, 143
Kroll, Jerome, 80, 97–98

Kubiak, Anthony
  Stages of Terror, 5
Kubota, Shikego
  Vagina Painting, 83–84

Lalou, Elizabeth, 42, 93
Laureys, Steven, 87
Le Geu Saint Denis, See *Geu Saint Denis, Le*
Le Mystère de Saint Sébastien, See *Mystère de Saint Sébastien, Le*
Liebermann, Matthew, 142
Lieutenant of Inishmore, The (McDonagh), 32, 68, 73, 74, 158
Liotard, Philippe, 121
Lips of Thomas, The (Abramović), 10, 77, 80, 81, 82, 83, 84, 85, 86, 88, 90
Little, Lester, 111
Lochrie, Karma, 96
Loomis, Ronald, *See* Fakir Musafar
Louis IX, 51
Lovers, The/Great Wall Walk (Abramović), 87

Machinal (Treadwell), 67
Mad Max (film), 127
Madonna, 120
Mangolte, Babette
  Seven Easy Pieces (film), 77, 115
Manzoni, Piero, 116
Mapplethorpe, Robert, 4, 119, 120
Marioni, Tom, 82
Marshall, Louise, 106, 110
martyrdom, 2, 9, 10, 22, 42–43, *See also* Apollonia; Denis; Sebastian
  gender and, 90–95
Martyrdom of Saint Apollonia, The (Fouquet), 10, 78, 90
Martyrdom of Saint Sebastian and Scenes from His Life (Giovanni del Biondo), 10, 104, 105
Martyrs and Saints (Athey), 114, 124

McDonagh, Martin, 162
  Beauty Queen of Leenane, The, 73
  Cripple of Inishman, The, 73
  Lieutenant of Inishmore, The, 32, 68, 73, 74, 158
  Pillowman, The, 9, 49, 50, 71–76, 158
McGill Pain Questionnaire, 15, 21
McNamara, Jo Ann, 97
medical anthropology, 18–19
medicine
  gender and, 95–96
  history, 43–46, 50–51, 95–96, 106–107
medieval
  execution, 52–60
  history, 50–52
  humor, 41–42, 63–66, 149–53
  urban culture, 46–47, 111
  vision theories, 43–45
Melzack, Ronald, 12–15, 18, 28, 67
Merback, Mitchell, 43, 53, 58, 109, 112
Meredith, Peter, 90
Mills, Léonard, 146, 149
Mills, Robert, 110
Miltner, Wolfgang H.R., 87
Mishima, Yukio
  Confessions of a Mask, 105
Modern Primitives (Juno, Vale), 122
Molinier, Pierre, 114
Montaigu, Jean de, 54
Montana, Claude, 120
Monty Python and the Holy Grail, 23
Morrison, India, 32
Mueller, Roswitha, 84
Mystère de Saint Sébastien, Le, 6, 132, 144–53, 162–64
  elements of the grotesque, 10, 132, 144–46, 149–53
  humor 149–53
  vertical hierarchies, 144–46

mysticism, 79–80, 96–101, 109, 112–13, 129, 156–57, 161
   gender and, 79–80
   in work of Marina Abramović, 86–89

Namuth, Hans, 116
National Endowment for the Arts, 101, 113, 120
Naumann, Bruce, 81
Body Pressure, 81, 89
neuroscience, 11–15, 16–17, 20, 30–32, 43, 48, 67–68, 80, 86–87, 110–11, 141–42, 165–66
New York Times, 3, 4, 36, 82
T Magazine, 161
Newbigin, Nerida, 93
Nightsea Crossing (Abramović), 86
Novick, Rebecca, 122
Ntshinga, Norman, 35
Ntshona, Winston, 9, 25, 27–30, See also *Island, The*; *Sizwe Banzi is Dead*
Nussbaum, Martha, 30–31, 68

O'Dell, Kathy, 118
Obrist, Hans Ulrich, 88
One Life to Live (TV soap opera), 120
Ono, Yoko, 83
Orlan, 89, 115
Orléans, Duke of, 51
Our City Dreams (Clemente), 115

Paik, Nam June, 123
pain
   biomedical perspectives, 5–6, 11, 43–45
   communication of, 2, 16–20, 27–29, 155
   definitions, 11–15
   gender and, 9–10
   history of, 20–23, 98–99, 121–23
   philosophy and, 16–18
   science of, 11–15
   self-inflicted, 1, 2, 9, 74, 84, 125, 134, 159
   theories, 16–20
   medieval, 20–23
   Scarry, Elaine, 16
   Sontag, Susan, 69
Pain Journal (Flanagan), 123
Pane, Gina, 81, 84, 85, 115, 160
   Conditioning, The, 81, 85
   Contraction, 85
   Rejection, 85
   Self-Portrait(s), 85
Paparazzi (film), 128
Parisian Journal, 50, 53–59, 75, 107, 153, 164
Parker, Sarah Jessica, 89
Parsifal (Wagner), 114
Passion of the Christ, The (film), 127
Pearl, Daniel, 4
Peters, Edward, 37
Petit de Julleville, Louis, 91, 92
Phaedra's Love (Kane), 138, 143–44
Philbrick, Jane, 90, 92
Philip IV, 94
Philip VI, 51, 109
Philoctetes (Sophocles), 114
Pillowman, The (McDonagh), 9, 49, 50, 71–76, 158
Pink Narcissus (Bidgood), 114
Pitts, Victoria, 126
pity, 33, 41, 69, 129, 141, 143, 147, 155–58, 158, See also compassion; empathy; politics of pity; sympathy
Plato, 21, 44
Plesch, Véronique, 42, 145
pneuma, 43–45, 50–51, 66, 95–96
politics of pity, 9, 27, 34–38, 41, 47, 155–56, 165–66, See also Boltanski, Luc
Pollock, Jackson, 84, 116, 118
Preston, Stephanie, 31
Pulp Fiction (Tarantino), 2

226   Index

queer theory, 113–15, 116–22

Rabelais, François, 100
   Gargantua and Pantagruel, 152
Ramanchandran, V.S., 14
Reagan, Ronald, 67
Records of Early English Drama
   (REED), 91
Redbook, 120
Régy, Claude, 140
Rejection (Pane), 85
Rey, Roselyne, 20
Rich, Frank, 4, 75
Road Warrior (film), 127
Role Exchange (Abramović), 83
Rose, Sheree, 122–23
Rosenwein, Barbara, 111
Roux, Simone, 45–46, 95
Runnalls, Graham, 40, 63, 92

S/M culture, 4, 116–22
Saalfield, Catherine Gund
   *Hallelujah! Ron Athey: A Story of
   Deliverance*, 113, 121
Sacher-Masoch, Leopold von
   Venus in Furs, 119
saint plays, 6, 8, 11, 22, 27, 40–42, 47,
   60, 76, 79
   male vs. female protagonists,
   91–94
Saints, *See* Apollonia, Denis, Sebastian
Sarat, Austin, 68
Saved (Bond), 136
Savran, David, 116–17, 120–21, 127
Scalia, Antonin, 38
Scarry, Elaine, 34
   Body in Pain, The, 16
Schiavo, Terri, 6
Schneemann, Carolee, 84, 101
   Interior Scroll, 84
Scorpio Rising (Anger), 119
Sebastian, Saint, *104*, 105–107, 114,
   129–30, *132*, 146–51, 162
Seedbed (Acconci), 81

self-harm, 122–26
   cutting, 1, 97, 125–26
Self-Portrait(s) (Pane), 85
Seven Easy Pieces (Abramović), 80, 85,
   89, 90, 101
Seven Easy Pieces (Mangolte: film), *77*, 115
Sex in the City, 89
Shoot (Burden), 117, 118
*Sick: The Life and Death of Bob
   Flanagan, Super-Masochist*
   (Dick), 123, 124
Silverman, Kaja, 126
Singer, Annabelle, 136
Singer, Tania, 31
Sizwe Banzi is Dead (Fugard, Kani,
   Ntshona), 34
Smith, Adam, 68
Snapper, Juliana, *103*, 114, 115
sodomy, 109
Solar Anus (Athey), 114, 127
Solomon R. Guggenheim Museum, *See*
   Guggenheim Museum
Somalia, 3
Sondheim, Stephen, 67
   Assassins, 67
   2004 revival, 75
Sontag, Susan, 4, 69, 80, 81
Sophocles
   Antigone, 29, 34
   quoted in *The Island*, 29–30
   Philoctetes, 114
South Park, 128
Spierenburg, Pieter, 52
Spivey, Nigel, 105, 106, 110
Stages of Terror (Kubiak), 5
Stalin, Joseph, 100
Stiles, Kristine, 100
Stuhlbarg, Michael, 71
Summa Theologica (Thomas Aquinas), 88
Symes, Carol, 47
sympathy, 6, 8–9, 21, 50–51, 68, 75,
   135, 141, 155–58, *See also*
   compassion; empathy; pity;
   politics of pity

Tailby, John E., 90
Tarantino, Quentin, 2, 138
terrorism, 5
  state-sponsored, 3–5, 74–75
Thomas Aquinas, 42–43, 88
  Summa Theologica, 88
Thompson, Louisa, 134
Tierney, Matt, 138
torture, 2, 7, 16, 22
  dramatized, 27–30
  of saints, 42
  state-sponsored, 3–5, 37–38, 114, 129
  Abu Ghraib, 3–4, 5, 37, 114
  Guantánamo, 37, 69, 114
  South Africa, 34–38
Trans-fixed (Burden), 81
Treadwell, Sophie
  Machinal, 67

Ulay, 86, 87

Vagina Painting (Kubota), 83–84
Vale, V.
  Modern Primitives, 122
Van Gogh, Vincent, 116

Vawter, Ron, 114
Venus in Furs (Sacher-Masoch), 119
Versace, Gianni, 120
virgin martyr, 90–94, 164
vision
  medieval theories, 43–45
Visiting Hours (Flanagan), 123
Vogue, 120
Vogue Italia, 161

Wagner, Richard
  Parsifal, 114
Wall, Patrick, 12, 15, 18, 28, 67–68
Watson, Ariel, 142–43
Weiss, Thomas, 87
Wild One, The (film), 119, 127
Wilke, Hannah, 101
Wilson, August, 159
Wit (Edson), 19–20
Wogan-Browne, Jocelyn, 91, 93
Wojtyla, Karol, *See* John Paul II, Pope
Woolf, Virginia, 18, 19
  "On Being Ill", 16

You Always Hurt the One You Love (Flanagan), 123

GPSR Compliance
The European Union's (EU) General Product Safety Regulation (GPSR) is a set of rules that requires consumer products to be safe and our obligations to ensure this.

If you have any concerns about our products, you can contact us on

ProductSafety@springernature.com

In case Publisher is established outside the EU, the EU authorized representative is:

Springer Nature Customer Service Center GmbH
Europaplatz 3
69115 Heidelberg, Germany

www.ingramcontent.com/pod-product-compliance
Lightning Source LLC
LaVergne TN
LVHW011815060526
838200LV00053B/3792